In Sunshine
& in Shadow

In Sunshine & in Shadow

A Daughter's View of Homesteading and Beyond

Catherine A. Smith & Jean Smith Mottershead

ISBN 978-0-9958014-0-0 (hardcover)
ISBN 978-0-9958014-2-4 (paperback)
ISBN 978-0-9958014-1-7 (PDF)

This book has been self-published by the authors. To reach them, please send correspondence to:
    PO Box 291
    Quathiaski Cove, BC
    V0P 1N0
    insunshineandinshadow2017@gmail.com

Purchasing information at insunshineandinshadow.wordpress.com

Cover and text design by Iva Cheung
Cover image: *Red Cross Kitchen Cabin* by Dorothy L'Heureux. The cabin was Cathie and Danny Smith's first home together. This painting, by a local artist, herself a daughter of pioneers, hangs in the home of Rick and Janet Smith.
Printed and bound by IngramSpark
Unless otherwise credited, all photos are from the family's collection. All previously published photos are reprinted with permission.

Contents

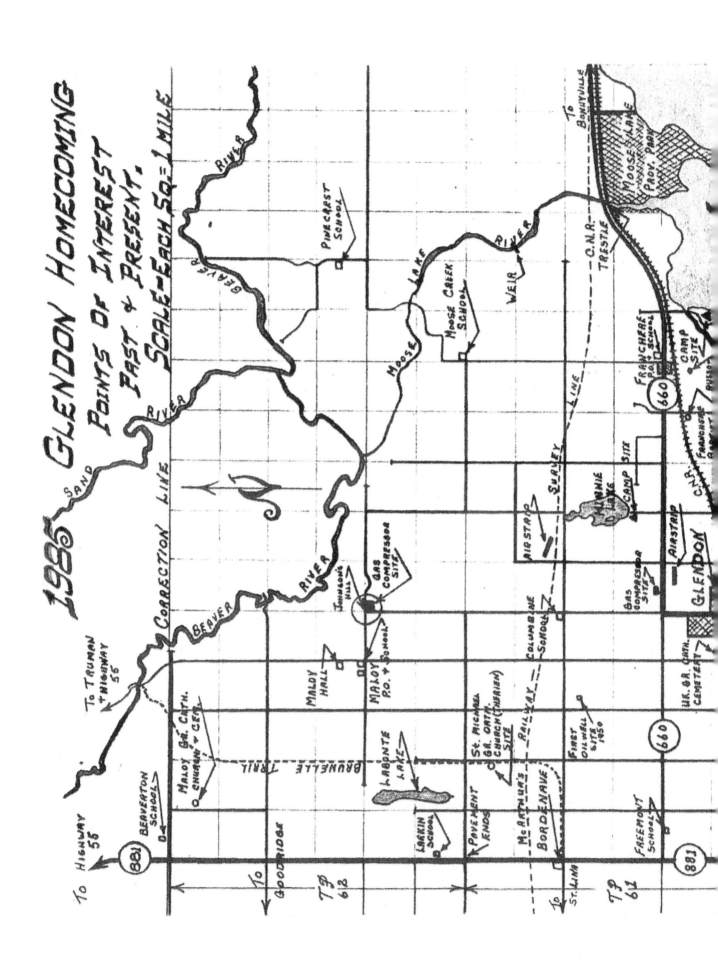

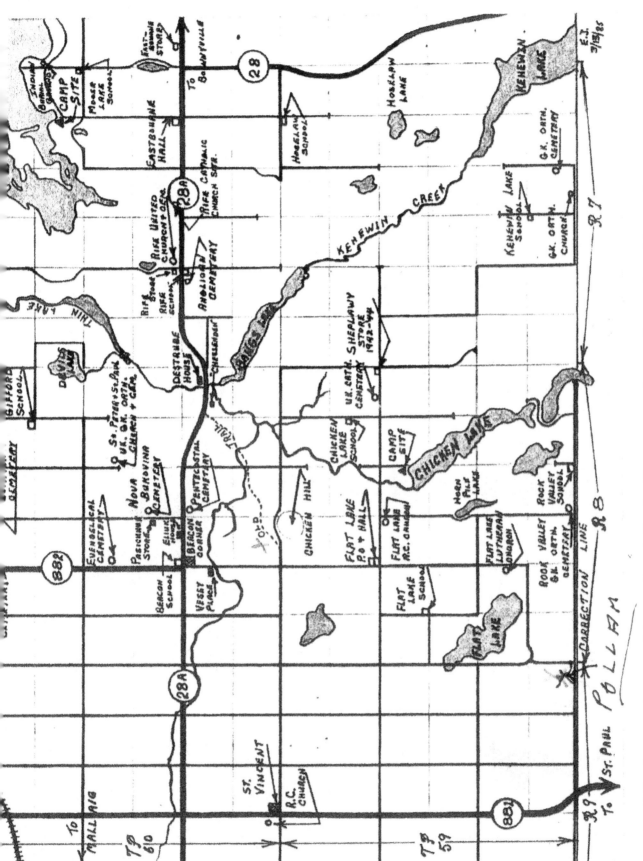

Map of Glendon area. A section of the map "1985 Glendon Homecoming—Points of Interest Past & Present." Courtesy of the Glendon Homecoming Committee.

Me, Cathie Smith, with my husband, Danny Smith, on our 55th anniversary.

Introduction

When I was 85, I had the temerity to start writing my memoir. I had written a few short articles about pioneers for local newspapers and community history books, and I had collected genealogical material on my forebears from the time of their entry into this country, so I thought I was ready to do the job. I wrote a dozen or so pages, then, feeling overwhelmed, I decided I was too old to tackle such a project. I put my pages in a trunk.

Ten years later, when I was 95, I got my pages out of the trunk and showed them to my daughter, Jean (Smith) Mottershead. By this time, I was the only living biological member of my generation of the Ross–McClure family. I realized that if my parents' experiences as pioneers were to be recorded, I was the person to do the job. I had the most first-hand knowledge of my parents' joys and sorrows, successes and setbacks. Jean encouraged me to start writing again. She suggested I write down my recollections in a few paragraphs each day. She offered to type, edit, and organize my material to be published in the form of a small booklet. I wanted to have a dozen copies of the booklet to present to eleven descendants of my parents—my four children and my siblings' seven children.

The project quickly ballooned with three expansions. First, Jean's daughter-in-law, Iva Cheung, a professional editor, suggested our booklet be placed in Ottawa's archives as part of the 150-year celebration of Confederation, planned for 2017. We—Jean and I—suddenly felt added responsibility to provide more context, history, and insights into community and country. Second, Jean thought focusing on only my side of the family—Rosses and McClures—would be too limited. Didn't I, she wondered, after 66 years of marriage to her father, Danny Smith, know enough about his family, the Smiths, to include them in my memoir? With her help I ventured into telling the Smith story, a more dramatic one than that of my Scottish ancestors. Third, Jean and I realized most of our readers would find our booklet more interesting if we lengthened its time period to include the names of their family members up to the time of publishing. We also realized we had to limit the project. We forsook the idea of making a giant family tree, choosing instead to simply list the names of descendants in family groupings. **We also agreed to simplify captions on photos by not repeating the surname "Smith" over and over. Unless otherwise indicated, readers may assume someone without a surname in a photo caption is a Smith.**

For over a year, the project has taken us on a journey back in time, and occasionally forward. The journey has been as broadening, exhilarating, and sobering as a ride in a hot-air balloon. We saw, like a patchwork of landscapes seen from above, a patchwork of different eras; different generations, with many beginnings and endings of life, many sorrows and joys; and constant change. Jean called her cousins to get updates on their experiences, greatly enjoying all the renewed contacts. Many people gave her stories—always interesting and sometimes humorous. She called me nearly every evening to share and discuss these stories, and I was often able to add context and details. We both feel humble and grateful to have had such enthusiastic participation from our relatives. We had a lot of fun and learned a lot.

We are astounded that our intended "booklet" turned into a volume of several hundred pages. We are pleased, however, that the book is now going out to more than eleven people. We hope this memoir conveys some of the goodwill and sparkle we encountered as we chatted with many of you and learned more about our shared bonds.

Acknowledgements

We—Jean and I—gratefully acknowledge the many people who made generous and valuable contributions to this memoir. Their enthusiasm and support inspired and sustained us. Mainly they are my relatives—nieces, nephews, my sons, and their spouses. They are descendants of either the William and Helen Ross family or the Charles and Esther Smith family, or, in the case of my sons, descendants of both. These people are the following:

- Edgar White; Diane (White) Brown; Lynne (White) Sutherland; Ross White
- Elsie Ross; Laurie "Louie" Ross; Allan Ross
- Mack Smith, Sid Smith, and Rick Smith
- Stella (Spence) Mills [through letters written to Elaine (Smith) Doonanco]
- Peter Metcalfe
- Joan (Smith) Doonanco-Gray; Frances (Smith) Kuori
- Mervin Smith; Elaine (Smith) Doonanco; Allan "Jeep" Smith

(We did not have recent addresses or phone numbers for descendants of the Charles Smith—aka Bill Davis—family and the Allan Smith family, so we do not have direct input from them. We have, however, included some information about these families.)

We value everyone's input, but we must mention several people who made special contributions. Some spent dozens of hours gathering information, documents, and photos, all of which enriched our book.

Dorothy Hill took time from supervising the three remaining Hill's Native Art stores, in Vancouver, Nanaimo, and Koksilah, to talk about her parents, Lloyd and Frances Hill, and their remarkable legacy. Engaging information about her father's background appears in Chapter 9's section about our circle of friends. Dorothy provided other valuable and dramatic information, which, along with material from many letters Lloyd and Frances wrote to Danny and me, was incorporated into a 20-page chapter on the Hills. In the end we omitted that chapter, deciding it should be expanded and published separately as the Hills' story.

Mack and Diane Smith willingly tramped around in the snow photographing Chicken Hill, the Rife United Church, tombstones, and other things. Their daughter **Danielle Smith-Weeks** emailed us many of these and other "pics." Mack and Diane also sent us historical documents and maps.

Rick and Janet Smith, along with **Bob and Lynne Sutherland**, travelled to Prince Edward Island and photographed the Ross ancestral home and several tombstones. They also met with a genealogist, Donna Johnston Collings, who shared her information about the Ross family in PEI and eagerly recorded new information about Rosses who had gone west. Dozens of times Janet emailed scanned documents or photos to us. Rick dug up relevant data and discussed it on the phone and in person.

In England, **Peter Metcalfe** collected information about his mother, Margaret Smith Metcalfe, and her family in England. He sent more than 30 family photos on a memory stick and emailed a set of captions to accompany these photos. He also scanned and emailed documents, such as his mother's baptism record. Peter also wrote sketches of his siblings, David and Pauline, whose lifespans were sadly short. He also provided interesting documents, one signed by Queen Elizabeth.

Joan (Smith) Doonanco-Gray came to a Smith Reunion in 2007 with a marvellous photo taken at Truman in 1947. In it the children of Tommy, Danny, and Reg are lined up against our Pontiac car. Sixty years later, that photo led to a similar but updated photo. Both photos are used to introduce Chapter 14.

Allan "Jeep" Smith, probably inspired by the two photos of lined-up cousins, prepared a package of photos as gifts for cousins in the photo. Along with 8½ × 12–inch prints of the cousins, he included rare and special photos, such as the house where the Smiths lived when they arrived in Canada. He meticulously prepared Post-it notes to go with the photos, providing dates and comments. He also helped write the story of his wife, Grace, who died at an early age.

Elaine (Smith) Doonanco said she would go to her archives and see what she could find for us. What she found was pure gold, which she generously shared with us. Her material includes the following:

- a set of genealogical sheets on four generations of Smiths,
- information from her childhood correspondence with Mary Davis (daughter of Charles Smith Jr., aka Bill Davis),
- letters to Elaine from her cousin Stella (Spence) Mills, daughter of Ettie, the eldest member of the Charles and Esther Smith family, and
- photos of the Allan Smith family and the elder Charles Smith.

Elaine's material reveals family members who were only vague shadows in our consciousness as attractive, capable people. A photo of Charles Smith Sr. holding his small grandson's hand takes the old man from the category "missing person" to "gentle grandfather." It is a privilege to have access to Elaine's material and to share it with our readers.

Iva Cheung, Jean's daughter-in-law, first raised our aspirations by sending us information about putting this memoir in Canada's Archives in Ottawa, and in so doing she made our book better. Later, Jean's son Jeff suggested we consult with Iva, his wife and award-winning professional editor, about finishing the book according to best publishing standards. We were pleased and privileged to have Iva's expert guidance throughout the final stages of our project. We greatly appreciate Iva's creation of the index and her impeccable handling of our sometimes quirky material.

Don Mottershead, Jean's husband, helped us every step of the way with his supportive stance and technical expertise with computers. Don's help was vital in bringing our project to fruition.

CHAPTER 1

McClure and Ross Family Origins in Canada

I begin my memoir with a photo of my parents, William MacKinnon Ross and Helen Brooke McClure, on their wedding day, June 27, 1911. They are in Nelson, British Columbia, on the frontier. They look pleased with themselves, William even triumphant. The federal government is also pleased. Confederation took place less than 50 years ago, and the government wants energetic young people to marry and help populate the Canadian West. My parents' marriage lasted 52 years, until death parted them. Though their life was not quite idyllic, they fared well, without any tragedy within their immediate family.

At the outset of my writing, I did not plan to delve into genealogy, but I found myself wanting some context for my own and my parents' existence. I limited my search back in time to the McClure and the Ross families' arrival in Canada. At the end of this chapter you will find a streamlined family tree showing only my ancestors and me, without any siblings. In this chapter I present first the McClures and then the Rosses.

The McClures

Hanging on the wall of my parents' home was an intriguing object—a framed, four-foot-long, black-and-white photo of an event reported in the Toronto *Empire and Globe,* June 16, 1922. In the photo are three tiers of people, over 150 people per tier. According to the accompanying newspaper article, the photo shows the "Grand Reunion of McClures of Peel County… 500 Strong." The newspaper goes on to say that the 500 McClures who came to the reunion were descendants of three brothers—James, John, and David McClure—who arrived in Canada in 1820. Dr. William McClure, a physician who spoke at the reunion, had traced the McClures back to Norse and Scottish ancestry. He said that in Scotland the McClures, who were Presbyterians, refused to "take the

The First Century of McClures in Canada

Opposite: *Nelson, 1911. Mama and Papa on their wedding day.*

oath of the Covenant" and give up their religion. To escape persecution they moved to Castleton, Ireland. There the family became oppressed by "landlordism, high rents, and poverty," so the three brothers decided to immigrate to Canada. Given their more than 500 descendants, we know the brothers thrived in their new country.

Three Outstanding McClure Careers

The McClures thrived not only in terms of numbers of descendants. Some of them had notable careers. An example is James McClure, one of the three immigrant McClure brothers. James became well known in Ontario as a cabinet maker. I was so fortunate as to receive a chest of drawers he made. My cousin Edith Jennings, who lived in Ontario, offered to send the chest to me if Danny and I would pay the freight. Massive and beautiful, it is no ordinary piece of furniture. It was originally finished with oxblood, but when my son Rick and his wife, Janet, received the chest, they employed a professional restorer of antique furniture to reveal its beautiful walnut wood.

Home of Rick and Janet Smith, Rife, 2016. Chest of drawers made by James McClure after he immigrated to Ontario in 1820.

Another notable career was that of the doctor who spoke at the reunion, Dr. William McClure, who was a medical missionary in China and the family historian. Even more outstanding than William's career was that of his son, Dr. Robert Baird McClure (1900–1991). Robert practised medicine in many countries, became Moderator of the United Church, and in 1971 was named Companion of the Order of Canada. His biography, written by Munroe Scott, is published by Penguin.

James McClure and his wife, Martha Ann (Wilson) McClure, were my great-grandparents and parents of my mother's father, Joseph McClure. A big, kind man, Grandpa McClure won the hearts of his grandchildren when he visited us in Alberta in 1923. Unfortunately, his wife, my grandmother, Mary Elizabeth (White) McClure, died of cancer a few weeks before I was born. I knew her only through her letters, which Mama had kept and often reread. In her last letter, in 1919, Grandma McClure wrote that she would "dearly love" to see Mama and be with her when she gave birth later that year. As it happened, Mama gave birth that June to twins— me, Catherine Anna, and my brother William Alexander. Sadly Grandpa McClure travelled alone on his only trip to visit our family.

The Sad Side of Pioneering

Flat Lake, Alberta, 1924. Grandpa McClure with my twin brother, Alex, in the sheep pasture. Grandpa called Alex "a fine chap."

Watford area, Ontario, about 1875. Joseph McClure's farm and buildings. Mama and all her siblings were raised here.

A Trip to Mama's Childhood Home

When I was 19, Mama and I visited Mama's sisters and other relatives in Ontario. I noticed the warmth and goodwill of the McClure family, and I saw the family home where Mama and all of her siblings grew up. According to Mama, the original McClure immigrants made house building a priority and so did not spend many years in log cabins. The photo of Mama's home was taken on a grey day after the snow was gone, before any green leaves had appeared. The photo makes the farm seem a forlorn place. In fact, the home was spacious and comfortable, a pleasant place to live.

List of McClure Siblings

Daughters did not farm in those days, so the McClure sisters left home, marrying or adventuring to other places. My mother and her sister Lillian adventured together to faraway British Columbia. Below, listed with biographical data, are the six daughters and two sons of the Joseph McClure family. (A granddaughter, Muriel, was raised as a daughter.)

- Frances Lillian (1876–1967), teacher, m. Charles McLane; lived in San Diego, California

- Edith Lavinia (1877–1961) m. Alex Watson; lived in Petrolia, Ontario
- Joseph Leonard (1878–about 1944) m. Clara Dodd then Alice Longley, from Maine; lived at Chicken Hill, Alberta
- Mary Ethel (1880–1973) m. Ben Williamson; lived in Petrolia, Ontario
- Helen Brooke (1883–1968) m. William Ross; lived at Chicken Hill, Flat Lake, and Rife, Alberta
- Alexander (1886–about 1918) died of rheumatic fever, leaving wife, Edna Winson Bissell, and two young sons; lived in Sarnia, Ontario
- Jessie Olivia (1887–1976) worked and lived in Detroit, Michigan
- Muriel (1895–about 1975) m. Frank Kinmond; lived in Rochester, New York

Aunt Jessie's passport photo, about 1925. Mama's unmarried sister, Jessie, worked in Detroit, saved money for gifts and travel, visited parents, siblings, nieces, and nephews—a boon to the family.

Joseph McClure (1865–1924) and Mary Elizabeth (White) McClure (1865–1919). They lived on the farm near Watford, Ontario, and raised two sons and six daughters, including Mama.

The Rosses

My father told me that near evening on August 7, 1803, our ancestors arrived on the ship *Polly* from Portree, on the Isle of Skye. How these people came to settle on Prince Edward Island is a well-documented story of conflict and intrigue. In it a generous benefactor helps 800 Scottish workers escape the yoke of rich and powerful landlords.

Eight Hundred Settlers Recruited

According to Professor J.M. Bumsted's article on *Wikipedia,* some turmoil and some good luck were involved in the settling of PEI. The Earl of Selkirk, a magnanimous and honourable man, was sympathetic to the plight of Scottish Highlanders who were being threatened by their landlords. (The Earl was also looking for a way to make a name for himself and so win a seat in the British House of Lords.) The British government promised to give him land in Upper Canada if he could recruit hundreds of settlers for the land. The Earl quickly recruited 800 Scottish farmers on the Isle of Skye, but he ran into unexpected hurdles.

Attempts to Thwart Selkirk and Settlers

As it happened, the people who accepted the Earl's offer were among the most ambitious and prosperous citizens on the island. Proprietors in the Highlands, realizing the emigration of these settlers would cost them their labour force, persuaded the British government to withdraw the offer it had made to Selkirk—land in Upper Canada. Selkirk had to quickly and privately buy land somewhere else. That land turned out to be on Prince Edward Island. The panicking Scottish landlords were not done fighting to keep their work force. They succeeded in getting the cost of passage to Canada made prohibitively high for the settlers. Their ploy was foiled when Selkirk used his own money to offset the increased price of passage for his settlers. Despite his generous expenditures, Selkirk had not yet won the hearts of all his settlers. Some would-be settlers, upon discovering they were not going to Upper Canada as expected, initiated court action. As a result of that action, the emigration was delayed and did not get underway until mid-summer of 1803.

Donald Ross (1848–1923) and Mary (MacKinnon) Ross (1854–1943). They lived on Prince Edward Island and raised three daughters and six sons, including Papa.

Surviving and Prospering in the New World

Arriving at their destination in August, the settlers had to plunge into cutting down trees to build log houses for themselves before winter. Selkirk reported that before he left that fall all the families were housed. Through his thoughtful planning, Selkirk had laid the foundation for a prosperous, congenial society. He had surveyors lay out long, narrow parcels of land with access to the sea so settlers could fish. Potatoes grew well between the trees, cattle had lush pasture, and men could earn extra cash by harvesting trees for the timber trade. Selkirk, who spoke Gaelic, advocated that the people retain their language and culture, and so the idea of the Canadian mosaic was born. The settlers quickly prospered and by 1824 had built the lovely St. John's Presbyterian Church, which is still in use. Lord Selkirk, as the Earl became, had brought his settlers to a nearly ideal new land.

My Branch of the Ross Family

My branch of the Ross family began when Donald Ross and his wife, Margaret (MacDonald) Ross, settled in the district of Valleyfield, PEI. Their son John Ross and his wife, Rachel (MacPherson) Ross, were among the first generation of Selkirk settlers' descendants born in Canada. John and Rachel's children (second-generation descendants) included my grandfather, Donald Ross. A third generation, children of Donald and Mary (MacKinnon) Ross, included my father, William Ross and his siblings. (See list and partial family tree at the end of this chapter.)

Crowding and Consumption

When John Ross died in 1874, his wife, Rachel (MacPherson) Ross, aged 55, became the matriarch of the home, living there for 37 more years, until her death at 92. For some years Rachel's role was an onerous one, managing her family of seven older children in a modest house. A terrible worry was that two of her children, Alex and Christie, had tuberculosis, then known as "consumption." The names of Alex and Christie Ross are on the tombstone of their mother, Rachel. Before the death of his father, John, Donald Ross, eldest son, had taken over running the farm. After a year or two he brought his bride, Mary MacKinnon, to join the family. Over the next 21 years Donald and Mary had up to nine children living in the family home. At first, the couple shared the house with four of Donald's siblings. Eventually these siblings either died or lived elsewhere. Alexander died in 1876 at age 22 and Christie died, probably in hospital or a sanatorium, in 1893 at age 32. The census of 1901 shows twelve occupants in the house—Donald, Mary, all nine of their children, and Grandmother Rachel. At peak occupancy the old house must have been crowded, but a greater concern must have been that tuberculosis was in the house for more than two decades. No one else contracted the disease, but illness and untimely deaths must have darkened the atmosphere in the house.

A Beautiful Home Built Too Late

By 1907 Donald and Mary had built the spacious home shown on the opposite page. Regrettably, the house was built too late for most of their children to enjoy it. By then, five of them had left PEI to seek their fortunes in faraway places. To her parents' delight, one daughter, Rachel, had married and lived nearby, raising children who were destined for higher education and professions. Sadly, within a decade after the house

The Donald Ross home built in 1907. Photo by Janet (Lay) Smith, 2015.

was built, two of Donald and Mary's sons had died in war. Their youngest daughter, Florence, had married and moved to Alberta with her husband. Only one son remained with his parents in the big house.

After my grandfather Donald died, in 1923, my grandmother Mary became the family matriarch, a position she held for 20 years, living in her home with her youngest surviving son, Malcolm (Mac), and his wife, Bessie Matheson. I never met my Ross grandparents, but I felt a warm regard for "Grandma Ross"—so much so that our first son, MacKinnon, is named after her. She knitted socks, mittens, and other items and sent them as gifts. From an early age I wrote thank-you letters to her. Years later I realized that my letters amused my grandma in a way I could not have guessed.

Mary (MacKinnon) Ross, a Beloved Matriarch

In the 1970s my husband, Danny, and I visited Uncle Mac and Aunt Bessie in the big Ross home on PEI. We enjoyed their gracious hospitality and Bessie's lively sense of humour, which became apparent as soon as we walked into the living room. I was surprised to find a photo of me on

Visits to PEI

the mantle. Aunt Bessie laughingly told me about one of the thank-you letters I had written to my grandmother. It had a blot of ink on it, and beside the blot I had written the helpful information that under the blot was the word "and." I was pleased to have been a source of mirth, remembered for half a century. Danny was astounded by how much Uncle Mac looked like my father, and I felt closer than ever to my departed grandmother.

In 2015 my son Rick and his wife, Janet, along with my sister's daughter Lynne and her husband, Bob Sutherland, visited the Ross home in Valleyfield. They found

Valleyfield, PEI, 1940. Grandma Ross with grandson, Jackie McLeod, who, as Reverend McLeod, worked in Vancouver.

people there were "as friendly as you would ever want." The new owners of the Ross house welcomed the Ross descendants and their spouses from the West. A genealogist, Donna Johnston Collings, who happened to be on hand, gave Rick and Janet pages of genealogical data, and she recorded new information about the Alberta Rosses.

List of Ross Siblings

Following is a list of Donald and Mary Ross's offspring with some biographical information:

- John (1877–?) lived somewhere in USA
- Alexander (1879–?) named after Donald's deceased brother; lived somewhere in USA

- William MacKinnon (1881–1963) m. Helen McClure; lived at Chicken Hill, Flat Lake, Rife, and Bonnyville, Alberta
- Rachel Ross (1884–1965), named after her grandmother, m. Angus McLeod; lived in Valleyfield
- Catherine Anna (1886–about 1983) named after Mary MacKinnon's mother, Catherine McQueen; unmarried, lived and worked in Boston, USA
- Daniel (1888–1917) had left home early, was 28 when killed in WWI
- Flora (Florence) (1891–1973), named after Donald's sister, m. Alex MacLean; lived at Rife, Alberta
- Malcolm (Mac) (1894–1972) m. Bessie Matheson; lived in Valleyfield
- John Murdock (1898–1917) was 18 when he was killed beside his brother in WWI

Prince of Wales College, PEI, about 1916. John Murdock Ross. Donald and Mary Ross's youngest son, John M., was preparing to become a medical doctor before he enlisted to go to war.

Valleyfield, about 1916. Brothers going to war. L–R: John Murdock Ross (1898–1917), Daniel Ross (1888–1917).

Although they died before I was born, I seem to have always known that two of my father's brothers lost their lives in World War I. John M. Ross and Dan Ross lost their lives at Lens in the Battle of Passchendaele. John M. died in the hospital just a few days after hearing the Allies had won the battle, but Dan's body was never found. Many years after the

An Amazing and Moving Coincidence

war, by coincidence these two men touched our lives again. My brother Donnie was in Bonnyville's Duclos Hospital to see a doctor from PEI who had come to relieve the shortage of doctors at the hospital. When Donnie gave his name, the doctor asked, "Where did that name originate?"

Donnie replied, "It was the name of my grandfather on PEI, Donald Ross. I was named after him."

"Did you have two uncles killed in the war?"

"Yes," Donnie said. "John M. and Dan."

"Well, I was standing beside those fellows when Dan was blown to pieces. I knew those fellows."

The doctor's story affected all of us in the family. Even though most of us had never seen the two lost brothers, they suddenly seemed close to us, and we mourned their deaths. We felt the horror of war and the gloom that comes with hearing about young men being blown to pieces. I realize that knowing about previous generations broadens our experience of the world.

Left: Valleyfield, 2015. Tombstone of my great-grandfather, John Ross (1815?–1874). Photo by Janet Smith.

Opposite, top: Valleyfield, 2015. Tombstone of my great-grandmother, Rachel (MacPherson) Ross, and two of her children. Photo by Janet Smith.

Opposite, bottom: Valleyfield, 2015. Tombstone of my grandparents, Donald and Mary (MacKinnon) Ross and two of their sons, killed in World War I. Photo by Janet Smith.

Rosses Who Left PEI

I have wondered what motivated my father and six of his siblings to leave PEI. Perhaps some felt their home on PEI had been a gloomy place. Perhaps Papa was not satisfied with his job as a teacher and thought life on the frontier would be more exciting, maybe more lucrative. Mac MacLean, Uncle Alex's brother, and also a migrant from PEI, cast a different light on Papa's leaving. He said my father had been in a horse-and-buggy race in which he forced the competing horse and buggy off the road. Threatened with court action, Mac said, my father quickly left PEI and headed west. In 2015, a local Valleyfield citizen revived the story, telling Rick and Janet he had heard Papa fled because he feared the opposing driver would die from his injuries. The driver survived, but young William went westward to stay.

Maintaining Family Ties

I wonder how people felt as they left their parental home and community, perhaps never to return. Many tears must have flowed at partings. With luck, letters and occasional reunions helped to maintain ties. Papa occasionally wrote letters home, once with news that his first son was named Donald, after Papa's father. Like the McClures, the Rosses also had a beloved unmarried sister, Aunt Catherine, who occasionally visited family members, showering them with gifts. After an absence of about 35 years, Papa and his sister Florence returned to PEI to visit their mother, by then in her eighties. Florence also brought her young son Kenneth on the trip. Our grandmother reported being too excited to sleep the night before they arrived. I am glad that after the terrible grief of losing two sons in battle, my grandmother finally had the joy of seeing Papa, Aunt Florence, and her Alberta grandson before she died.

Mama and Papa's Compatibility

A desire for adventure took Mama and Papa thousands of miles from home to BC. There they met and married, by chance choosing a spouse of whom their parents would approve. Their two families were much alike, though a McClure man was more likely than a Ross to win the caber toss, and the McClure girls' auburn locks out-dazzled the Rosses' dun-coloured hair. Both were large and prosperous Celtic families with conservative values. Each was headed by a mother and father who believed marriage was for life. Both families valued education and membership in a Protestant church. Love of poetry and music ran through both families. In fact, Mama and Papa were very compatible.

Ross–McClure Family Tree

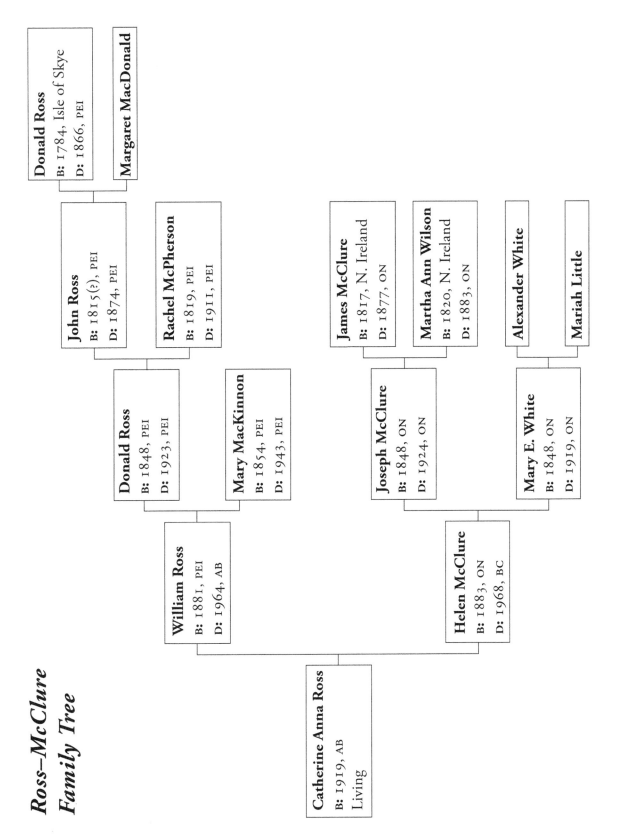

Donald Ross
B: 1784, Isle of Skye
D: 1866, PEI

Margaret MacDonald

John Ross
B: 1815(?), PEI
D: 1874, PEI

Rachel McPherson
B: 1819, PEI
D: 1911, PEI

James McClure
B: 1817, N. Ireland
D: 1877, ON

Martha Ann Wilson
B: 1820, N. Ireland
D: 1883, ON

Alexander White

Mariah Little

Donald Ross
B: 1848, PEI
D: 1923, PEI

Mary MacKinnon
B: 1854, PEI
D: 1943, PEI

Joseph McClure
B: 1848, ON
D: 1924, ON

Mary E. White
B: 1848, ON
D: 1919, ON

William Ross
B: 1881, PEI
D: 1964, AB

Helen McClure
B: 1883, ON
D: 1968, BC

Catherine Anna Ross
B: 1919, AB
Living

CHAPTER 2

 ❯❯❯

Introducing My Family

Christmas, 1930. Back row, L–R: Donnie Ross, Papa (William Ross), Mama (Helen Ross), Aunt Alice McClure, Len McClure (Mama's brother). Front row, L–R: Alex Ross, me, Vivian Ross, Muriel McClure.

To introduce my family of origin and some descendants, I use two family photos, the first taken in 1930, the other in 1944. Both photos were taken on a Christmas Day at the "Armstrong Place," which my parents had bought in 1928.

In the first photo, my twin brother and I are nine years old. Mama's Christmas feast was ready, but before we could sit down to it, Mama arranged for Lester Story, our hired man, to use her new camera to take a family photo. We gathered in the snow outside to get good light for the photo.

In the back row, Donnie, who is only 13, is looking unusually tall and pleased with himself, possibly because he is standing on tiptoe. You can see Papa lurking in the back with his cap shading his eyes and Mama in the big lace "bertha" that she really doesn't like but fell heir to. She is trying to dodge the bright winter sunshine, and she wants to get her dinner on the table. Beside Mama, Aunt Alice, who had long been a single teacher, looks calm and secure in her roles as second wife to stalwart Uncle Len and stepmother to Muriel. If Aunt Alice knew the sadness and struggles that lay ahead for her, the expression on her face might be quite different. In the front row Alex and I look as usual—generally pleased with life. At this time, we twins are still near the same height, but that will change. Vivi had cabbaged some lipstick and an eyebrow pencil and succeeds in looking dramatic yet demure. Beside her, Muriel looks determined to take on the world. Her mother, Clara Dodd, had died in childbirth, and Muriel was raised for five years by foster parents, until her father, Uncle Len, remarried. She had learned how to fend for herself, which she did throughout her tumultuous life.

The 1930 Photo

Above: Christmas, 1944. Back row L–R: Donnie Ross, William Ross, Danny Smith, Ray White, Alex Ross. Middle row, L–R: Helen Ross, Vivi White, me, holding Sidney Smith. Front row, L–R: Diane White, Edgar White, MacKinnon (Mack) Smith, Jean Smith.

The 1944 Photo

In this second photo you may recognize only Mama, Papa, and Vivi. We see Papa and Mama looking different, a little more worn. Papa has started shrinking in height, and his hair has thinned. Mama's hair is whiter. Vivi looks more grown up. I am there too, looking very much more grown up, holding my youngest child, Kenneth Sidney. My other two children, Daniel MacKinnon and Catherine Jean, are standing in front of me. My kids and I have the surname "Smith." Helen Diane White and William Raymond Edgar White are standing in front of their mother, Vivi White. Vivi's and my husbands are also in the photo; they are the tall men, Danny Smith and Ray White, looking like twins as they peek over Mama's and Vivi's heads. My twin brother, Alex, has grown into the tall fellow on the right, and Donnie, nearly as tall, is on the left. The little Smith and White cousins enjoy playing with each other, except Siddie is still too young to join in much. Still called "chickadee," he attracts attention for his blond curls and his energy. On this cold winter day, Diane is the only one who had the foresight to grab a coat and a present.

Introducing Danny and Ray

I met Danny in 1928 when he came to work for Papa during haying season. He was 14 and had recently arrived with his parents from England. Twelve years later he and I were married. Our romance is a long story, told in Chapter 9.

A few months after the 1930 Christmas photo was taken, the "Southerners" arrived from Youngstown, having given up on their drought-stricken farms in southern Alberta. Papa's sister Florence, and her husband, Alex MacLean, simply appeared at our door. Even more significant for our family was the arrival a few days later of an English immigrant, charming Ray White. When he met my sister, Vivi, Ray was immediately entranced, and six years later he married into our family.

Those Who Remain

Of the people in the 1930 photo, I am the only one still living. From the 1944 photo, I am the only member of the older generation still living. Mama and Papa, Vivi, Donnie, Alex, Ray, and Danny are missing, and sometimes I feel like "The Last Rose of Summer." Happily, all of the children in the photo are alive and well—a little wrinkled but healthy and full of enthusiasm for life. I delight in following the lives and achievements of the present Ross and Smith generations.

Browning house lawn at Rife, 1954. Jean, babysitter, age 13, and Rick, age 15 months.

Ross Grandchildren Born Later

Soon after the 1944 photo was taken, the family continued to increase in number, eventually producing 11 grandchildren for Mama and Papa. Donnie married a kind and attractive woman, Olive Munroe, from Apple Hill, Ontario. Over the next several years they had three children, Elsie, Laurence (Laurie) "Louie," and Allan. Vivi and Ray added Madelyn (Lynne) and Ross to their family. Danny and I added Richard to ours. Of course all the newcomers were welcomed and loved. To introduce our Richard (Rick), born in 1953, I use a photo of him about 15 months old, sitting outside, on Jean's lap. In one of my fondest memories of him as a little boy, he is wearing the red short-pant suit I knitted for him, standing on the stage at Eastbourne Hall belting out "Rudolph the Red-Nosed Reindeer."

I have a similar memory of Laurie Ross, who was in my grade one class. At the school Christmas concert, his voice rang through the loudspeaker as he sang "All I want for Christmas is my two front teeth" and showed with his fingers where his teeth had been. Happily, Rick and "Louie" have been best friends all their lives. But who would have thought sweet little Rick and Louie would one day startle Louie's teetotalling mother by performing a rowdy, raucous version of "White Lightning" at Eastbourne Hall? Their "Tubs and Scrubs" band had a limited repertoire, but what crowd pleasers they were!

Bonny Lodge, about 2010. L–R: Olive Ross, me, Pat Williams, Louie Ross.

Ross White, my sister Vivi's son, took this charming photo. It is great to have good photographer on hand to capture good times.

CHAPTER 3

Seven Years at Chicken Hill

The cabin on Chicken Hill, Alberta; summer 1919. L–R: Uncle Len; Vivi, Mama; newborn twins, Alex and me; and Donnie.

On the right you can see some of the fence built to keep sheep and deer out of Mama's vegetable garden. Mama loved this cabin and was not eager to leave it when Papa wanted more and better land.

Union Work in BC

Born in 1881 in Valleyfield, Prince Edward Island, William Ross, my papa, trained as a teacher at Prince of Wales College in Charlottetown. He taught school in PEI for a few years, but, whatever his reason for leaving there, he ended up on the west side of the continent. For a while he did some prospecting in Washington State, USA, but he soon returned to Canada, stopping in Greenwood, BC. There he became Secretary of the Miners' Union.

Department of the Interior, Washington State, USA; March 19, 1910. Papa's stake on timber and mineral rights in Washington.

Meeting and Marrying Mama

In Greenwood, BC, Papa met Helen McClure, my mama. Born in 1883 in Sutorville, Ontario, Mama had accompanied her sister Lillian to Greenwood, where Lillian had accepted a job as a teacher. Mama worked as a milliner there and sometimes as a waitress. Papa may have met Mama in church, but more likely he was captivated by the slim, blue-eyed girl as she served food in the hotel restaurant. On June 27, 1911, Papa and Mama were married in Nelson, BC.

Getting a Homestead

About 1912 Papa's friend Jim Fraser told Papa he had invested $10 to file on a "homestead," 160 acres of land, in Alberta. He suggested Papa do the same, which Papa did.

In 1913, when Mama was expecting their first child, the couple decided to move to the Alberta homestead on which Papa had filed. Papa resigned his job and began collecting a railcar load of "settlers' effects" to be sent by train to Edmonton.

Birth of Vivian in Ontario

Mama took the train to her family's home in Ontario to await the birth of their baby. On March 1, 1913, she safely delivered her baby, whom they named Mary Vivian, Mary being the name of both grandmothers. They called her Vivian, which was shortened to Vivi most of the time.

With Mama in Ontario, Papa worked alone on the move to his homestead, a quarter section of land on Chicken Hill. In April, along with his carload of settlers' effects, Papa travelled by train to Edmonton. That carload included a wagon and four horses, Dan, King, Bird, and Silver Bell. Upon arrival in Edmonton, Papa harnessed the four horses (with harness he must have brought), hitched them to the wagon, loaded up his possessions, and made the five-day trip to his homestead. During the night he slept either under the stars or under an umbrella. (Years later Papa commented he could always find his horses at the end of the pasture closest to BC.)

After he arrived at Chicken Hill, Papa's first priority was to build a cabin. He was fortunate in hiring Wallace Kriaski to help him. Wallace, who lived only a few miles away, was a dandy axeman and carpenter. The two men soon built a neat cabin from hewn logs. The cabin had two small bedrooms and a good-sized kitchen/dining room, all partitioned off the living room. It was near the bottom of the hill, beside the road, which you can see in the photo as a barely visible short, white line above some dark trees.

Chicken Hill, 2016. Photo by Mack Smith.

Steeper than it looks in this photo, Chicken Hill looms over the prairie landscape. It was probably formed of glacial till after the last ice age. Some of the soil may contain a lot of gravel and rocks.

Inviting Mama to Come

After the cabin was built, Papa felt ready and eager to have his wife and baby daughter join him. Printed below is the last page from one of his letters to Mama. In the missing first part of the letter, Papa apparently advised Mama to save money by buying a train ticket from Ontario to Vegreville rather than to St. Paul. From Vegreville she would go by stagecoach to St. Paul.

Here is the letter Papa wrote to Mama in 1913:

> [They will] charge you double for a special trip. If you can find out, before you leave, when your train will be in Vegreville and let me know, I will have an idea when I should go to St. Paul to meet you. It is eighteen miles from here to St. Paul. I am afraid you will have a tiresome trip with her Ladyship [baby Vivian] to look after. But we should have nice weather after all the rain, and the mosquitoes should have returned to the field by that time. Hear the Railway is building again. Should be through here by next summer. It will really look good when it comes. Never was in a place where the time flies like it does here. Think you will like it here even though it is rough and unhandy. Will be looking for an early reply.
>
> With all my love, remain yours ever,
>
> Will
>
> P. S. Mail comes here Tuesdays, Thursdays, and Saturdays. If you come to St. Paul on Friday, I could drive in on Fri. and come back on Sat., but it does not matter much about that. Will

Mama's Rough Trip

Papa was not on hand to meet Mama in St. Paul des Metis (as the town was then called) when she arrived on a September day in 1913. Mama sometimes reminisced that when she got off the stagecoach which had brought her from Vegreville to St. Paul, the first person she met was a prominent businessman, Alphonse T. Brosseau. (One of Alphonse Brosseau's stores still exists in Bonnyville, still owned by the Brosseau family.) She also met Jim Demers, the man who clerked in the Brosseau store and who welcomed her to Alberta. She asked questions and made arrangements to get to Chicken Hill.

On the final leg of her trip to Chicken Hill, Mama must have realized that she indeed would be pioneering. She travelled by covered buggy, with the intrepid Hector Landry from Durlingville handling the horses. To people used to prairie landscapes, Chicken Hill seems a mountain, but the climb up the hill was only part of the challenge. In some places the roads were flooded, and as the wheels sank into the mud, water washed over the floor of the buggy. Mama had to lift up her feet to keep them from getting wet. And all the while she was holding her baby tightly in her arms. Fortunately, the buggy's route went up to Chicken Hill and by the door of the Ross cabin. Finally, Mama and baby Vivian arrived at their new home. The cabin pleased Mama, and she was confident she could make it a comfortable home.

An Empty Larder

Papa, perhaps deterred by muddy roads, had not made his planned trip to St. Paul to buy provisions for his wife and new baby. Mama never expressed disappointment that Papa did not meet her in St. Paul. (Perhaps she had not communicated her travel plans early enough.) She did, however, mention his lack of provision of food for her and the baby. On the day she arrived, the only food Papa had in the house was some old potatoes from a neighbour's garden of the previous year. He had no garden, and they had to go to a neighbour's place for milk for the baby.

A Full Larder, an Inviting Home

Mama would change things! She would not be without chickens for meat and eggs; vegetables, berries, and fruit for canned preserves; and flour, sugar, and yeast for breads, pies, and cookies. Her family would be well fed.

Along with caring for her small baby and cooking, Mama immediately started improving their home. For their first Christmas, she and Papa bought some building paper in St. Paul. It would provide insulation from the cold and would improve the look of a room. On Christmas Eve, 1913, Mama and Papa stayed up all night putting the paper up in the kitchen/dining room. At 7:00 am, while Papa got some sleep, Mama put on her apron and began cooking Christmas dinner for company. Lucy and Jim Fraser were guests for the first Christmas in their new home.

Mama must have been a wonderful helpmate. Her cooking and housekeeping made the cabin an inviting home. Outside she also helped with chores, including holding the lantern at night so Papa could see to pound nails into the stable he was building.

Friends and Neighbours

Flat Lake, about 1916. Back row, L–R: "Grandpa" Fraser, Mr. Wirgen, Jim Fraser, William Ross. Middle row, L–R: Mrs. Blais, Lucy Fraser, Nellie MacKenzie, Helen Ross, Stanley Mack. Front row, L–R: Jimmy Fraser, Vivian Ross, Margaret Fraser.

In pioneer times, people were wise to have good relations with their neighbours, which Mama and Papa had. Their nearest neighbours were the Laddishes and Harasym Mack, and on the other side of the hill were the Doonancos and Harborenkos. Their closest friends were the Frasers and the MacKenzies, who lived about six miles away.

Right: *Glendon, about 1995. Elaine and Peter Doonanco with a chair once owned by Jim Fraser. Now restored, the antique chair graces their home.*

In 1915 Papa became the first teacher at the newly built Nova Bukovina School, later called Beacon School. The 19 children in attendance all spoke Ukrainian and very little English. They were all eager to learn and made good progress, so Papa enjoyed teaching them. Teacher's pay was meagre, however, and Papa was keenly aware that during the war years farmers were getting high prices for their products. He was eager get out of the classroom and back into farming.

A Brief Return to Teaching

Baby Donnie Is Born

Chicken Hill, early spring, 1918. Papa holding six-month-old Donnie. Grandfather Fraser kneeling. Five-year-old Vivi only half in the photo.

In 1917 Aunt Jessie, Mama's sister, came from Ontario to stay with Mama, who was expecting another baby. On October 4, the Rosses' first son was born, named John Donald after the two Ross brothers, John M. and Dan (also known as Don), who were killed in 1917 at the front in World War I.

After nearly five years as "Her Ladyship," little Vivi probably felt supplanted by the important baby boy who would "carry on the Ross name." Years later she still seemed to feel some ire about being only half in the picture, noting the fact on the back of the photo and writing on the front of the photo itself.

Battling Loneliness

Homesteading pioneers, if they were realistic, expected years of back-breaking work and little income. But some may not have anticipated other possible challenges, such as crop failures, accidents, illness, and loneliness. Especially in the evening, pangs of loneliness would creep into their quiet times. A year brought only a few occasions, such as dances and Christmas, when people could socialize with neighbours and make friends. Rare as they were, such occasions helped build a sense of community and lessened loneliness.

Maintaining family ties by mail helped many pioneers cope with loneliness. News that a relative from home was coming to visit or live in their area would typically be met with great joy. Mama and Papa were each fortunate in having an unmarried sister who came to visit every few years. Aunt Jesse McClure and Aunt Catherine Ross, beloved letter writers and visitors, were vital in maintaining family ties.

Len McClure Comes to Chicken Hill

About the time Mama and Papa settled on their homestead, Mama's brother, Len McClure, came to work in the hayfields around Chicken Hill. Uncle Len was a widower, having lost his wife, Clara, three years earlier, when his daughter, Muriel Merle Dodd McClure, was born. Unable to care for an infant while earning a living, Uncle Len had no choice but to put the baby into foster care. He chose to seek his fortune close to where his sister Helen lived. He acquired a quarter adjacent to Papa's quarter. Mama was fond of her brother and pleased to have him nearby. The two siblings helped each other handle the sad news in the spring of 1919 that their mother had died on her birthday, March 31.

The country was still sparsely settled, and people wanting to socialize had to put some effort into finding friends. Social mores at the time dictated that men had men friends and women had women friends. Furthermore, having grown up with five sisters, Mama especially yearned for female company. Nellie MacKenzie and Lucy Fraser were valued friends, but they lived far enough away that casual get-togethers were rare. When Aunt Jessie came to help when Donnie was born, Mama schemed about finding a husband for her and so keeping her in the community. Papa's friend Tom Passingham, a nice but rather shy neighbour from Ontario, was often at the Ross house. He showed an interest in Aunt Jessie and even drove her to St. Paul when she was leaving. But Aunt Jessie was like some confirmed bachelors, not interested in marriage. Charlie Petersen, another worthy bachelor, showed an interest in her, too, but again, no dice. Jessie simply preferred her work as a domestic in Detroit over marriage.

Aunt Jessie Avoids Marriage

If Aunt Jessie left Alberta thinking homesteading was a precarious business, she was right. Money was always scarce, and there was no insurance for crop failures, accidents, or disease. Mama and Papa were comparatively lucky in that they had both had saved some money when they were in BC, and Papa had some income as a teacher.

Money, however, did not help much when the terrible influenza pandemic of 1918–1919 raged over the world. It was especially hard on strong, young people and caused the death of half of the American soldiers who died in World War I. Estimates of flu deaths worldwide ranged from 20 to 40 million people.

One spring day in 1919 Papa and Tom Passingham were returning by horse and wagon from Vegreville when Tom got so chilly that Papa said, "Here, take my coat." Papa did not realize he and Tom were coming down with the flu. Papa was in bed with the flu for weeks. Mama, who was near the end of a pregnancy, was nearly worn out looking after Papa and her two young children and doing chores inside and outside the house. Miraculously, Papa and Tom survived. So did Mama, and the "baby" she was carrying, which turned out to be twins—Alex and me, born June 26, 1919.

Influenza Pandemic Strikes

Aunt Catherine Helps

Before her twins were born, Mama managed to write a letter to Papa's sister Catherine, telling her about the flu and the sad news of Mama's mother's death. In response, Aunt Catherine wrote the following comforting letter to Mama.

35 Hummewell Ave

Newton, Massachusetts

June 3, 1919

Dear Sister,

I was very glad indeed to get your letter yesterday, but sorry you have been having a rather hard time. I can't imagine how Will pulled through under those circumstances when people who had been attended to right away died by the thousands here. And you between looking after him and the children and everything—in your condition! It is just a miracle.

It makes me cross to hear of Will working in his condition. What good is money if you are not well? If he would rest now, it would make a lot of difference to him in the years to come.

I am so sorry for you in your trouble. It is hard to lose your mother at this time. How nice it would have been if she had been able to visit you this summer, to be with you. You must not worry too much. It will only hurt you and do no good. I know how hard it is to drop it.

Now Helen, I want you to write me as soon as you get this and tell me what you need for the baby. We can buy everything under the sun here readymade, and it would be foolish to try and sew and prepare things when you are not strong. It would please me very much if you would send me a list of things you need. The longer the better, it would suit me. I am crazy about children's things as well as children, and I would enjoy buying things very much. So please write right away. I am going home [to PEI] sometime in July. I have had the brothers' picture enlarged, and I am getting photographs made for you and Florence. I hope to get it all straightened out before I go home.

Florence has no children. She had a stillborn baby. She felt bad to lose it. They escaped the flu. So did I. I cannot tell how, as I was in the midst of it. It was something awful here last fall for a while. Nobody could realize the conditions without seeing them. I wish you could go East this summer while I am home. It would do all of you good, and you would be just as rich in the fall, even if you dropped everything this summer. This life is so short at the longest. People should be careful of their health and enjoy life as much as possible while they are here.

It is too bad Vivian is so far from school, although she is young enough yet. I hope someday I can study bookkeeping and go out West for a trip anyway.

Does baby [Donnie] walk yet? He is such a fat baby. It will take him longer to walk. He must be a dear baby.

It is very hot here. I am living alone here, so I can take it easy when it is too hot. Write soon.

With love,

Catherine

Aunt Catherine's letter must have given Mama solace at that time. In the next few decades, whenever Aunt Catherine came to visit us, she always brought generous and thoughtfully chosen gifts, but she would have been very welcome without them. I have always been pleased that I was given her name. An attractive, likable woman, she was like Aunt Jessie in preferring to remain single. Mama enjoyed Aunt Catherine's company, but she did not consider trying to find a husband for her.

Maple Ridge Store, early 1950s. Aunt Catherine with Diane and Edgar White standing in front.

Crisis at Alex's and My Birth

Mama seemed not to worry about giving birth a third time. Perhaps she was too busy to spend time worrying. Despite being so common, a birth is a dramatic and awe-inspiring event. The story of my birth and that of my brother Alex reveals something of the difficulty and danger of birthing in pioneer times.

Sometime in the early morning of June 26, 1919, Mama told Papa that the baby was coming. Papa hitched a team to a buggy and drove the five miles over to Jim and Lucy Fraser's cabin to ask Lucy to come and help Mama with the birth. Lucy left her warm bed and family to ride back with Papa in the buggy. There she found Mama stoically enduring contractions coming only a few minutes apart. About 8:00 am a good-sized baby boy arrived. Lucy washed him, dressed him in a diaper and gown suitable for the warm June weather and handed him to Mama. Lucy, who was not well herself, then left.

When Papa looked in on Mama, he found her still in some physical distress. He drove his buggy a mile away to the home of other neighbours, the Labines, and asked Mrs. Labine to come and bring her experience to the situation. When Mrs. Labine examined Mama, Papa reported her eyes were "as big as saucers" as she said, "There's another one coming!" In a few more minutes, I had made my entry into the world. Luckily there were a few more diapers and a gown to dress me in. (I later was heir to clothes outgrown by Lucy's two-year-old baby, Douglas.)

My newly born brother had been crying all the while I was getting born, and I soon joined him in crying. Mama tried to nurse us but she had no colostrum and no milk. We two babies cried and cried. Finally, probably worn out, I stopped crying, and my breathing was apparently imperceptible. Mrs. Labine regretfully told Mama, "The little girl is gone." Feeling she could do no more, Mrs. Labine left. And Mama cried.

After some minutes passed, Mama got out of bed to look at her dead baby girl. To her amazement and delight, a little hand moved. Mama found a heartbeat and rejoiced.

But there was still a crisis. Mama had no colostrum or milk. Uncle Len rode over and told Mama that a professional nurse from England, Mrs. Todd, lived not far away and might be able to help. At Uncle Len's urging, Papa hitched a team to the buggy and drove to get Mrs. Todd. She came back with Papa and found a situation she said she had never before encountered: Mama's breasts contained no milk or colostrum. Up to this

Opposite: Chicken Hill, 1919. Exhausted Mama holding newborn twins, me and Alex.

time, Mama had dared only to give us water, fearing that cow's milk might make us sick. Mrs. Todd had brought some barley and set about making barley gruel. She put small spoonsful of it into our mouths and watched as we swallowed it and opened our mouths for more. She put the gruel in baby bottles and watched us suck eagerly on the rubber nipples, which had belonged two-year-old Donnie. At last we were getting food. Mama learned how to make the gruel, and we were on our way.

We thrived. Alex died at age 93, and at 97 I'm still going strong. I still love gruel in its thicker form—porridge.

Mama Schemes a Marriage

After a few months, when Mama had worked out a routine for her three babies and Vivi, she turned her thoughts to her brother Len and his single state. She considered Alice Longley, a teacher from Maine, who taught at Rife School. As it happened, Alice herself was considering Len. While driving her horse and buggy to work one morning, she saw Len working on the land and viewed the widower with great interest. She lived close by with her father, Mr. Longley, and, perhaps with his help, she was introduced to Len. By arranging for Alice and Len to both be at her dinner table, Mama did what she could to help a romance develop. On June 2, 1921, Len and Alice were married. As soon as they could, they went to Saskatchewan to pick up Len's five-year-old daughter, Muriel, and settled into family life on Chicken Hill. Mama and Aunt Alice enjoyed a close friendship for the rest of their lives. For both of them, the friendship defended against loneliness. Alex and I grew up knowing kind Aunt Alice.

Right: Chicken Hill, about 1921. Len with his daughter, Muriel.

CHAPTER 4

Eight Formative Years at Flat Lake

Pullam place at Flat Lake, 1920. Alex and I as toddlers. We were already exploring the wonderful outdoors. We had not yet learned how to put on a smile for a camera.

Leaving Chicken Hill

As a teacher, Papa had not had much opportunity to clear and break the land of his homestead. He decided he wanted a different homestead, one with more fertile land and more cleared land. Mama was not eager to move. She had settled comfortably into the cabin to which she had brought the newborn Vivian and where her other three babies were born. With whitewash and pictures on the walls, she had turned the cabin into a pretty home. But Papa was persuasive, so in the fall of 1919, when we twins were only four or five months old, the family temporarily moved to the Frank Corbett place. It had better buildings for our family's few stock—some cows, sheep, and the four precious horses brought from BC. The Corbett place was available only for the winter, but Papa had plans and means to acquire another place.

Blissful Childhood Days

In the spring of 1920 our family moved to the Pullam place, at Flat Lake, where we were nearer family friends, the MacKenzies. Here Alex and I went through toddlerhood and started school. As soon as we were able to walk, Alex and I began exploring the wonderful world around us. In the spring, even before all the snow had disappeared, we could find crocuses to pick and bring home to Mama. In the summer we found lovely high-bush cranberries growing near the creek banks. Once in a while

Flat Lake, about 1926. Alex and me. A colour photo would have shown bright orange, yellow, and red nasturtiums behind us. Alex has learned to smile a little—but not me.

we would run into delicious dewberries, which we would pick and eat, even though we had to cope with their straw-like cores. Before we would leave a wooded area, we would search for that elusive cud of spruce gum.

Flat Lake picnic, about 1924. Back row, L–R: Hector MacKenzie, Muriel McClure, Vivi Ross. Front row, L–R: Donnie Ross (kneeling), Alex Ross, me, Eileen MacKenzie.

One time when we got home there was a package from Aunt Jessie. In it was a teddy bear for Alex, which I recall he loved immensely. There was probably a gift for me too, but what I remember was the great joy that bear brought to my beloved twin brother.

Finally the time came when Alex and I were old enough to walk, together with Vivi and Donnie, to the exciting place called school. Our teacher at Flat Lake School was Miss Madeleine Ryan, whom we adored. I still remember the song Miss Ryan had me sing at the Christmas concert over 90 years ago:

> Take me back to dear old childhood,
> Where the water lilies grow,
> Where the roses and the wildwood
> Seem to whisper sweet and low.
> I've a heart ache and a longing,
> For the days that used to be.
> Take me back to dear old childhood,
> Which in memory I see.

At that time, I did not know how poignant the words would seem to me now.

A Joyous Mix of Past and Present

Stepping into the present, I must say I feel very fortunate that my chain of friends includes links to Miss Ryan as well as to new, also treasured friends. Miss Ryan became Mrs. Robson Press, and when I became an adult, she was one of my best friends. Now her daughter Eileen and husband, Phil Walker (former city water commissioner), of Edmonton, are among my best friends. At least twice a year we have get-togethers. A most memorable one was on June 12, 2015, when guests included Eileen and Phil; new friends, Patricia and Ian Perry; my daughter, Jean (who had taught high school French to Pat Perry); niece Elaine Doonanco; and Eileen's cousin Brooke Bosefield. We enjoyed lunch at the Neighbourhood Inn followed by an afternoon of singing songs and reciting poetry. My photos are from 2015, but we had a similar party in 2016.

Bonnyville, June 2015. Above, L–R: Ian Perry, Pat Perry, Jean Mottershead, Phil Walker, Eileen Walker, and me. I am hostess. (I have learned to smile).

A Remarkable Coincidence

Returning to the past, I will tell you about a remarkable coincidence at Flat Lake. Because the MacKenzie home was very near the school, teachers usually boarded there. They added an interesting personality to the household, and sometimes a teacher would be involved in some little drama or amazing coincidence, as in the following story. When teacher Miss Gertrude MacKinnon came to board with the MacKenzies, people noted that she was from PEI, which they knew was also Papa's home province. Papa said he did not know anyone by her name. One day, however, when Papa rode his horse into the MacKenzies' yard, Miss MacKinnon looked out the window and said, "Oh my goodness! That looks like Mr. Ross." Nellie MacKenzie replied, "Well, it is Mr. Ross." It turned out that although Papa and the new teacher indeed did not know each other, Miss MacKinnon's sister had "gone out with" John Ross, Papa's youngest brother, killed in the Great War. Obviously John Ross and Papa had strongly resembled each other.

We were at the Pullam place at Flat Lake for eight years, but only a few photos, mainly blurry, were taken there, and they are all in black and white (because colour was not yet available). Even a sharp black-and-white photo could not do justice to my favourite image from Flat Lake. It is of Mama working around her brilliant red, orange, and yellow nasturtiums, such splendid flowers, so intriguing with their fresh fragrance and their edible, peppery petals and tails. Each summer Mama always managed to grow nasturtiums, planted with pea-sized seeds saved the previous fall. Nasturtiums always remind me of Mama, and they are dear to my heart.

Mama's Nasturtiums

There was much more to our lives at Flat Lake than lovely flowers. It was there that Alex and I learned about life. We formed our views of the world there. We learned to laugh and endure being laughed at. We learned about swearing—though not from Mama or Papa. We learned about scary things such as ghosts and sad things such as unintended deaths of lambs. We learned about the joy that music brings. Whether we listened to someone else's music or made our own, music enthralled us. We learned about right and wrong—that setting fire to a haystack is wrong. So is stealing. We also learned that in at least one indigenous culture, taking what you need is not stealing. We learned about the fragility of life and how people have to help each other in order to survive. We learned that a dog can save a life. We learned that some animals provide food and some help with the work. We learned that people have to work hard to earn a living or to manage a household. We also learned about the folly of running away from home.

Learning Experiences

Overall, I think our most important learning during our years at Flat Lake was that life can be full of joy. Part of our joy came from Alberta's beautiful cloudless skies. (Meteorological data report 325 sunny days per year in Edmonton.) Nearly every day Alex and I were out enjoying sunshine, even the cold sunniness of winter. On summer mornings we woke to see poplar leaves that fluttered in the sun and golden fields of barley. On winter evenings we saw the evening star, its steady light gleaming above blue-tinged white snowdrifts. When an occasional cloudy sky put our world in shadow, we were not down-hearted. Clouds sometimes brought thrilling thunderstorms. They also brought welcome

In Sunshine and in Shadow

moisture—in summer, rain for grain and berries; in winter, snow for tobogganing and spring runoff. Enjoying each other's company in sunshine and in shadow, we twins developed cheerful outlooks that served us well in the sunshine and shadow of our future lives.

Caterpillars Embarrass Me

As in most families, some of our experiences turned into amusing little stories that were told over and over again. One such story was at my expense when I was about four years old. I had a terrifying experience when Alex and I went out to explore the world in our bare feet. We were playing around the rocks by the gate to the home of our neighbours, the Rezels, when I suddenly realized something alive and furry was moving on my foot. When I looked down, involuntary screams burst out of my mouth. My screams brought Mama running at top speed down the long lane to rescue me—from harmless caterpillars. I survived the horde of furry larvae that were travelling over my foot, but being the butt of jokes and much laughter, however, shrank my four-year-old ego for at least that afternoon. And I still shudder at the feel of those caterpillars on me.

A Laugh at Papa's Expense

Although Papa enjoyed a laugh at the expense of others, his status in our family was such that he was rarely the source mirth—at least not openly. One time, however, he unintentionally gave us and the neighbours an opportunity to laugh. In the evening, a sound that seemed to signal all was well in our world was Papa's off-key whistling as he did the chores. "Star of the East" and "Back Home Again in Indiana" were among his favourites. One day Mrs. MacKenzie told us about hearing what sounded like a roaring bull in a field close to her house. When she went outside to check on the bull, she realized it was only Papa, a half mile away, rendering in his strong voice the Scottish song, "There's a Wee Hoose 'mongst the Heather." We kids were enormously entertained by Mrs. MacKenzie's story and her advice to Papa to stick to whistling.

Nellie's Hallowe'en Party

Mrs. MacKenzie, or "Nellie," as Mama called her, held parties to brighten the lives of children in the area. At her Hallowe'en party, as we bobbed for apples, our friend Bertha Knapp somehow slipped and broke her ankle. At first Bertha screamed, just as all we kids were capable of doing when in pain. When Bertha switched to cursing, though, she went far beyond our capabilities. She made our jaws drop with string after string of swear words, some of which were familiar to us. But other words were new to us, strange obscenities and blasphemies we had never heard before but which we were trying to store in our memories as fast as we could. Quite soon Bertha was carried out of the house, placed in Stanley MacKenzie's car, and rushed to St. Paul. There Dr. Decosse, a fine pioneer doctor, attended to her. Bertha's ankle healed very well. The Hallowe'en party was not what Nellie had planned, but it became famous in the community. For us kids it was a most memorable event. We relived it dozens of times, sometimes using Papa's huge Webster's dictionary in our attempts to acquire some of Bertha's amazing vocabulary. As news reporters would say, the Hallowe'en story "had legs."

A Heroic Rescue

A heroic story to which I was the only witness happened when Alex and I were out looking for lumps of spruce gum near Dog Rump (also called Dogrum) Creek. The spring runoff had turned the creek into a rushing river. By chance, we had with us a beautiful bluish collie dog called Rex. The dog, who was known for his good looks and love of children, belonged to a nurse, Miss E. Anderson, who ran the Rife Red Cross hospital. (How there came to be a Red Cross hospital in Rife is told in Chapter 5.) Miss Anderson had to be away for a few weeks and had chosen our family to take care of Rex. She knew he'd be happy with the supply of children at our house. Suddenly Alex, who could not swim, slipped off the bank into the cold torrent of the creek. Rex immediately jumped into the water, seized Alex's collar in his teeth and swam hard, towing him to shore. If the dog had not acted as he did, almost certainly Alex would have drowned. Instead, though chilled and shivering, Alex was able to walk home. Rex calmly shook the water out of his coat and walked close to Alex on the path to home. To this day, I marvel at the good luck of having Rex on the scene, preventing unending grief in our family.

Rescue at Dog Rump Creek, spring, 1923. Rex, the collie dog, pulls Alex from the flooded stream. Sketch by Blair.

Ghost Story

At Flat Lake we had a neighbour called Cecil Wakefield, a Welshman who had earned his living as a butcher in England before he immigrated to Canada. Mr. Wakefield tended to squander his time at neighbours' homes, so we saw more of him than any other neighbour. Being accustomed to seeing just blue or green eyes around us, we kids were fascinated by his big brown eyes. When he told ghost stories to us, we were transfixed by his eyes gleaming in the lamplight. As he slowly piled up details, we felt a ghost enter the room. One of his favourite tales was about a woman who had a golden arm, of which she was very proud. Before she died, she specified that the golden arm be buried with her, and her mourners followed her wishes. But someone dug up her grave and stole the golden arm. The woman's voice could be heard crying, "Bring back my golden arm." For years, Alex and I were afraid to walk by a graveyard at night.

Docking Lambs' Tails—Badly

Mr. Wakefield was unintentionally responsible for a disaster for our family. He was a somewhat rough-and-ready type of person. Papa had a little flock of sheep, and after the lambs were a few days old, their long tails were always cut off. (I still don't know why.) The cuts had to be made at the proper slant. One day, two lovely male lambs were innocently lying on their straw when Wakefield came along, grabbed them and slashed their tails off the wrong way. The mistake caused the lambs to shiver to death. The financial loss was hard for our parents to bear, as they needed every available dollar. They also felt sorry that the little lambs' lives were so short and had ended with suffering. Despite this unfortunate incident, Wakefield remained a welcome friend. In later years, when word came that his daughter was employed as a translator during World War II, we rejoiced at her achievement.

A Lethal Treatment

There was another unfortunate incident in the sheep fold, this one the result of ignorant misinformation or inexpert use of legitimate information—probably the former. Someone told Papa that administering iodine to pregnant ewes would prevent goitre. What the iodine did, as Papa had administered it, was kill the unborn lambs. Fortunately the ewes survived, but the loss of the lambs was a serious setback.

Besides hard work and setbacks, pioneer life had many sources of joy. For the Rosses, music was one such source. Realizing that Vivi was keen to learn a musical instrument, Mama and Papa decided that our home should have a piano. In St. Paul, Georges L'Heureux, editor of the *St. Paul Journal,* sold Mason and Risch upright pianos. He was willing to sell a piano on credit to customers who came with a substantial down payment. Papa ordered a piano, and Vivi and Mama began counting the days until it would arrive. Finally, one dark winter evening, we heard harness jingling and sleigh runners squeaking on the snow. We heard men's voices and then a knock on the door. A voice called, "We've brought your piano." Papa opened the door wide and went out into the dark to help the men bring the crated and blanketed piano into our home. Mama, Papa, and Vivi were bubbling with excitement, but my shrieking and jumping around soon made them realize that a four-year-old could be just as excited as they were. I was thrilled when Papa set me on the piano bench and I touched the keys. Now, more than 90 years later, the fascination remains. Through his generous entrepreneurship, Mr. L'Heureux provided pianos and the gift of music to many people in a large swath of northeastern Alberta, and I am happy to pay tribute to him.

The Ross family welcomed into their home anyone who could make music or simply loved music. Mr. Wakefield was one of the latter. He would often ask Mama to play one of his favourite songs on the piano. Being a Welshman, he would request "Men of Harlech," and sometimes, with a sheepish grin, he would ask for "The Hundred Pipers." It was a song that Papa also relished, especially if there was an Englishman around to be irked by it. Although they were in a new country, Celts were not likely to completely forget antagonisms of the old country. They gloried in the song's triumphant lyrics, suggesting that a hundred Celts blowing on their bagpipes had dumbfounded and defeated an English army, which ran away.

> Dumfoun'er'd the English saw, they saw
> Dumfoun'er'd they heard the blaw, the blaw
> Dumfoun'er'd they a' ran awa', awa'
> Frae the hundred pipers an' a', an' a'.

Sometimes the music was in neighbours' homes. On one occasion Mama and Papa took me to the home of Mr. and Mrs. Dunstan Smith. Mr. Smith stood at the organ, singing while playing "I Love a Lassie." His deep bass made a lasting impression on me.

Jigs from the Fields

Sometimes the music came from the fields. Papa employed Indians (as Indigenous people were called in those days) to do "brushing," the first step in clearing land. When he heard that one of the Indians had brought a violin with him, Papa invited the man, Adam Mountain, to come to our house to play his violin. Adam's music reminded Papa of the fiddling he had heard on Prince Edward Island when he was growing up. For us kids, it was an introduction to a very vigorous and fascinating kind of violin music. Our great favourite was Adam's "The Red River Jig."

A Lesson about Stealing

Also fascinating to us kids were the teepees that the Indians put up in Papa's fields. Our curiosity got the better of Alex and me, and one day when all the Indians seemed to be away from the teepees, we two brats invaded. We found a tobacco can filled with beautiful blue, red, and yellow needles, such an amazing curiosity that we felt we had to take it home with us. When we showed our loot to Mama, she told us that the needles were porcupine quills the Indians had dyed. They used the coloured quills to do beautiful embroidery on clothing such as buckskin jackets and moccasins.

Then Mama's voice got stern. She said what we had done was stealing and sent us back to the teepees to return the tobacco can of quills. When we got there, we were dismayed to find people in the tents. With our guilty heads down, we went to the opening of the tent from which we had taken the can.

When the old grandmother who was near the entrance saw what Alex had in his hand, she gave us a toothless smile, nodded and held out her hand. She said something in Cree that we did not understand, but the tone told us everything was all right. We later learned that in Cree culture it was okay to enter another person's home and take whatever one needed. Locking doors to keep people out of a house was the offense. In our case, however, we did not need the porcupine quills, and we had no right to take them.

Left: Flat Lake about 1923. We twins return a stolen can of coloured quills. Sketch by Blair.

About this time I committed another offense—one that no culture would condone. One day when I was about four I was left at home with Alex, Donnie, and Vivi while our parents were away for the day. Tommy Brennan, a bachelor friend of my parents, showed up at our place. He insisted on calling me "Kay." He was amused when he saw I did not like that name, and he started using it in nearly every sentence. Finally my frustration turned to rage. I grabbed the poker and ran after him. Someone disarmed me, and I ran off crying. I am still ashamed of my behaviour that day. But the incident should have been a lesson for Tommy that amusing oneself by teasing children is reprehensible.

A Bad Reaction to Teasing

Left: I react badly to teasing. Sketch by Blair.

People who had migrated from one end of the country to the other typically had an extra burden of grief when a loved one at home died. There were no tender deathbed scenes to remember. A letter carrying the sad news was all they had by way of a celebration of life. When Grandmother McClure died, just before Alex and I were born, Mama was sad that she was not able to be with her mother in her final days. She treasured the last letter her mother had written to her, and eventually I read it too, with its poignant sentence: "I dearly wish I could see you again." My grandmother's wish was never granted.

Grandmother McClure Dies

Happily, in 1923, when Alex and I were four years old, Grandfather McClure found the time and means to visit our family. He was a kind man, and his visit must have allayed some of the sadness in Mama's heart. I was young and stored away only two of his comments in my memory. On seeing Mama come in from milking five cows and carrying heavy milk pails down a long lane, he warned, "You'll kill yourself, Helen." Mama had to assure me his prediction would not come true. Grandpa McClure seemed to fancy Alex, whom he called a "fine chap." I was glad to hear my beloved twin described this way. Now, as an adult, I wonder whether our kind old grandfather was compensating for Papa's favouring of Donnie.

Grandfather McClure Visits

Flat Lake, summer 1923. Grandfather McClure in sheep pasture with Ross kids. L–R: me, Vivi, Donnie, Grandfather, with hand on Alex.

Coping with Health Crises

In times of crisis, survival often depended on help from neighbours or family members. In 1924, a neighbour, Charlie Petersen, was the Good Samaritan when Alex and Vivi came down with sore throats and a dangerously high fever. Papa rode to Charlie's house and asked for help. Charlie immediately started his car and drove over to our place, where the sick kids were loaded into his car. He sped them to Elk Point, where Dr. Ross made the fearsome diagnosis—diphtheria. The doctor treated them against the disease, and they soon recovered.

At this point, I must pay tribute to Dr. Ross and Dr. Miller. With their compassion and professional competence they performed heroically for many years in Elk Point. Many people had longer lifespans because of these two doctors.

Another crisis for our family came the next year, 1925. Mama had to go to Edmonton for a hysterectomy. During her two-week stay in hospital, the family member who took care of the three younger children and managed the cooking and cleaning was none other than our sister, Vivi. She was a competent 12-year-old, and we fared very well. We had a special treat when Aunt Alice came to visit and see how we were doing. Aunt Alice brought an iced cake sprinkled with tiny coloured candies. How beautiful that cake looked to us! How delicious it tasted!

A few days later Mama came home. How happy we were to see her again! How blue her eyes looked! At the time Louis Fedorus was our young and smiley hired man. He kindly told us not to make noise because, as he said, "Your mother is sick." Soon Mama was ready to play piano as Louis accompanied her on his violin, playing pieces such as "Snow Deer" and "Red Wing."

Aunt Jessie Arrives

About two years after Mama's operation we got word that Aunt Jessie was coming again for a visit with us and with Uncle Len, her brother, and Aunt Alice. On the appointed day, Alex and I went down to the gate at the end of our long lane to wait eagerly for the mail truck to come. At last the truck came and Aunt Jessie jumped out of it. She immediately took a pear out of her pocket, and Alex and I set about sharing the sweetest pear we had ever eaten.

Threshing Time Excitement

After a few days with us, Aunt Jessie was driven over to Uncle Len's house to stay for a few days. It happened to be threshing time, harvest time, the most exciting time of the year. To each farm on their schedule, crews of men came with a threshing machine and teams of horses hitched to wagons with hayracks on them. The hayracks were loaded with bundles of wheat or other grain and driven to the threshing machine. A long continuous belt stretched from a pulley on a tractor to a pulley on the threshing machine. When the belt moved, it produced a flurry of action in the threshing machine. Most spectacular was the action at the end of the conveyor belt, which carried bundles up to the intake place, where claw-like blades chopped ferociously at them. There was the big pipe that blew yellow stems and leaves into huge piles of clean and valuable straw, used mainly as bedding for animals. There was the smaller pipe out of which a light but steady stream of kernels dribbled into a waiting wagon box. There was the roar of the tractor and the rattle of the threshing machine. There was the clean smell of chaff in the air and the pungent but good smell of sweaty horses. From the wagon boxes the precious kernels were shovelled into wooden granaries to be stored for use as food for people and animals and for seeding next spring. Some of the grain would be taken to an elevator and sold for cash.

A Woman's Role at Threshing Time

Harvest time was a busy time not just for the threshing crews. Women had the task of preparing huge amounts of meat and mashed potatoes, vegetables and pies for the hungry men. Three times a day the women washed cutlery and tall stacks of plates, saucers, and cups. No one had hot running water, so the metal dishpan often was put on a moderately hot part of the cook stove to keep the dishwater warm. Menus had to be carefully planned in advance, and all provisions had to be on hand. After the men had gone to their sleeping places, the weary woman's last task at night would be to lay the table for breakfast in the morning. She would be up as early as four in the morning, ahead of the men, to cook breakfasts of porridge, pancakes, eggs, and bacon. Having another woman to help with the cooking was almost a necessity, so it was kind of Aunt Jessie to offer to help Aunt Alice in the house during threshing time.

A Preposterous Plan

On a remote farm, a threshing crew might need to be lodged in the farmhouse or a hayloft. The McClure home was one such place. It had a large living room/dining room, where several men from the threshing crew were slated to sleep. It also had one bedroom, where Aunt Alice and Uncle Len slept. Aunt Alice suggested Aunt Jessie sleep in the living room. Aunt Jessie was outraged! Uncle Len made a firm decision on the side of his sister. In the end, the two women slept together in the double bed in the bedroom, no doubt as far apart as they could be without falling out of bed.

To this day no one can explain the behaviour of Aunt Alice, normally a kind and thoughtful woman. Some have suggested she simply was not worldly enough to realize the impropriety of her planned arrangement. Nowadays some of the younger generation would wonder what Jessie's problem was.

Runaway Kids

As soon as the threshing was over, Aunt Jessie came back to our place. Unfortunately she had to contend with strange behaviour there—mine and Alex's. I cannot remember exactly what prompted us to set out to see the wide world, but that's what Alex and I did. We had only got halfway to the Knapps' when who should pull up but the infamous master of profanity himself, George Knapp. (He was father of Bertha Knapp, who had given us the demonstration of swearing at Mrs. MacKenzie's Hallowe'en party.) He stopped his horse and asked us where we were going. He soon realized what we were up to. He asked why we were running away and we replied,

Left: Flat Lake about 1926. L–R: Alex and me. I show off "the biggest mushroom in the world."

"They are too mean to us. Aunt Jessie is too bossy." He told us to get into his buggy. Alex hopped in readily, but I hung back. George reported to Mama, "The little woman didn't want to get in." I then suddenly felt that we had been little ingrates in attempting to run away—especially "the little woman." How that description of bothered me! It made me want to stay with good people like Mama and Aunt Jessie and just be a child for a while longer before I ventured into the wide world.

Prospering By Hiring Men

During our time at Flat Lake, Papa made his property more valuable by hiring men to clear more land. His objective was to sell the Flat Lake place for enough money to buy more land with a better house on it. Perhaps his most highly regarded hired man for clearing land was Carlson Tollefson. Alex and I liked Carlson too, especially for the way he always greeted us kids with kind words and a smile. He was one of the newcomers who worked for a while as hired men and eventually went on to either file on their own homestead or start a business. In Tollefson's case, it was a successful boat rental and fishing enterprise on the west shore of Moose Lake.

The Lure of Rife

Papa was also looking in the direction of Moose Lake, in particular toward Rife. A newly named community about a dozen miles to the east of Flat Lake, Rife had attracted some outstanding new settlers. Much of the land there was more fertile than what Papa had on the Pullam place. And word was that killing frosts came later in the fall there. Our time in Flat Lake was about to end.

CHAPTER 5

A Brief History of Rife (1908 to the Present)

Eastbourne Hall, 2015.

As a place for socializing, Eastbourne Hall, built in 1940, was comparatively late to arrive. It was the result of cooperative efforts of people in three school districts: Rife, Hoselaw, and Moose Lake. It was given a new, distinctive name and became a vital part of all three communities. It remains thus in 2017. Because of its great success in the community, I chose it to begin this chapter, rather than the older and also important United Church.

During the 1930s, Rife had earned the nickname "Holy Trinity" because of its three churches, United, Anglican, and Catholic. This abundance was probably not so much the result of intense religiosity in the community but more the result of competitiveness among influential people with differing views of propriety. The United Church, built about 1932, is Rife's only remaining church. For many years Olive Ross kept the floor clean and the pews dusted. It is still well kept but rarely used.

A Dream Come True

By the end of 1927, Papa had found the place to expand his farming—the recently named community of Rife. Rife's fertile land, gentle hills, broad valleys, and sparkling lakes had long appealed to him. When he heard that Harold Armstrong's house and land in Rife were for sale, he jumped at the opportunity. When Mama saw the Armstrong house, she readily agreed to uproot the family and move. What neither Mama nor Papa had anticipated was the liveliness and progressiveness of the community they were joining. Several Rife citizens had earned a reputation for entrepreneurship. They had visions of what they wanted in a community and the money, energy, and experience to realize their ambitions. Rife was indeed an alluring destination for the Rosses.

Unstoppable Change

With the hindsight of old age, I can tell you that when the Ross family arrived there in 1928, Rife had reached the zenith of its glory days. Change was coming fast. People who had a car or a truck could go to town for supplies and no longer needed a store just a buggy ride away. Farmers with tractors could farm more land, so they began to amass quarters, even whole sections, buying out their neighbours. Inevitably farm populations began to dwindle. Farm houses and barns, stores and livery stations were abandoned and slowly decayed. Only larger towns with a railroad running through them were likely to survive. Rife had no railroad. Eventually railroads were also abandoned, once an unthinkable possibility. Change is inescapable, and, from what I've seen, it is largely unpredictable. Although the name "Rife" has all but disappeared, a vibrant community remains. In this chapter, I tell you about the rise and fall of Rife and how the community flourishes today.

An Outstanding Leader

Maurice Destrube, who arrived in 1908, was probably the most important early settler in the area later known as Rife. He was not the only successful entrepreneur to come to Rife, but his story, both triumphant and tragic, is compelling and inspiring. His book, *Pioneering in Alberta: Maurice Destrube's Story*, was published in 1981 by the Historical Society of Alberta. With his drive, intelligence, and high principles, Maurice prospered and contributed greatly to the community. Much of his pioneering work was done before the Ross family moved to Rife and before I was born, but when my husband and I came to know him in his later years, we felt honoured by his friendship.

Born in England to a French father and English mother, Maurice was raised in London, where his father was a wealthy banker. Enticed by posters advertising free homesteads of 160 acres of fertile farmland in Alberta, Maurice left his promising job in the bank to adventure in the new world. He had decided to try his hand at farming and gained experience by working on the farm of his uncle, his mother's brother, in Missouri. By 1908 he was ready to file on a homestead in Alberta and for that purpose travelled to Edmonton. He chose a quarter in the most picturesque valley of the area. A small river, with various names—Bangs, Valley, Thin, and Tyne—ran through the valley's broad floor.

Three Brothers Arrive

Soon two of Maurice's bothers, Guy and Georges, joined Maurice and filed on nearby homesteads. A fourth brother, Paul, settled in Edmonton to work in a bank. The three homesteading brothers chose their land carefully, securing fertile quarters near each other. They quickly met the requirements for "proving up" homesteads and so were entitled to file on additional homesteads in the area. The three adventurous brothers cooperated with each other, planned carefully, and worked hard. After a few years they together owned 12 valuable quarters of land and a herd of cattle. They lived well-rounded lives, scheduling time for recreations such as swimming, tennis, and snowshoeing. They also took time to socialize with people living nearby, natives and settlers, and had some connections with officials in Edmonton.

When he was in Missouri learning about farming, Maurice had met beautiful Maggie LeBow, with whom he corresponded while he established a home at Rife. When he was ready, he proposed and she accepted. The couple were married in Missouri in 1909 and resided for five years in the little sod-roofed cabin Maurice and Guy had built.

By 1910 the Destrube brothers, along with Maurice's wife, Maggie, recognized a need in the community and began bringing in essential items for sale. After a while they established the Destrube Bros. Trading Post. It flourished, providing quality products for hundreds of customers until 1936.

Through astute business practices and hard work, the Destrube brothers prospered at whatever ventures they chose. However, it would be a mistake to think they had no hurdles to overcome. In 1913 a man calling himself Sam Eldridge filed on a quarter section two miles from the Destrube Trading Post. He boasted that he, in partnership with a local man, would build a store to put the Trading Post out of business. These two men set about building their competing store. As the store went up, terrible things started happening to the Destrubes. First their two beloved collie dogs died of what the veterinarian said was strychnine poisoning. Then their store was broken into and robbed. Then several of their horses died mysteriously; the government analyst found arsenic in their stomachs. Then one autumn night all the Destrubes' haystacks, except for one near their buildings, were set on fire. Without hay, the brothers had to sell nearly all of their cattle. Other people complained that Eldridge stole furs from their traplines and valuables from their homes

At first the St. Paul police were unable to lay charges. Then Georges Destrube told the Alberta Attorney General, a friend of the family, about their troubles. The ensuing investigation found stolen items in Eldridge's cabin and evidence that the name "Sam Eldridge" was in fact a stolen identity. The culprit was actually Jim Henderson, an American outlaw. When police attempted to apprehend him, there was a scuffle in which Henderson was wounded. He died on the way to the hospital in St. Paul. As far as I know, Henderson was the only completely nefarious person ever to come to Rife.

Marriage and Entrepreneurship

A Vicious Enemy

An Architectural Treasure

After living for five years in a sod-roofed cabin, the Destrubes decided it was time for more spacious housing. Georges, trained as an artist and architect, drew up plans for a stately two-storey house built of hewn logs. By 1914 the brothers had completed the house, and for a brief and joyful time Maurice and Maggie, Guy, George, and their older sister, Sylvie, lived together in the beautiful new house.

St. Paul Alberta, 2011. The Destrube house during restoration. The house was designed by Georges Destrube and built in 1914.

About 1977 Esther Sandmeyer suggested the Destrube house be designated a historic site. It was painstakingly restored by the St. Paul Historical Society and is now part of the St. Paul Museum.

With the outbreak of war in 1914, Paul, Guy, and Georges enlisted. Maurice, who wanted to go with them, was persuaded by his father to stay at home to keep the trading post going and give his brothers a place to return to. He promised to share whatever profits he made with his brothers when they returned. He formed a partnership with Arthur Kennedy, his cousin from Missouri, who was by then married to Maggie's sister, Nora. The Kennedy family arrived in 1916, with two little daughters, Margaret and Esther. The partnership was productive, increasing the ranch from 800 to 2000 acres and the cattle herd from 60 to 400 by the time the war ended.

War Breaks Out

The arrival of the two little Kennedy girls inspired Maurice to call together interested community members to organize the first school district at Rife, with trustees, a secretary-treasurer and a teacher, Miss Margaret Chamberlain. The school, situated at the Rife crossroads, had the minimum required five pupils.

Establishing a School

Although life was going well in Rife, worry about loved ones at war hung over the community. As it took the lives of men in the trenches, World War I destroyed hope and happiness at home. Guy and Paul were killed, and Georges was gassed and impaired for life. In Flat Lake, Papa and Mama mourned the loss of Papa's two brothers, Dan and John.

The Scourge of War

For Maurice, the war's terrible toll was not the only tragedy. In 1918 his beloved wife, Maggie, died in childbirth, along with their infant daughter. No wonder in Maurice's book, the chapter telling about these losses is called "Armageddon."

Death in Childbirth

Despite the devastation caused by his losses, Maurice was not yet finished contributing to the Rife community. As before, he did not work alone. His sister introduced him to a friend of hers, Pevensey Wheeler. Pem, as she was called, had been the matron of a hospital in England and was a very capable, community-minded person. In 1921 Maurice and Pem were married. Pem had a philanthropic bent and energy to match her husband's. Together the couple made things happen.

A Second Marriage

A Hospital and a Church

Pem used her influence and fundraising efforts to get a Red Cross hospital built in 1924 on the west slope of Rife Valley. In 1936, with labour input from Maurice, she also had the small but charming St. John's Anglican Church built at Rife corner, three miles east of the hospital. She also funded the building of a large white house, which she described as a "Swiss chalet," for Maurice and herself on the west bank of Rife Valley. It was the first house in the community with indoor plumbing. Pem and Maurice lived there happily for 25 years.

Later the Arthur Kennedy and Oliver Sandmeyer families made it their home, and Cathie and Frank Sandmeyer live there now, 2017.

Moving the Red Cross Hospital and Kitchen

Pem Destrube's newsworthy achievement—a hospital in pioneer country—was known throughout many communities. However, the hospital did not exist for long, abandoned in 1928, probably because of progress in Bonnyville in the form of Duclos Hospital. The main part of the Rife hospital was moved and used as a house on property homesteaded by Georges Destrube. Some years later my husband bought that property.

Eventually two of our sons owned the land and used the hospital building as a grainery. Finally, wanting to use the land where the building stood, they burned the building down.

The kitchen that had served the Red Cross hospital was a small log building. It was moved to another quarter belonging to Maurice Destrube and turned into a one-bedroom cabin. Surprisingly, the small log structure was more challenging to move than the lumber-framed Red Cross hospital.

Dutch Smith was the teamster who moved the kitchen. He was reported to have used 32 horses in tandem on the move. My guess is that he did not use all 32 horses at once but instead harnessed them in teams of 8 or 16 to take turns at pulling the heavy load.

The former kitchen was the rented home to which my husband and I brought our first-born baby, Catherine Jean. After

Danny in front of the Red Cross kitchen, about 1980.

about a year there, we bought our own farm, the Jones place, with a bigger house. The cabin then served another family, the Duncans, for many years. When our farmer sons bought that property, they put a match to the cabin in order to use the land on which it stood.

We were pleased to be able to buy the "Jones place" with its well-built barns and house. The Jones had come in 1914 from Pennsylvania to farm at Rife.

Opposite: *Rife, 1982. Despite the dilapidated state of the Red Cross hospital, our sons were sentimental enough to take a photo of it before burning it.*

Jones place at Rife, December 24, 1943. Jean, 3 years old, steadies Mack, 20 months old.

Fate of Rife's Churches

Only a small graveyard remains where St. John's Anglican Church once stood. The Anglican church, the product of great effort by Maurice and Pem Destrube, Jack and Dorothy Browning, and a few others, was moved in one piece to St. Paul. Set among the poplars, this graceful building was beautiful. It still looks graceful in its urban setting.

Left: St. John's Anglican Church at Rife, about 1935. Photo from M. Destrube's book, Pioneering in Alberta, *and reprinted with permission. Set among the poplars, this graceful building was enchanting.*

Below: The Rife United Church still stands. Photo by Mack Smith, 2016.

Similarly, St. Ann's Roman Catholic Church, which had been built primarily through the efforts of Georges Destrube's wife, Suzanne, ended up in Bonnyville. It had originally perched on a hill a mile east of Rife corner. Now located next to Bonny Lodge, it is used as a chapel.

Although the Rife United Church is intact and well kept, it is rarely used.

Other Influential People

The Destrubes had more influence on the community of Rife than any other family, but a number of other prominent people also settled in Rife. A discussion of their lives is beyond the scope of my memoir. At this point, however, I will mention a few people who made a difference to my life.

Mrs. Evelyn Thurston gave Rife School a library, which enriched my school years. She also donated generously to the building of Eastbourne Hall, earning the privilege of naming the hall after her home in England.

Canon Browning instigated building of the Rife United Church, which I attended and which still stands, its graveyard still in business and still has resting places for a few more people. When Canon Browning came to live with his son and daughter-in-law, Jack and Dorothy Browning, the spacious "Canon room" was added to the house to accommodate him. The Brownings were our friends and next-door neighbours when I was growing up, and later my husband and I and our family lived for many years in the "Browning house." I often had to explain to visitors that what they heard as the "Cannon room" was not the place where we stored our big gun, only the place where an Anglican church official, a Canon, had lived.

Browning house, Thanksgiving, 1989. After the Thanksgiving feast, men retire to the Canon room for coffee and cake while women clean up the kitchen, which they messed up while cooking the feast. L–R: Danny Smith, Alex Ross, Donnie Ross, Allan Ross, Don Mottershead.

The Hills, Lloyd and Frances, are next on my list of prominent people from Rife. Lloyd came from a family that manufactured pipe organs in London, but he left England to homestead in Alberta. He met and married my friend Frances Hillary. After a few years of farming at Rife, Lloyd and Frances moved their growing family to BC, where they bought a store and post office. We kept in touch through visits and letters, and I saw that Frances was far more than the kind and energetic farm wife I already knew and liked. Her business acumen was astounding. We expect the story of how Frances came out of the woods and built her chain of seven "Hill's Native Art" stores will be told in another publication.

Why Didn't Rife Thrive?

Considering all the clever and industrious people who established businesses and amenities in the Rife area, some have wondered why Rife never became a town. Others point to the fact that the railway passed through Franchere instead of Rife as part of the reason that Rife shrank rather than grew. (On the other hand, Franchere did not grow much, either.) Now all that remains at Rife corner is the little white United Church (photo on page 59), with its surrounding graveyard.

Funded at first by Canon Browning's former parish in England, this church was expected to be Anglican. That plan went awry, and the dedication was to the United Church. In 1931 Evalyn Jones and Leslie Knapp were the first couple to be married in it.

Disappeared Buildings

While the United Church has remained and Eastbourne Hall and resort are thriving, other pioneer establishments have vanished. Three buildings—St. Ann's and St. John's Churches and George Destrube's house—are preserved in other locations, but the following have disappeared, going from west to east on Highway 28A:

    Red Cross hospital
    Turcotte Livery Barn
    Destrube Bros. Trading Post and house
    Rife Post Office at Boyd's General Store
    Aylesworth Livery Barn and Stopping House
    Rife Post Office (at Aylesworth's)
    Rife School, for grades one to eight
    Corbett's General Store

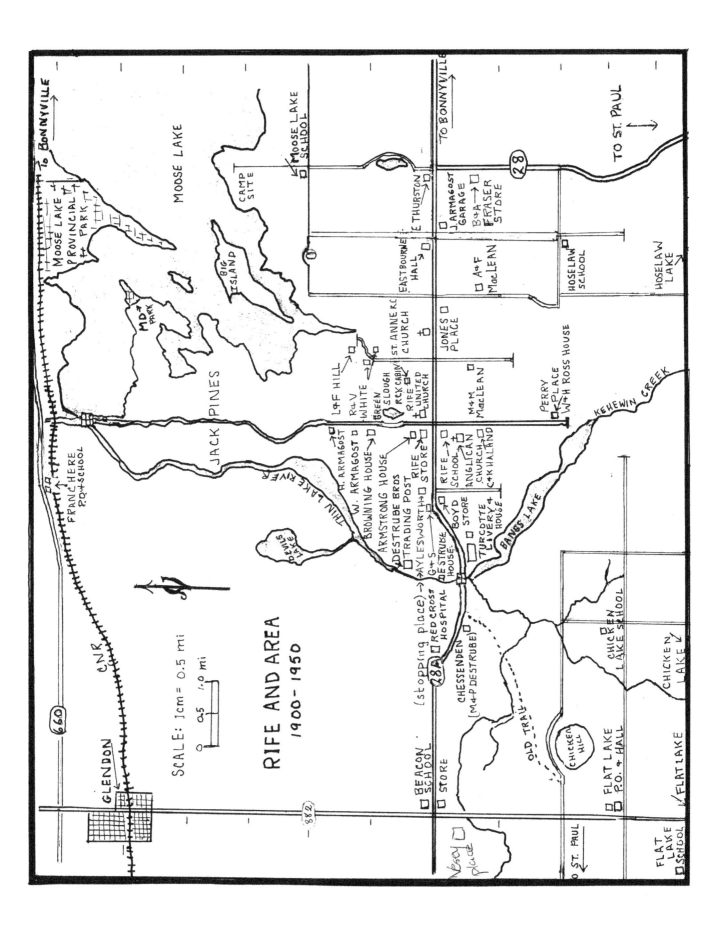

RIFE AND AREA
1900-1950

SCALE: 1cm = 0.5 mi

0   0.5   1.0 mi

Hoselaw School
Jarles Armagost's Garage
Moose Lake School
Fraser Store
Modern Eastbourne Community

Opposite: Map of *Rife and area, between 1900 and 1950.*

It's a very different story for Eastbourne Hall, four miles to the east of Rife corner. Built in 1940, the hall survives and expands, thanks to community spirit and cooperation among descendants of original pioneers and newcomers to the area. It is a popular centre for wedding receptions, dances, and other events, an example being the recent (summer of 2015) celebration of the hall's 75th year as the heart of the community. A few miles to the north, in conjunction with Eastbourne Hall, on the shore of Moose Lake, people from the community of Rife and other districts have built a lovely semi-private resort. The resort includes generous camping spaces, ball diamonds, bleachers, playgrounds, a tennis court, washrooms, and a building for concessions and for meetings and other gatherings. Both the hall and the lakeshore property are managed and maintained by hard-working Hall Committee members, including several Smiths and Rosses.

People in my age group often regret change and long for the adventure and neighbourliness of pioneer times. But the forces of change can seldom be resisted. Mechanized farming has enabled a successful farmer to handle greater and greater stretches of land. Mechanized travel eliminated the need for little schools and little stores scattered about the countryside.

Hoping for Constructive Change

Future change, whether for better or worse, is inevitable. I do not expect to live long enough to see how the world changes in response to degradation of the environment. I recall the landscape I grew up in, with its abundance of trees, wild berries, game, and song birds. Nowadays I seldom see a red-winged blackbird and never an oriole. On TV I hear about oceanic gyres of plastic—what we thought were harmless bags and bottles—that never decompose, remaining forever to damage sea life. I worry about the environment that my great-grandchildren and one little great-great-granddaughter will have. I hope our leaders learn from the past. I hope the changes that come undo some of the damage already done to the planet.

Present Everyday Life

I will now use photos, mostly of Smith family members, to show how pleasantly life goes on in the Rife area today, specifically in the Eastbourne Community. The first sets of photos are from the campground/resort called Eastbourne Ball Diamonds. ("Smith" surname is usually omitted in photo captions.)

Lorene Lay-McCaig, Samantha, and LeeAnn in a hard-fought bean bag game.

Top: *Blair Mottershead, me, Jeff Mottershead. My grandsons enjoy dwarfing me.*
Bottom: *Janet and Rick enjoy doing dishes at camp.*

Moose Lake, 2003. Danny's 90th birthday celebration—waiting for supper.

Top: *L–R: Janet; Mikayla, Jeff and Jayden Weeks; Mack; Danny.*

Centre: *L–R: Rick, Jeff Mottershead, Iva Cheung, me, Blair Mottershead.*

Bottom: *L–R: me, Blair Mottershead, Diane, Denise Charawich, Danielle Smith-Weeks.*

Left: Moose Lake, 2003. Supper time. L–R: Tom Charawich, Lorene Lay-McCaig, me, Danny.

Moose Lake, 2014.

Left, centre: Vern "Didi" Vachon gets breakfast ready; Terry gets smoked.

Left: Enjoying the peace of the lake. R–L: Jeff Mottershead, Iva Cheung, Janet.

Top: *Moose Lake, July 2014. Cousins with same Ross–McClure great-great-grandparents. L–R: Morgan Gillis, Brooklyn Vachon, Devlin Mottershead, Lachlan Gillis, Jerzey Vachon.*

Centre: *Moose Lake, July 2014. Warming up after a swim by playing cards in the sun. L–R: Jerzey Vachon, Lachlan Gillis, Devlin Mottershead, Morgan Gillis, Brooklyn Vachon.*

Bottom: *Moose Lake, about 1995. An earlier generation warms up after a swim. L–R: Denise, Jonathan Ross, LeeAnn, Janet, Jeff Mottershead, me.*

Samantha and Brian's Wedding

I want to tell you about a unique and joyful Eastbourne wedding, partly to reveal the charm of the community and partly to introduce some of my descendants. In the spring of 2015, Samantha Smith, Richard and Janet's eldest granddaughter, and her partner, Brian Mare, sent out invitations to a "Red Neck Wedding." The wedding took place outdoors on June 13 at the Eastbourne ball diamond where Samantha and Brian first set eyes on each other. All members of the wedding party wore cowboy boots, including the bride, resplendent in a beautiful long white gown. The flower girl, Kaylee Mare, not quite two years old, daughter of the bride and groom, also wore cowboy boots—tiny pink ones.

An intermittent light rain did not deter the wedding party from holding the ceremony as planned, under the flower-bedecked arbour at home plate. Most of the 200 invited guests attended, cheerfully wiping off the wet benches which had been set up on either side of a broad, grassy aisle. As the ring bearers, Brooklyn and Jerzey Vachon, led Kaylee to the arbour where the groom waited, the little flower girl called out joyfully, "Dad," and ran to wrap her arms around her father's legs. When a friendly stray dog appeared, however, she single-mindedly pursued it, much to the delight of the seated guests. After the bridesmaids and groomsmen were in place, the bride's father, Terry, walked down the aisle with Samantha on his arm. The bride's grandmother, Sandra Salzl, a marriage commissioner, performed the wedding ceremony. After the ceremony, everyone gathered at Eastbourne Hall for a reception and dance.

Prior to the wedding, Sid and Shirley's daughter Kim, along with her husband, Ray Parenteau, held a luncheon for Kim's parents; her sister, Heather, and family; members of the bride's family who were free to attend; and guests from BC. The BC guests included Vivi's daughter Lynne, her husband, Bob Sutherland, and my daughter, Jean Mottershead, the bride's great-aunt.

The photos on the next pages show more than my words can tell.

Above: *Kim Parenteau's home, June 13, 2015. Guests at a luncheon before Samantha's wedding. L–R: Heather Hebert, Shirley Smith, Hostess Kim, Bob Sutherland.*

Right: *Eastbourne Ball Diamond, June 13, 2015. L–R: Guitarist Dylan Hansen, Courtney Nicholson.*

Left: Guests at the wedding: Lorene Lay-McCaig, Janet, me, Kyd.

Below: More wedding guests. Back row, R–L: Heather Hebert, Ray Parenteau, Great-Grandpa Rick Smith. Front row, R–L: Terry, Marci, Kyd, Vern Vachon, Kim Parenteau, LeeAnn Vachon, Halle Hebert, Macie Parenteau, Shirley, and Sid. Front: Kaylee Mare.

Above: *Groom, Brian Mare, and marriage commissioner Sandra Salzl waiting for the bride. All is ready for the wedding. The rugged altar is decorated, and the carpet is in place. The plastic cover will be lifted off the table to provide a dry surface for signing the marriage documents.*

Opposite, top: *Ring bearers Jerzey (left) and Brooklyn (right) Vachon escorting flower girl Kaylee Mare (centre) to the altar. Kaylee has just caught sight of her dad and is calling out to him.*

Opposite, bottom: *Anson Smith taking time from hockey to attend his sister's wedding. He gives his little niece, Kaylee, a warm, secure place from which to watch the wedding. Guitarist Dylan Hansen looks on.*

Left: *Terry with his daughter, Samantha, on his arm.*

Above: *The wedding. L–R: three bridesmaids; maid of honour, Courtney Nicholson; marriage commissioner, Sandra Salzl; the bride, Samantha Smith; the groom, Brian Mare; best man, Steve Mare, peeking over his brother's shoulder; three groomsmen behind; Brooklyn and Jerzey Vachon. Relaxation and fun to follow.*

Above: *Eastbourne Hall, 7:00 pm, June 13, 2015. Wedding reception and dance. Above, L–R: Courtney Nicholson, Samantha and Brian Mare; Steve Mare. (Beautiful smiles!)*

Right: *Terry and Marci Smith with their son, super emcee, Kyd Daniel Smith.*

CHAPTER 6

‹——·——›

My Decade at
the Armstrong Place

Armstrong house at Rife, Christmas, 1939. Vivi and Ray White proudly presenting William Raymond Edgar White, called Edgar after his grandfather on the White side. Edgar, later "Ed," was Mama and Papa's first grandchild. The Armstrong house is partly visible behind the leafless lilac bushes.

Papa's Judicious Purchase

By Christmas, 1927, Papa had completed a deal to buy the Armstrong place at Rife corner. It included several fertile quarters and a spacious log house located a short walk away from the Rife intersection. Harold Armstrong, who homesteaded the property, was born in England and raised in Ontario. About 1910, with the help of two experienced Norwegian builders, Gervase Koppang and Olaf Larson, he built the main part of the house. Although he never married, Mr. Armstrong had a well-kept house, yard, and garden, thanks to the work of his two unmarried sisters, who shared the home. According to Maurice Destrube, the Armstrong house was used as a place of worship before any of the three Rife churches were built.

In this chapter I talk first about work and play in and around our new home and then in the community.

Room for Family and Hired Help

Early in 1928 our family moved into the Armstrong house. We were all pleased with our new home. Papa was pleased with the well-built barnyard buildings. Mama, Vivi, and I were delighted with the house. The original part of the house was a well-built bungalow with a generous windowed attic, a design sometimes called a storey and a half. This large rectangle originally was the whole house, but by the time we arrived, two lean-to additions had expanded the house. These provided two private bedrooms on the north side of the rectangle and a large kitchen on the south. Before long, Papa added a long lean-to on the west side, providing sleeping quarters for Alex, Donnie, and the hired men he usually had on hand.

The dimensions of the main room allowed for a table to be set for 20 people in the dining area. That space, along with the kitchen, later accommodated 70 people at Vivi's buffet-style wedding reception. The attic above the main rooms was accessed by opening a door to a stairway at the north end of the room. Under the slanting roof there was a long, narrow space for two double or single beds, a few chairs, and cloth-covered orange-box night stands. After the men's addition was built, the attic was designated sleeping quarters for females, including guests and hired girls. In a partitioned-off room, Vivi and I shared a double bed and a closet.

Convenience and Versatility in the Kitchen

Left: A "range" or cookstove like the one Mama used in the Armstrong house.

This blue antique stove is in the gazebo or "yurt" that Sid and Shirley built. Mama's stove was bigger, less ornate, and pale yellow.

In the kitchen Mama enjoyed having a large "range" or cook stove, with a warming oven above the cooking area and a large hot-water reservoir attached to the warm side of the stove, away from the hot fire box.

Mama had the luxury of two cupboards, a pretty corner one with glass doors, and plainer one, built by a local carpenter. That man, Jack McIntosh, had perished in World War I. Mama especially valued the latter cupboard, with its sizable space for storing pots and pans and wide counter for rolling out pie dough and kneading bread. Mama said she often thought, as she kneaded bread, about the talented builder of the cupboard, another victim of war. Near the east windows a table stood, and opposite, near the outside door, was a wash stand with a basin and soap, either aromatic Lifebuoy soap or Mama's potent lye soap.

Armstrong barnyard about 1930. Papa with cattle. Papa was pleased with the sturdy barns.

Cream Separator

An essential machine in many pioneer kitchens was a cream separator, and ours occupied a corner of the kitchen, near the outside door. Twice a day Mama and later Alex and Donnie or hired men would bring in pails of cows' milk to be separated into cream and skim milk. The machine was operated by turning a crank, which ran the milk through a set of discs and let out a flow of cream on one side and skim milk on the other. A large pot placed on a round platform attached midway up the separator caught the cream, and milk pails on the floor caught the skim milk. The speed at which the crank was turned determined the consistency of the cream—fast for whipping cream, slower for lighter cream. In later years, cream was put in a big metal "cream can" and picked up weekly by the Bonnyville or

Glendon Creamery truck for cash. The cream had to be stored in a cold room during the winter and put in the "ice house" in summer. With the addition of scraps from the kitchen, the skim milk was turned into swill, a nutritious food for pigs.

In the depth of winter people used saws to cut huge, heavy cubes of ice out of frozen sloughs and lakes. In the ice house, sawdust, obtained from sawing wood for stoves, was piled on and around the ice to insulate it from the heat of warmer seasons. The ice remained all summer and provided excellent refrigeration. The ice could also be used along with salt in making ice cream.

The cream separator had to be kept very clean so cream did not sour. Usually twice a day the apparatus had to be taken apart and washed in different water from what the dishes were washed in. The cleaning job, which became my responsibility, was time consuming, with what seemed dozens and dozens of little metal discs to be meticulously cleaned. Occasionally, in cool weather, if Mama needed me for some other job, she would suggest I just rinse the separator by operating it with a pail of cold water going through it.

You may be wondering where and how laundry was done; butter made; meat, eggs, and vegetables preserved. The kitchen was the place where such work was usually done. The equipment would be brought in from our store room, which was outside, a little wooden building about ten feet square, not far from our kitchen door.

Laundry

Initially, to do the laundry we used two galvanized circular tubs, one with suds from Mama's lye soap, the other with clear water for rinsing. Using a glass scrub board, one could rub and scrub the laundry into cleanliness. Eventually Mama got a washing machine with a wringer attached to it. The machine was a barrel-like tub with a lever on one side. The tub was set into a frame so that if you pulled the lever back and forth, the contents of the tub were agitated, eliminating the need for a scrub board. To operate the wringer you turned a crank. We used clothespins to hang the laundry on a clothesline. In winter the items quickly froze on the line but they would have lost some of their moisture by the time we brought them in to hang on a wooden clothes rack in the living room.

When the laundry was dry, many items were sprinkled and rolled up to dampen evenly for ironing. Shirts, blouses, skirts, tablecloths, napkins, handkerchiefs, pillow cases, even sheets were ironed. The ironing board was stored in the kitchen, fitted in between the big cupboard and the wall. Three or four flat irons were kept in the bottom of the cupboard. In preparation for ironing, the flat irons were placed on suitable parts of the stove to get the right temperature for each fabric. To use a flat iron, you would snap a metal and wood handle onto it and lift it from the stove. As soon as that iron had cooled too much to be useful, it was placed back on the stove and another iron chosen. And the ironing went on.

Making Butter

When we needed butter, the churn would come out of the store room. We would pour cream into it and operate it somewhat like a smaller version of a washing machine. Quite soon we would hear the sound of balls of butter swooshing around in the buttermilk.

Rife, about 1932. Alex and Donnie are in style with their riding britches.

Mama preserved a lot food. She salted pork, preserving it so well that some of us were not excited about eating it. Anyone wanting to eat the salt pork had to have it thoroughly parboiled to make it palatable. Mama put some meats in the smokehouse to preserve them. In making our favourite preserved meat, Mama browned beef, made gravy to cover it, and canned it in quart sealers. She put eggs into a big ceramic crock full of "water glass." When the hens all stopped laying to concentrate on hatching chicks, the eggs were fished out of the water glass and used. Mama stored root vegetables such as potatoes, beets, parsnips, turnips, and carrots in a cellar under the kitchen floor.

Preserving Food

Mama also canned many fruits and some vegetables from the garden. When the snow melted in the spring of 1928, Mama was thrilled to find a weed-free, well-cultivated, and fertilized garden spot. In it Mama and we kids planted cut-up potatoes and seeds for carrots, peas, beets, parsnips, and spinach. When the weather was warm enough, we set out the tomatoes, cabbages, and celery that Mama had started indoors early in the spring. The garden made us appreciate the Armstrongs' love of gardening, so typical of English country people.

Bounty from the Garden

Even if their clothes were shabby, pioneers with the will to work hard at gardening, hunting, butchering, and preserving were usually very well fed. They dined almost entirely on food that would nowadays be classified as organic.

Not long after we had moved into the Armstrong house, Mama made improvements to it. The logs of the main structure had been meticulously peeled. When Mama and Vivi applied a coat of varnish to them, the logs took on a beautiful sheen and a rich copper colour that contrasted nicely with the unusually white chinking between the logs. Many pioneers used cow dung as chinking, a suitable substance for that purpose. It produced sturdy, odourless, grey-brown protection against the cold winds. The Armstrong house, however, had been chinked with a white cement-like substance. The chinking worked well and brightened the rooms with lines of white.

Improvements to the House

Another creative improvement Mama made was to have a sliding skylight installed above her stove in the kitchen. During the day, the skylight added a cheerful brightness for anyone slaving over the hot stove. When it was opened, the skylight let out smoke from the wood fire or (heaven forbid) from scorched food. Though Papa predicted the skylight would leak in rain or snow, I believe it never did. After a few years in the Armstrong house, Mama and Papa covered the rough wooden floors of the main room and kitchen with good-quality beige linoleum. The upgrade brightened the rooms and made cleaning the floors much easier.

Papa's Part-time Job

Sale of cream and pigs made some cash flow, but Papa had the good fortune to be offered a job as a property assessor for the area between St. Paul and Bonnyville. To do that job he felt he needed a car with a roof. He sold his topless Model T Ford to Wade and Edna Armagost for $135 and bought the Model A Ford shown below.

Papa with his 1929 Model A Ford.

Foraging for Berries

As spring turned into summer in our first year at the Armstrong house, Alex and I were delighted by the lovely lilac bushes standing tall and fragrant around the board fencing of the yard. We were thrilled to find black and red currant bushes loaded with fruit. At nine years of age we still foraged for wild berries, but now we were expected to come back with substantial amounts to be canned or used in pies.

One day Alex and I managed to fill a big granite cup with wild strawberries. The berries were precious—delicious but tiny, only the size of small peas. We decided to put our cup down and walk over to where the men were cutting hay. We stayed only a few minutes, but when we got back to where we had left the cup of berries, we found no cup. We looked and looked, but it never turned up. It was a bitter loss for us—one that Alex and I never forgot.

Then there was the day that we walked as far as the home of neighbours, the Horbans, picking wild raspberries on the way. Alex, always so generous, would call me over to share the best berries the moment he found them. We managed to fill a two-quart bowl with the tasty red berries. About 4:30 pm we were happily heading home when a car with three men in it pulled up. The driver asked us if we would sell our berries to them. We were trained to avoid interacting with strangers, so we said, "We'll have to ask our mother first." The men went on their way, and we had the great treat for supper ourselves. The incident remained in our minds—our first brush with the possibility of working for profit.

Possibility of Profit

Another day we had a struggle to get even a pint of raspberries, and we ended up about four miles away, at the home of neighbours, the Charltons. Mrs. Charlton must have realized we were hungry and tired. She cut off a slice of fresh bread and spread it with raspberry jam. My, that was a treat! As you see, I still remember Mrs. Charlton's kindness. That was one of our first brushes with the charity of others.

A Kindness Not Forgotten

I cannot talk about berries without mentioning saskatoons and blueberries. Saskatoons, which grew in grape-like clusters on bushes everywhere, were so plentiful that many people considered them too ordinary—like dandelions. Townspeople seemed to appreciate them, however, and so did my friend Frances Hill, who canned them for healthful wintertime desserts. Blueberries were king of the berries. They were located only in particular spots, such as the jack pines north of the Armstrong place and on an island in Moose Lake. Every summer Alex and I walked into the jack pines and picked bushels of the tasty, nutritious, and mouth-staining fruit.

How thrilled Alex and I were one day when Lindsay Lamb and Hervey Jones arranged to take us, Vivi and Ray, and Vivi's friend Elsie Reed by boat to pick blueberries on Moose Lake's island! We packed picnic lunches and spent a full day harvesting the bounty of the island. Someone had brought fruit nappies and spoons along with cream and sugar to use in making a raw blueberry dessert for everyone. It gave us all blue teeth, but who cared? Food of the gods!

A Social Outing in the Island Blueberry Patch

Arranging to go home from blueberry picking on the island turned out to be quite entertaining when Hervey and Lindsay jostled with each other to see which one would get to sit in the boat with Elsie on the way home. Lindsay owned the boat, so he prevailed. Eventually he and Elsie were married.

Work and Play at Home

Male and Female Roles

In subtle ways we were moving toward grown-up interests and concerns. We spent a good part of our waking hours either at school or attending to chores at home, but we seldom considered the work drudgery—except perhaps washing the cream separator. Mama wanted her daughters to be competent housekeepers and cooks, but she did not require us to do everything she could do, such as killing and butchering chickens and spinning yarn from sheep's wool. In her first years on a homestead she had worked at farm chores, but both she and Papa considered most field and barn work to be men's work. With two sons and a hired man or two to handle the outdoor work, we females focused on work in the house and garden. Simply putting three meals a day on the table for seven or more people consumed many hours a day, and there were plenty of other jobs. Mama wanted Vivi and me to acquire feminine graces, to learn how to knit, crochet, embroider, and sew. She loved music and made sure to give her daughters and an interested son time to practise on piano, violin or,

in Alex's case, the saxophone. She also taught us to dance to music on the radio at home and orchestra music at community dances. We had plenty to keep us occupied.

Above: Rife, about 1935. L–R: me, Mama, and Vivi.

We also had some fun with Papa. When we were younger, he occasionally gave us a treat by reading aloud from our school books. A favourite story was "One Eyes, Two Eyes, Three Eyes." He had a dramatic reading voice and always captivated us. In later years he also sometimes read to us from the lovely poem "Evangeline."

Stories and Poems

In our first year or two at the Armstrong house, Mama sometimes would tell Alex and me stories, supposedly to help us settle down to sleep. We would often clamour for the one that started, "In the Black Forest of Russia, where snow lies on the ground nearly nine months of the year…." We would be breathless as she told about the man, his wife, and their little daughter travelling with wolves around their sleigh. One by one, three of the four horses were cut loose for the wolves to eat. Just at the crucial moment, the one remaining horse managed to get them home. (I used to worry about whether that last horse got safely into a barn. Later I began to wonder about the voracious appetites of those wolves. How could they polish off three horses so fast?) Even though we might have heard the story a hundred times, I don't think it ever induced much sleep.

Vivi seemed to enjoy memorizing poems, and I had the good fortune of listening to her recite as we were lying in bed, supposed to be getting to sleep. One of her favourites was "The Red River Voyageur." Another was "The Highwayman," who came riding on the ribbon of moonlight up to the old inn door. I used to wonder about that man—so romantic yet so bad.

Occasional Visitors

Now and then we'd see Uncle Len, Aunt Alice, and Muriel coming down the long lane for a visit. Muriel had a way of adding excitement. The visits were fairly short, especially in the fall and winter, when darkness descended early. Once dinner was over, they would soon start the long buggy ride home.

Rife School

The school year was more than half done by the time we had settled into the Armstrong house, but Mama and Papa said Donnie, Alex, and I would be joining the Rife School class in mid-term. Thanks to the work of Maurice Destrube and the committee he formed, the Rife School District had been organized in 1916. The first Rife School was held in what Maurice described as "an empty Indian cabin," and it served only five students. In 1920 the Destrube brothers donated three acres of Georges's homestead to be used as a site for a more permanent school. By the time we attended the Rife School, the building was a sturdy, spacious frame building, with a classroom for about 30 pupils in grades one to eight and a good-sized cloakroom. It was located at Rife corner, which was the junction of the road to Franchere and the road from St. Paul to Cold Lake, now Highway 28A. I believe this was also the location of the first Rife School.

According to government regulations, a school district had to be not more than five miles square, and the school had to be centrally located in the square. Fortunately for us, our new house was less than half a mile from the school. Mama walked with us up the hill to the school and introduced herself and all three of us to the pleasant young teacher. Sadly, the teacher, Mrs. Gartley, was not to be our teacher for long. Her husband was killed or disappeared a few weeks after we started school, and Mrs. Gartley went back to her home community. Miss Sedgewick was our next teacher, and we enjoyed having her teach us for the remainder of that year and the next.

High School and Teacher Training for Vivi

Vivi was already eligible for high school when we moved to Rife, but instead of attending school that spring, she studied Latin through the Alberta Correspondence School. In September 1928, she left home to go to school in St. Paul. At first she boarded with a family there, but after a

Opposite: Three former residents of the Armstrong house. L–R: Vivi (Ross) White, me, Olive (Munroe) Ross. Photo about 2000.

Vivi lived at the house about five years, leaving to attend high school and Normal School in Edmonton. She taught at Moose Lake until her wedding in 1936. I lived there nearly ten years, leaving in 1938 to work in Detroit until my wedding in 1940. Olive came here as Donnie Ross's bride in 1948 and lived in the Armstrong house and eventually a new house nearby until Donnie died, in 1994. (This photo is probably a copy of one David White had pinned up in his office.)

few months Mama and Papa decided that if she boarded with Catholic nuns, she would have more opportunity to advance her piano skills—and would be subject to the nuns' strict rules. After two years in St. Paul, Vivi chose to go to Edmonton, where she lived in the boarding house home of Papa's cousin Rae McPherson and attended Victoria High School. Vivi enjoyed her life in Edmonton. After graduating from high school there, she took a year of teacher training in Edmonton.

Rife School Building

Rife School served Donnie, Alex, and me very well. The building itself was probably built by a local carpenter, Mr. Scheldro, renowned for the excellence of his work. It was sturdy and well designed, but it was a school house for only about 30 years. In 1951, changes in society dictated that dozens of school districts in Alberta had to be consolidated into more economical school divisions. Rife students were bussed to Glendon, and a year or two later the Rife School building was sold and moved to serve as a house. That house may still be standing.

In 1928, as the teacher rang the bell to summon us into school, we walked or ran up four or five steps to the cloakroom. There we hung up coats and scarves and put mitts, overshoes, and lunch pails on a shelf below our coats. Near the door was a stand with a pail of water and a dipper for anyone who was thirsty. Also on the stand was a basin into which one could pour some water and use a bar of soap to wash hands. (One might or might not want to use the towel.)

The school room was bright with a long line of fairly large windows on the east side and two small higher windows on the west side. With its high ceiling, the room had an airiness about it. With a heater and brick chimney at the back, it had a coziness about it in winter. In cold weather, an older student was designated as the fire starter and had to come early enough to get a crackling fire going in the heater before the rest of us arrived. The fire starter during the winters I was in school there was Olive Armagost. In cold weather, pupils were sometimes allowed to move tables closer to the heater. In very cold weather, they understood that they did not have to come to school.

The school was well equipped. There were built-in cupboards at the back of the room and shelves of books near the front of the room, most books donated by Mrs. Thurston. For the Christmas concert, some of the fathers would come and build a temporary stage at the front of the room, and the mothers would supply sheets to be strung up on a wire high above the stage to serve as curtains. In the corner, opposite the teacher's wooden desk, a pump organ stood. It was used for the Christmas concert and for music classes. I was thrilled when I was designated the organist for such events.

School Equipment and Furniture

The pupils were seated on chairs lined up at long tables. These tables were very versatile compared with the more up-to-date classroom furniture that landed in schools a dozen or so years later. Those "modern" creations were heavy, cumbersome chair-and-desk combinations—black, curly-cued, enamelled iron frames with wooden seats and tops. They were eventually replaced by light individual tables and chairs.

With its two outdoor toilets, one for boys, one for girls, discreetly placed far apart among the poplar trees, the school provided for nearly every need. One problem with the boys' toilet was that sometimes salt-seeking porcupines chewed on the urine-soaked boards, requiring replacement of boards. After a few years, a small horse barn made of logs and a small frame teacherage (small house for a teacher) appeared on the school lot. Only students who rode a horse to school were supposed to go into the barn, but when no horse was there, it was a great place to sneak into for play. The teacherage must have been a mixed blessing for the teacher— convenient but giving students access to information about the teacher. By examining the trash pile outside the teacherage, one could, for example, get an idea of the teacher's diet—canned stews, canned pineapples, or whatever.

Outdoor Facilities

When Alex and I were 11, a new teacher arrived at Rife School—a jovial young man from Camrose. We instantly warmed to him, which was lucky because he was to be our teacher until Alex and I finished grade eight. Mr. Malmo was not a strict disciplinarian, so we responded by being

Mr. Malmo Teaches at Rife

perhaps a little too familiar with him and occasionally rowdy. We enjoyed school, though, learned a lot from Mr. Malmo, and adored him and his sense of humour. One memorable time we must have been especially noisy, for he called out, "Silence in the pig market! Let the old sow speak first." We were silenced—but not for long.

Teacher's Other Duties and Pay

Besides putting up with us and teaching us, Mr. Malmo had a list of other duties, such as bringing a pail of drinking water from the pump into the school, sweeping the floors and cleaning the blackboards. For all his efforts, he was paid $40 a month, $15 of which went to his landlady, Mrs. Aylesworth. Papa was treasurer of the school board and sometimes did not receive funds from the government soon enough to pay Mr. Malmo on time. Poor Mr. Malmo just had to wait.

We girls used to play on the organ and sing the following cheeky little ditty: "Mr. Malmo so they say, goes a-courting every day. Sword and pistol at his side, he takes Frances for a ride." Frances was his fiancée back in Camrose. We thought Mr. Malmo's wit was scintillating when he finally commented, "That organ will soon be playing that song by itself."

Relationship between Teacher and Student

I believe at least one of the grade eight girls would have been pleased if Mr. Malmo had gone a-courting her. But, as Mr. Malmo had made clear, he had a fiancée. Nevertheless, hopes such as his student had were within the realm of reason. Had a male teacher wanted to choose a spouse from among his older female students, the community would not have objected—providing his intentions were honourable. Anyone my age is likely to know of several marriages between a male teacher and his student. The easy acceptance of such courtships in those days stands in stark contrast to what I see nowadays. Now, a male teacher dating a female student could end up in court, possibly jail, with his license to teach withdrawn. He would be deemed to have violated his position of trust. Paradoxically, I see today's society is far more accepting of casual sexual behaviour among young people than in pioneer days.

To partially understand why courtship between a male teacher and students has gone from acceptable to reprehensible, we need to realize how different courtship was in pioneer days compared with the present. In older times, dating might consist of meeting at church and sitting together or dancing together at a community dance. Both student and male teacher would consider sexual intimacy out of the question during courtship. There was no birth control pill, so sexual intimacy carried the risk of pregnancy. And pregnancy of an unmarried girl could bring disaster down on her head. She would typically be sent away to have the baby somewhere else and give it up for adoption. Sometimes pregnant girls were simply abandoned by their families. With such heavy sanctions, a female student would be inclined to resist intimacy. I do not know of any male teacher causing pregnancy of a student, but had it happened, marriage would have been the only honourable course.

Courtship in Pioneer Days

As for female teachers, they were subjected to more restrictions than male teachers. Sometimes they had early evening curfews except when attending a school-related event. In a few districts they were told they would lose their job if they married. In most districts a married teacher who became pregnant was required to resign. Despite the rules, single female teachers in pioneer Alberta were targets for eligible bachelors, and many of them married prosperous farmers in the community.

Restrictions on Female Teachers

My Aunt Alice was one such teacher, marrying Mama's brother Len in 1922. Childless, she continued to teach at Chicken Lake for a number of years. However, she did not have complete control over what went on in her classroom. She told of an astounding incident that apparently was replicated in other Alberta schools. She came to school one day to find a medical team had arrived to take tonsils out of the pupils. Not prepared to participate in the operations, she went home. When she came back to school the next day, she found the premises had not been properly cleaned. Surprisingly, some of the students had come to school, but Aunt Alice closed the school. She drove her horse and buggy to a school board member's home to complain about the condition of the school. Someone cleaned the school, and apparently all the children survived the operation. Such was the authority of the medical profession that Aunt Alice could not stop the needless and dangerous operations.

Tonsillectomies at Aunt Alice's School

Preparing for the "Christmas Tree"

When Alex and I were attending Rife School, it was the hub of social life in the community. The highlight of the year was the Christmas Concert, commonly called "The Christmas Tree." To raise funds for it, socially active community members organized all sorts of events. There were crib parties and whist drives (both involving playing-card competitions), chicken suppers and dances, most with small entry fees–usually a quarter from men and a food item from women.

Just before the concert date, things got exciting. We seemed to be living the story of the "Shoemaker and the Elves." We'd come to school and find something had gone on after we'd left the day before. First would be a temporary stage built out of lumber. Then a freshly cut Christmas tree might be erected. One morning we would arrive and find the school had been transformed into a wonderful theatre. The tree was majestic, decorated with balls, shining blue, gold, green, and red; garlands, gracefully drooped from branch to branch; and tinsel, which shimmered and fluttered when someone walked by. Crepe paper stringers, red or green, swooped down from places high up on the walls then up to meet in the centre of the ceiling, where a cluster of honeycomb paper bells was hanging. The effect was magical, like a tent from an Arabian tale.

Program at the Christmas Tree

Every pupil in the school had an item or two on the program—a poem to recite, a song to sing, a role to play in the Christmas story. Older students could be Mary, Joseph, a shepherd, or a wise man; younger children could be angels on high or possibly animals in the stable—as long as they played their roles with appropriate decorum. A humorous play was always popular.

Here is the "Welcome Song" Mr. Malmo had us sing, with appropriate actions, to open one of our concerts:

> At last, my friends, the time has come for our program to begin,
> And so with quaking hearts we welcome you, brace up, and now begin.
> For though we've learned our parts, you see, our fortitude may flee
> And leave us with stage fright before such distinguished company.
> Welcome, welcome, welcome. It's well that you have come.
> Well we welcome you. We will try to make things hum.

And we welcome you well, we do.
We've a welcome, welcome, welcome, welcome, welcome,
    welcome,
For you and you and you.

As we sang the last line, we pointed enthusiastically at our special people.

Treats and Gifts at the Christmas Tree

After the program ended, always to thunderous applause, there were still more thrills to be had. Santa was coming! There was the usual delay, during which bells would ring outside and someone would report, "He's getting near." We older pupils knew that a jovial father was putting on a white beard and dressing up in the Santa costume.

Even if we didn't believe in Santa, we all were excited about getting our loot bags—usually two each. Several weeks earlier, one of the mothers would have written a letter to Eaton's telling the ages of all the boys and girls in the class. Just on time for the concert, a parcel from Eaton's would arrive at the Rife Post Office. It contained bags of non-perishables—butterscotch and mint candies, Brazil nuts and almonds, and a small gift for each child. Then Santa would hand out bags prepared in someone's kitchen just before the concert. In them we'd find a fragrant McIntosh apple and perhaps two exotic and delicious Japanese oranges—all wrapped in tissue. There might also be popcorn balls, brownies, and other specialties made by some of the mothers.

Finally, Santa would call out names and we'd step forward and receive our Christmas gifts—a bracelet, plasticine, checkers, Snakes and Ladders. Every child received a suitable gift. All the gifts, paid for out of funds raised in the community, were of nearly equal value. How well our community treated us!

Christmas Tree Dance

While the children devoured treats and played with their gifts, their parents quickly transformed the school room into a dance hall. Tables and chairs were pushed to the sides of the room. A copper boiler, half filled with water, was heaved onto the heater. When the water boiled, several cups of ground coffee were added. After the brew simmered to eye-opening potency, volunteer servers brought it to tables. The sound "ting, ting, ting" meant the musicians were tuning a violin or guitar and the dance was about to start. For a while children mixed with parents and other adults on the dance floor. As they wearied, children were placed to sleep on makeshift beds with coats and blankets. Dancing went on non-stop until around midnight. It would halt briefly as dancers and musicians shared the sandwiches and cakes they had brought and drank yet more of the potent coffee. After "lunch" a lively crowd would resume dancing for a while, but eventually men would go out to hitch teams to cutters. Women would get sleepy children into coats, boots, and caps and wrap scarves around necks and heads, leaving slits for breathing and seeing. Carrying sleeping children, urging others to come along, parents disappeared into the cold night. The dance might continue for another one or two hours, but the dancers were wise not to linger too long. The next night, and the night after that they could well be at similar events at other schools.

Competition among Schools

Life is never much like the idyllic heaven described in some sermons. It involves conflicts and battles of some sort. Even in our warm-hearted community, competition reared up, creating winners and losers. A teacher's reputation hung on the Christmas concert. When Mr. Malmo asked me to be the organist for the Rife School's program, I felt the underlying tension of competition. People evaluated every concert, comparing it with previous ones.

When Rife was joined by newly built schools in Hoselaw and Moose Lake, the competition intensified. People in the community entertained themselves by going to all three Christmas concerts—and judging. In her first year of teaching, my sister, Vivi, was the first teacher in Moose Lake School. She was keenly aware of the competition and put her considerable talent and much school time into preparing for the Christmas concert. When the Ross family attended that concert, they concluded that, yes, the Moose Lake concert was the best of the three. I was glad that by then I had finished with Rife School and was not in the competition. I confess I was also glad when all three Christmas Trees—Rife, Hoselaw, and Moose Lake—were over. They occurred as consecutive events in the three days before school ended for Christmas holidays. "Half-dead" was how many people in the community described themselves after a three-day Christmas Tree marathon.

Dances–Exhilarating and Socially Important

Even when there were no longer any Rosses attending Rife School, we were still often at the school for evening events. For me, dances were the most exciting of all, and they were held in other schools besides Rife. Throughout pioneer days, dances served important functions in the community. There were no telephones and few radios, and TV did not exist. Life on a farm could be lonely. Dances gave people of all ages and religions opportunities to connect with other people. They gave young people a chance to meet their partner for life in a way that was exciting and enjoyable, probably more fun than joining an online dating club. Dances brought music and the joy of dancing to all ages. Almost as soon as children could walk, they were encouraged to get out on the dance floor and learn to dance. A friendly older child or adult would act as the dance partner. When we were new to Rife, Stella Armagost came to where I was sitting at a dance and offered to teach me to dance. And a good teacher she was, introducing me to the intricacies of several popular dances.

Dance as a Form of Art

Dancing in pioneer days was much more of an art form among ordinary people than it is nowadays. There were so many dances to learn. Some were slow and graceful, such as the Norwegian waltz and the stately French minuet. Many were lively and athletic, such as the run-and-skip schottische, a variation called the Highland schottische, the heel-and-toe polka, and the Russian troika. When the Knapp brothers—Norman, Leslie, and Casey—came from Flat Lake, we had the fun of square dancing. As our versatile musicians played the tunes, the Knapp brothers called the square dances. Leslie Knapp would always choose frisky Valmai Nordstrom to dance the round polka with him. Some dances, such as the log cabin two-step and the round polka, were challenging workouts for the fittest among us. The dance partner of a sturdy farmer would sometimes find her feet leaving the floor, but she had no fear of falling. The muscular man would quickly tighten his arms around her until she regained her footing.

A Live Band at Every Dance

Rife was fortunate indeed to have talented and generous musicians who brought us live music. There was Alma Armagost (mother of the Harry Armagost family) on violin, her brothers Nels and Alfred Koppang on violin and guitar, respectively. On many occasions there was also Jack Nicholson on violin. Even if a person was not up to dancing, he or she could sit on the sidelines enjoying the show and the music. Simply attending a dance made one a part of the community, and possibly a financial contributor. Musicians often donated some of their "take" to community causes such as the Christmas Tree.

People who especially loved dancing often ventured out beyond their local community to other venues. Glendon was one such venue, favoured especially when word was out that the band included a drum. Wherever the dances were held, the musicians signalled the end of the dance by playing "Home Sweet Home." Unless they were utterly exhausted, dancers regretted the end of the fun. Sometimes they would persuade the musicians to continue playing until four in the morning. One time, the whole Ross family, including Mama and Papa, arrived home with the sun in their eyes at seven in the morning.

Eastbourne Hall

School house dances at Rife, Hoselaw, and Moose Lake disappeared after 1940, the year Eastbourne Hall was completed. The dance tradition simply moved into the big hall with the new name. The building committee had agreed that to avoid hard feelings, they must not name the hall after any of the three district schools. When Mrs. Evelyn Thurston made a large donation to the building of the hall, committee members gave her the task of naming the hall. With the name "Eastbourne," Mrs. Thurston not only memorialized her hometown in England, but she gave the hall an appealing name that suited it well. The hall was situated near the eastern boundary of the three school districts. Eastbourne Hall was and still is well located at the crossroads of Highway 28A and the road leading to Moose Lake on the north and Hoselaw on the south. The hall's expansive and polished hardwood floor soon attracted dancers from farms and towns in a much wider circle, from Bonnyville to St. Paul and beyond.

When pioneer people wanted entertainment other than dances, they usually had to create it themselves. People with special talents or interests

Left: Glendon, about 1995. Grace and Allan "Jeep" Smith dancing in traditional style.

might be involved in a play or a "talent show." The latter could consist of recitations, songs, gymnastics, juggling or other acts. Eastbourne, with its built-in stage, became a favourite venue for such shows, including those from Glendon and elsewhere. By the late 1940s, however, new technologies were sweeping away old ways.

A new and exciting entrepreneurial venture arrived in the Eastbourne community. Every two weeks for several years, Jack Doonanco brought movies to Eastbourne Hall and other halls in the area. Jack's selection of family movies, for example, westerns with Randolph Scott, Alan Ladd, or Audie Murphy, and comedies with Jerry Lewis and Dean Martin, delighted young audiences and sparked much chatter and laughter the next day in school. The movie business was probably not a great money maker for Jack, but, for a few years, it provided popular entertainment to the community.

Inevitably the ways we played, studied, and worked were changing. Jack's movies were a sign that we were moving out of pioneer days and do-it-yourself entertainment into an era of advancing technology. Competing with many other forms of entertainment, dancing gradually became less important in the social life of a community.

The way we educated our kids was also changing. By 1951 school busses, including Jack Doonanco's, were bussing students to more economical "consolidated schools" in Glendon or Bonnyville. Rife School was just an empty building to be disposed of.

The way we farmed changed as well. Farmers were acquiring trucks and machinery such as tractors so they could farm sections of land rather than mere quarters. Inevitably small farms were sold, swallowed up by bigger ones. Many former farmers found jobs in towns or cities, usually working for employers rather than managing their own operations.

Few, if any, of us had enough imagination to predict that technology would revolutionize everything. We had no idea that computers would enable free communication between people all over the world and instant access to information. We had no idea that technology would put smog in our sky and plastic in our oceans.

The year 2015 brought the 75th year anniversary of Eastbourne Hall. The event was marked by a float in the Bonnyville Canada Day parade, a ball tournament at Eastbourne Ball Diamonds, and a dinner and dance at Eastbourne Hall. It was a chance to look back at pioneer days. We had a rich life then. In summer we could frolic at a beach at Moose Lake or play pickup softball at the nearby ball diamond. In winter we cleared snow off the sloughs and lakes for skating and pickup hockey. And in all seasons we danced!

I am happy to see many of these traditions live on, with some changes. People still swim in Moose Lake, but now they also water ski on it, pulled by motor

Left: *Glendon, July 1995. Granddaughter Denise Elaine Smith and Tom Charawich's wedding reception and dance. Denise's gown was made by her mother, Diane.*

Lively wedding dances, such as this one, with its old-time band playing waltzes and polkas as well as some jive music (but no hard metal), gave Danny and me the joy of dancing together one last time. A song says all good things must end some day. So it seems, but happy memories linger on.

boats. At Eastbourne Ball Diamonds, teams in smart uniforms play in league tournaments. More than ever, people, including girls and women, still skate and play hockey but mainly in town, on artificial ice. At Eastbourne Hall people still dance on New Year's Eve and at weddings and anniversaries, sometimes even getting beyond gyrating and flailing to manage a waltz or a two-step. Hmm—maybe I should set up a dance studio.

CHAPTER 7

⊂⊃≍⊂⊃

The Smith Family at Flat Lake

As the Ross family was moving away from Flat Lake to Rife, a family of settlers from England was arriving there. In April of 1928, Charles and Esther Smith left their two married daughters, Esther and Margaret, in Yorkshire, England, and brought their five sons, Jack, Thomas, Daniel, Reginald, and MacDonald to Alberta. These sons ranged in age from early twenties to six years. The Smiths' eldest son, Charles, had immigrated to the United States a few years earlier. I bring the Smith family into my memoir because for over 65 years I was happily married to Danny Smith. Getting back to 1928, the Smith family had left England on the ship *Newfoundland,* sailing out of Liverpool and docking two weeks later in Halifax. From there they travelled by train to St. Paul, Alberta. In St. Paul they were directed to the office of Francis McAcheran, who was, I believe, in charge of placing newcomers on Soldier Settlement property. Mr. McAcheran drove the Smiths out to Flat Lake, to what seemed a suitable place for a family of seven, including parents, three young men, and two boys.

Opposite: *An urban area in England, about 1919. L–R: Smith brothers Tommy, Jack, and Danny. The boys are dressed in kilts for some occasion.*

Left: *The house at Flat Lake, to which the Smith family came in May 1928.*

In May, when the Smiths arrived, the property at first may have seemed almost the promised land. A large two-storey frame house stood on the property, and a lake sparkled nearby. More than ten acres of land had been cleared for crops, and there was a sizable hay meadow.

Mixed Feelings

Closer inspection revealed that the house was roughly finished and not insulated. Worse, the soil turned out to be thin and rocky. Within the family there were mixed feelings about the new country. Some of the sons, including Danny, saw it as a wonderful land of opportunities, not the least of which was the freedom to hunt and fish without fear of being charged with poaching. On the other hand, Esther told me years later that when she thought about what they had left behind, she had felt like crying. Charles must have immediately seen that working on a neighbour's farm, in accord with Soldier Settlement Plan rules, disastrously delayed spring work on his own farm. Furthermore, his attempt to become a landowner rather that a renter had burdened him with debt, something most of his homesteader neighbours had avoided.

Ellington, Yorkshire, England, between 1928 and 1945. This was the sturdy farmhouse the Smiths left behind.

Nearly all the neighbours around the Smiths' new property had obtained their land under the generous terms of federal legislation popularly called the "Homestead Act." That act, in effect between 1872 and 1918, was designed to populate Canada's prairie provinces. According to its terms, a man could, for a $10 administration fee, "file" on his choice of a quarter of land (160 acres). In three years, after clearing at least ten acres, putting up some buildings, getting some animals and living on the land for at least half of each year, the man was eligible for title to the land. At that time, he could file on another quarter of land, usually near or adjacent to his first quarter. He then became the owner of 320 acres of land—the only costs being two $10 administration fees and three years of hard work. According to a *Wikipedia* article, under the Canadian Homestead Act, the government gave away about 480,000 square miles of land.

Homestead Act

Coming too late for free land under the Homestead Act, the Smiths apparently were accepted as immigrants under the terms of the Soldier Settlement Plan. A similar plan in Australia accepted immigrants to that country, but the Smiths chose Canada. The Canadian plan was established in 1917 to replace the Homestead Act and help veterans of World War I get set up on farms. The first veterans to access the plan were eligible for free land available under the Homestead Act, but that provision was scrapped in 1918. By 1928, when the Smiths became involved with it, the plan in Canada was nearing the end of its existence, likely because by that time applications from soldiers had dwindled. Probably in an attempt to dispose of land designated for the plan, authorities apparently waived the requirement that settlers be military veterans. In this situation, Charles, with no military experience was considered eligible for Soldier Settlement property. Unfortunately, by then the choice properties had been taken. After less than total success, the plan ended in 1930, when the federal government turned control of public lands over to the provincial governments.

Soldier Settlement Plan

The terms of the Soldier Settlement Plan made more demands of applicants than the Homestead Act had. Settlers in the category of immigrants to Canada after World War I—that is, the Smiths' category—had even more onerous requirements. According to a *Wikipedia* article, they "were required to work on a Canadian farm for a time to prove that they had the capability to farm on their own, to have sufficient capital to establish themselves, and to make a down payment of 20% for land, stock, implements and buildings." If they wanted a loan, which the Settlement Plan could provide at 5% interest, they were "investigated as to their fitness, moral character, assets and abilities." Once they had settled on a property they were "regularly visited by field supervisors to check on their progress and give advice."

The Smiths had sold most of their possessions before they left England, so we can assume they were able to make the 20% down payment on their property. The remaining cost of the property would have been handled through a 25-year loan, essentially a mortgage. Under terms of the plan, Charles would be required to work on a Canadian farm to prove his capability to farm. We do know that he and his son Danny worked at picking roots on the farm of Emmet Davidson. This backbreaking job was involved in turning land covered with trees into fields for crops. For a man who had farmed successfully for many years in England, the requirement to pick roots for someone else before he could set to work on his own property must have been galling.

Baptism card for Margaret Smith, dated August 5, 1901. Margaret's baptism at Kippax Parish Church suggests that Charles and Esther lived near Kippax, where there were coal mines in which Charles probably worked.

I never met Charles, and I heard only a few anecdotes about him from my mother-in-law, my husband, and sister-in-law Charlotte, who was married to the youngest Smith son, Allan MacDonald Smith. In England Peter Metcalfe also supplied biographical data. Charles was born in Glasgow in 1877 and lived part of his childhood on a farm. He had a sister Isobel, with whom he had limited contact. He was working as a miner in County Durham when he met Esther Greening. After their marriage, which took place about 1900, they may have lived in the mining town Kippax, which is where, in September 1901, they baptized their newborn daughter, Margaret. A few years later, Charles and Esther rented a farm at Heighington, County Durham, where they farmed for several years. When the opportunity arose to rent a farm from Lord Swinton in Ellington, North Riding of Yorkshire, they seized it. With help from his growing sons, Charles prospered there, and that is where the family was living when they decided to adventure into a new country.

Introducing Charles Smith

My information about Esther comes mainly from my own observations and conversations with her, but also from Danny and Charlotte. Born in Nottingham in 1879, Esther was beautiful, quick witted, and very talented musically.

According to Charlotte, Esther was Jewish and had been raised among Jews. After her marriage, Esther did not observe any Jewish traditions, attended the Wesleyan Methodist Chapel, and sent her children to Wesleyan Methodist Sunday School. Despite such evidence to the contrary, Danny believed his mother was Jewish, and he recalled an incident in which a Jewish storekeeper in Glendon, Mr. Wintrobe, jokingly suggested she was Jewish, to which Esther replied, "Many a truth is told in jest." I am not positive that Esther was Jewish. According to the Internet, the name "Greening" is Anglo-Saxon. However, her mother may have been Jewish.

Esther's mother, a widow, was head housekeeper for a wealthy Jewish family. In this home Esther had access to early education, partly as an onlooker while the employer's children participated in lessons from a governess. When her mother's health failed, Esther and her mother moved to the home of an aunt who operated a large boarding house in Durham. In her aunt's home, Esther continued to receive an education in literature, business practice, elocution, and music, including singing lessons. Again

Introducing Esther Greening

she was partly an onlooker as the governess taught her cousins (one of whom became an announcer for the BBC). By the time Esther was 12, she had learned to sight sing, which is the ability to read an unfamiliar song sheet and correctly sing the notes without any accompanying instrument. If she wanted accompaniment when she sang for an audience, she could play her mandolin, which she always had at hand.

Hammond, BC, about 1947. Esther is about 68 years old.

In Hammond she was active in the Women's Institute, and in Haney, where she lived for the last four years of her life, she was director of the Haney Women's Institute.

Anyone who heard Esther sing realized she had been blessed with a very special voice, ranging from soaring soprano to moody contralto. A temporary boarder in the aunt's house was a man from New York who worked in the music industry. One day he happened to hear 12-year-old Esther singing and asked her mother to let him take the girl to New York to advance her singing career. Esther's mother, who had not long to live, declined the offer. But Esther had found the passion of her life and was determined to take every opportunity to sing for audiences. Not long after her mother's death she left her aunt's home and found employment in business—possibly in retail sales. Knowing Esther's love of singing and her confidence in herself, we can assume she seized opportunities to sing at the music halls which were popular in Durham at the time.

A Passion for Singing

It was probably at one such event that Esther caught the eye of a rugged young miner from Durham. About two years older than Esther, Charles Smith had the self-confidence to set out to win the beautiful and talented singer as his bride. Esther probably was attracted to the virile-looking young man who admired her, and who, as one photo shows, was a dapper dresser. Insightful as she was, she probably recognized his character strengths—ambition, willingness to work hard, and generosity. He was handicapped, however, in that he had never attended school. According to Esther, he was certainly intelligent, having somehow learned how "figure"—that is, to do arithmetic—including using decimals and percent, without ever being in school. Esther was well aware that culturally he was not a suitable match for her, but she settled on marriage with the young miner who wanted her hand.

Settling on Marriage

The truth was that Esther had a limited choice of suitors. As an orphan, she had no wealth to bring to a marriage. More than that, she had a barrier to marriage in the form of a two-year-old daughter, also named Esther (Ettie). The little girl had been fathered by a man to whom Esther had been engaged, a man she described as a "gentleman." He had applied to immigrate to South Africa, and Esther expected to go with him as his wife. According to Esther, her fiancé took offence when she waved in a friendly way at his brother on a bus. (This was not the only time Esther's friendly ways would have negative consequences for her.) When Esther became pregnant, her fiancé went to South Africa as planned but never arranged for her to come with him.

A Limited Choice

Charles Smith, somewhere in Western Canada, about 1945—many years after he had left the family. On the back of the photo is written, "Lovingly, Dad."

This was a time when unwed mothers were shunned by society and often by their families. Many were forced to go into a workhouse of some sort during their pregnancy and forced to give up their baby for adoption. Esther, however, decided to keep her baby. For her to do so would have taken tremendous determination, courage, and resourcefulness in those days. She had the crucial advantage of secure employment before and after her baby was born. Her action under the circumstances presages the strong maternal feelings she had for all her children.

A Courageous Choice

Marriage was a mixed blessing to Charles and Esther. Together they took some bold steps that brought financial success, but they also had interpersonal conflicts and a tragic loss. They shared a vision of what they wanted for their family and the drive to reach their goal. Thanks to Esther's education and knowledge of business, the couple were able to complete the paperwork involved in renting a farm at Heightington, County Durham, where the family lived for several years. It was in Durham that Danny was baptized. Renting the Swinton farm in Yorkshire a few years later was an upward move for the family. They moved into a two-storey stone farmhouse with seven fireplaces. Charles knew how to cultivate the land, produce crops for sale, and take good care of cattle and other animals. The family profited from the fact that the market town of Thirsk was nearby, arranging for sons to sell milk and other farm products there on market days. Charles worked hard and demanded the same of his sons, and the family prospered on the farm.

Financial Success

 The Smith family farmed in the part of Yorkshire that is the setting for the highly acclaimed TV series, *Downton Abbey*. Also James Herriot's well-known books, such as *All Creatures Great and Small,* are set in the same area—in particular, Thirsk, where the author had his veterinary practice.

By all accounts, Charles was a good father, though occasionally he used severe corporal punishment on the boys—as was common in those days. He was generous with his wife and family, falling in with his wife's wishes for their children to be educated, to go on holidays, and to have some experience with music, books, and the outside world. He also expected his children to be good workers, and he taught his sons the skills involved in farming.

Charles and Esther as Parents

Perhaps in part because of all the hard work he did, Charles had unusual physical strength. He confidently handled challenges, especially physical ones. A story that followed him from England was of his saving a friend and neighbour, Mr. Middleton, from being gored by a bull. As the bull charged at his friend, Charles leapt forward and grabbed the bull's horns and turned the animal away from the man, much to the relief—and almost disbelief—of the Middleton and Smith family members who witnessed the feat of strength.

Charles Smith in Canada, about 1948, looking as though he could still take a bull by its horns.

In the stone house, Esther expertly managed the household, which usually included two hired girls. The children were sent to bed at seven o'clock (whether sleepy or not) and were up early to do chores and get to school on time. On Sundays, depending on their age, they went to Sunday School or Chapel. The family had time and funds for holiday excursions. Some of the sons felt some resentment that hunting was restricted to the upper class. But mainly life was good, with wholesome food, cricket and football, and friends such as the Middletons and Veritys in the community.

Both parents valued and loved their children—the five sons who emigrated with them, the two married daughters they left behind, the eldest son, who emigrated ahead of them, and one more, a two-year old named Joseph, whom they left behind in a grave in England, probably in Durham.

A Grievous Loss

Both parents grieved when their sturdy little Joseph succumbed to a gastrointestinal infection. Unfortunately they did not help each other deal with the tragedy, and their marriage suffered. Even years later, Esther still talked about the loss and how it happened. According to her, the little fellow was just getting over diarrhea and regaining his appetite when his father insisted that Esther give him a dish of rice pudding. The mother disagreed, feeling that a diet of broth and gruel should be maintained a little longer, but she deferred to her husband. Severe diarrhea returned and the child died. As she told the story to me, I realized she still blamed her husband for the loss of the little boy.

Leaving England

About 1927 Charles and Esther applied to immigrate to Canada. Their two daughters had found husbands. Margaret was married to Reg Metcalfe, the superintendent at Leighton dam, where the couple lived in a spacious stone house. Esther (Ettie), who had trained as a nurse, was married to Lawrence Spence and living in Leeds. (Ettie kindly invited Danny for a two-week holiday, and there, in the big city, he had his first experience with homesickness.) Charles, the eldest Smith son, had immigrated to the United States, where he changed his name to "Bill Davis." (The name change seems to have been whimsical.) To Charles and Esther the time seemed right to go with their five sons and seek adventure and prosperity in a new country. Sadly they never saw their eldest three children again.

When the five Smith brothers gathered for their mother's funeral in 1954, Charles (aka Bill Davis) gave Tommy an account of how his name was changed: Charles was involved in rodeo work and traded his name and ID with a cowboy called Bill Davis. My nephew Jeep retold the story.

Like other migrants, the Smiths held a sale of their livestock, farm machinery, and household furnishings. In 1967, when Danny and I visited his friends and family in Yorkshire, we saw a handsome solid wood buffet, which the friend said she had bought at the Smith sale. Looking at that buffet and comparing it to the plain pioneer furnishings in their Canadian home, I began to understand why Esther felt like crying when she made the comparison. I wonder whether, as their ship sailed out of port, Esther and Charles knew what a gamble they were taking. Knowing Esther as I did, however, I knew she would refuse to be overwhelmed by misgivings.

Objects They Brought

The Smiths came with several trunks of clothing and household essentials. Each family member was allowed to bring a small package of their most prized possessions. Esther packed her collection of song sheets and her mandolin. Eventually I fell heir to the song sheets, which I treasure to this day. The songsheets, most bought for two shillings each from Boosey & Co in London, are in a variety of genres. There are songs about families, such as "Wyoming Lullaby (Go to Sleep My Baby)," which Esther had sung to her babies and which Danny sang to ours. Another song sheet in that genre is "Daddy," on which is written the note: "Margaret used to sing this." There are love songs such as "Love's Old Sweet Song" and "Till the Sands of the Desert Grow Cold." Esther must have loaned the latter song sheet to my sister, Vivi, for on it in my sister's handwriting is this note: "Papa loved to hear Ettie hit the high notes at the end." There are ballads such as "Rory Darlin'," an Irish lament about being forced off the land: "there's a stranger at the door...the land is ours no more." There are many sacred songs, "The Holy City" being one often requested by Esther's audiences. Another sacred song, "Looking This Way" will be discussed in Chapter 14.

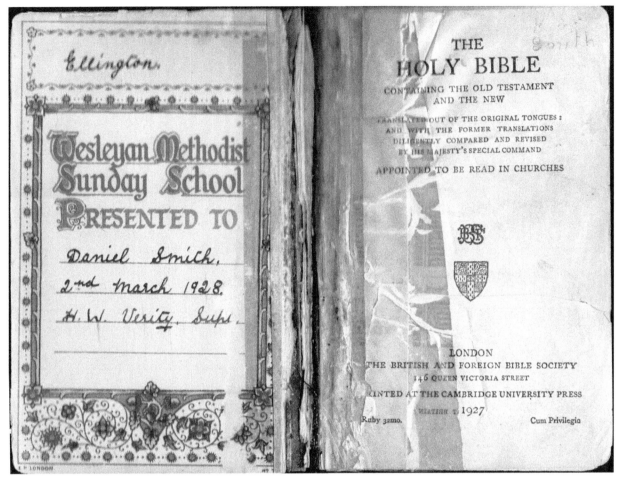

Danny chose to bring three books and a photograph with him. One book was the Bible, which had been presented to him only a month before they sailed away. The Ellingstring Wesleyan Methodist Sunday School Super, Herenza Verity, gave Danny the Bible for perfect attendance in Sunday School. The other two books are inspirational tales: *Sturdy and Strong,* by G.A. Henty, and the fairy tale *Dick Whittington and His Cat.* (Author Henty is mentioned in *Downton Abbey*.) The photo Danny brought is of a black-and-white cat walking on a stone wall. Danny told our kids the cat was a pet and he wanted a reminder of it.

Above: *Presentation Page of Danny's Bible.*

Opposite: *Sheet music for "The Holy City." This song was often requested by Esther's audiences.*

Though Danny loved horses and dogs, he also had a soft spot for cats. He would sometimes give a barnyard cat a treat at milking time by squirting a stream of milk into its mouth.

Memories of Life in Yorkshire

Life seemed good for the Smiths in Yorkshire. The chapter-opening photo of Jack, Tommy, and Danny dressed in traditional Celtic costumes was apparently taken on some holiday occasion. Although the three boys do not appear thrilled by their costumes, the photo indicates their parents had money to spare and an interest in costumes and culture. Danny's recollections of life in "the old country" were mainly happy ones. Esther saw to it that all their children received at least the standard grade eight education, and Danny recalled the fun of his school days—a run down to the river at lunch time to have a quick swim, cricket games, stops at the spring on the way home to drink the refreshing water. He was impressed by the discipline in the school, such that the master required students working at their desks be quiet enough to hear a pin drop. A good student, athletic and bold, Danny had many friends at school.

A story from Danny's school days was shared 40 years later when we visited Yorkshire. Norman Verity, whom Danny considered his best friend from school days, was on Danny's list of friends he wanted to visit. As we sat in the comfortable living room of Norman's farmhouse, the two men compared farming in England and Canada. Then abruptly Norman asked Danny whether he remembered the time he took on Bully ___. Danny remembered the story, but Norman told it again. Twelve-year-old Danny decided he'd seen enough bullying of younger children by the burly 14-year-old, so he challenged him. Apparently the wrestling/boxing match was prolonged and covered a lot of grassy ground. Strangely, no teacher interfered. In the end, Bully___ gave up, and according to Norman, was never known to bully younger children again.

As must often be the case when people visit friends of their childhood, Danny often had to work to make his memory of an old friend square with the reality he found. During our trip to Yorkshire, we visited with Hazel Middleton, who had gone to school with him. I had heard more than enough times about Hazel Middleton's hair. After 40 years, Danny was surprised the former Miss Middleton no longer had shining blond hair tumbling over her shoulders and down her back. When he expressed his surprise about her hair, Hazel was a little indignant, saying she would look silly in her fifties with long hair. After a few minutes of chatting, the old friends were reminiscing and finding familiar ground, but Danny never mentioned her beautiful hair again.

Left: *Yorkshire, 1926. Wedding of Margaret Smith and Reginald Metcalfe. Back row: unknown. Front row, L–R: Hazel Middleton, flower girl; Reg Metcalfe; Margaret Metcalfe; probably Reg Smith, ring bearer. I am guessing the identity of the little boy. He certainly looks like Reg Smith, who would have been 7 years old at the time.*

Above: *Marriage certificate of Margaret Smith and Reg Metcalfe.*

Hard Times at Flat Lake

Though their fortunes eventually improved, the Smiths' first few years in Canada were far from idyllic. As mentioned earlier, the terms of the Soldier Settlement Plan put Charles Smith in debt and required him to work for a while on other people's farms instead of his own. In the fall of 1929, just over a year after the Smiths' arrival, the Great Depression began with the fall of stock markets in the United States. In Canada, wages for farm workers lucky enough to get jobs fell to as little as $5 a month, along with room and board. People could survive in such situations, but there was no hope of paying off debts.

Tension between Charles and Esther worsened the situation. Long-standing grief and resentment over the death of the baby Joe was only part of the cause of conflict. Some evidence suggests that husband and wife battled with each other over who was boss in the family. Esther told me about an incident in which she got a good bargain on the purchase of a milk cow, but Charles disapproved of her action, telling her, "I'se the master here." There was another long-standing issue, one that Charles probably hoped would be left in England. There, when Esther conversed with men, Charles was infuriated by what he saw as her unacceptably friendly manner. Esther attracted attention in Canada in the same way as she had in England. An incident Danny told me about seems to symbolize the wreckage of Charles's hope for a new and better life in Canada and his realization that for him leaving Yorkshire was a mistake. One day, as he was walking through woods, he was entranced by a pretty little black-and-white cat busily getting insects out of a log and eating them. He must have thought how great it would be to take home a beautiful cat, one which was such a wonderful hunter. He crept up to the cat, which was ignoring him, but when he attempted to put his arms around the cat, his eyes and nose were suddenly accosted by a mist of burning, stinking spray. He ran toward home, reeking with skunk's musk, the smell spreading out around him and reaching his house before he did. His wife and sons were repelled by the smell and put distance between themselves and him. Two days later, after laundering clothes and bathing, Charles no longer carried much of the skunk's scent, but the bad smell may have lingered in his mind as a pall over life in the new land. After a miserable time at Flat Lake, Charles left the family.

Reactions to Charles's Leaving

With Charles gone, Esther may have found the new situation quite satisfactory. She was left with a bigger than average house, three big sons, Jack, Tommy, and Danny, capable of running the farm, and two younger sons, Reg and Mac, to whom she could devote her attention and see to their education and wellbeing.

Tension in the family had been between the parents, however, not between the offspring and either parent. In England Esther's daughter Margaret wrote to her mother expressing regret at the breakdown of the marriage. When Esther told me about the letter, she indicated that she did not agree with her daughter. Much later I saw a note on the song sheet "Daddy," indicating that Margaret's relationship with her father was a warm one. Peter Metcalfe, Danny's nephew in England, tells of a ceramic ornament, a cat playing with a spindle, which Charles gave to his daughter Margaret, Peter's mother. According to Peter, Margaret kept the ornament on display throughout her married life and eventually passed it on to her daughter Joan, who still has it on display.

Like his sister Margaret, Danny also felt disturbed when his father left. He was working on a neighbouring farm at the time, and he had no chance

Charles's gift to his daughter Margaret. The ceramic cat playing with a spindle was precious to her and her family.

to say farewell. Weeks later, when he heard that a letter from his father, written by a hired scribe, had come in the mail for him, he went to his mother and asked for it. She replied that she had burned it, and, as far as I know, she never revealed the contents of the letter. Danny was bitter that his mother had interfered with his father's attempt to communicate with him. He returned to working for the neighbour, Charlie Brennan, a kindly family man, while Jack and Tommy ran the farm.

For years Danny heard almost nothing about his father. After about 20 years had passed, he was excited to hear some intriguing news from a neighbour: a man travelling on the train running between Edmonton and Cold Lake had asked about his sons, Tommy, Danny, and Reg Smith. The neighbour was able to tell the man that all three were married, had families, and were successful farmers. Years later we learned that Charles was in contact with his youngest son, Allan, and his family. Until recently, that was all I recalled of decades-old news about the father-in-law I had never met. A recent search of old documents, however, made me realize how imperfectly my memory had stored some information. At the end of this chapter you will find an update on Charles's life.

Romance Thwarted from a Grave

Some months after Charles left, Esther attracted the attention of Jim Fraser. In Chapter 3's old-timer photo, taken about 1916, Jim and his wife, Lucy, can be seen. By the time Esther appeared on the scene in 1928, Jim had been a widower for several years, Lucy having succumbed to consumption. Tall, educated, and comparatively prosperous, Jim would have been interesting to Esther. We Rosses met Esther when Jim brought her in his car to the Armstrong house and introduced her to Mama. Esther was lively and gracious and Mama liked her immediately. When Esther told Mama that she was looking to get a divorce, Mama decided to do Esther a favour. She said bluntly, "Mrs. Smith, Jim Fraser will never marry you." Mama then explained that Jim had promised his wife, Lucy, that he would never marry anyone else. I think Mama and others saw Jim's promise as noble and romantic. In my mind, if Lucy extracted the promise, she was controlling rather than noble. In any case, Jim kept his promise. He and Esther remained only friends. Years later, when Danny and I encountered Jim in BC, Jim asked Danny about Esther and where she was living. Danny later commented to his mother, "I think Jim will be coming to see you." Esther shook her head.

Jack's Story

With Jack and Tommy working on the farm, Esther expected the farm would provide a living for the household. Events in 1932 shattered her world.

His mother's favourite, Jack was the most handsome and dashing of the brothers. Esther was especially proud of him for having qualified for entrance to Ripon Grammar School. When I was ten or eleven, Alex and I saw Jack at a dance at Rife School. He flashed his brilliant smile at us and said, "I know who you are. Do you know who I am?" Alex and I had met Danny when he worked briefly for Papa soon after the Smiths arrived, but we had not seen him for a perhaps two years. I guessed, "I think you're Danny." I was wrong about Jack's identity, but I was charmed by him. About 40 years later, when Danny and I visited a Yorkshire friend of the family, the lady, after mistaking Danny for an American, cried out, "By gum, you're Jack Smith." She suddenly remembered that was not possible and said sadly, "Oh no. Now I remember. We heard what happened. So sad. Such a smashing lad." We turned the conversation to happier things as we enjoyed the famous Yorkshire hospitality.

What happened was that Jack had died by suicide. Apparently Jack was prone to depression. Many years later, when Danny was in his nineties and could bring himself to talk about Jack's death, he told about Jack having

Flat Lake, about 1930. Jack Smith. Jack's death by suicide caused lasting grief to his mother and brothers, and it still brings sadness to his nephews, nieces, and one remaining sister-in-law.

confided to him that he was thinking of killing himself—long before he actually did. Danny, astounded and shocked, replied, "That doesn't make any sense. You've got everything to live for." Danny's comment seemed correct when Jack became engaged to the teacher at Flat Lake School, Jean Campbell. But sometimes at dances Jack drank too much of the homemade liquor, "moonshine," that was readily available. That was the situation on the cold fatal night in March 1932. Probably Jack's fiancée had stated her concern about his drinking before that night. In any case, she took the diamond engagement ring off her finger and put it in Jack's hand. Jack put the ring in his pocket. When he got to Corbetts' home, where he had been working, he went into the garage, held the ring up, pulled the trigger on a gun, and drove the ring into his head.

Terrible Ramifications

Naturally, Jack's suicide had a terrible effect on everyone concerned. It was a shock to his fiancée, who was turned away by Esther when she attempted to attend Jack's funeral, held in the Smith farmhouse. It was an unimaginable horror for Danny, who, while he was washing his brother's body for burial, found the engagement ring in the head wound. For the Corbetts, there was the mournful experience of hearing their dog howl all night after the gunshot and the gut-wrenching task of washing away blood. For Esther, grief over losing her favourite son was locked away in her heart with grief over baby Joe's death.

Officials of the Lutheran Church in Flat Lake were willing to accept Jack's body into their cemetery. My son and I looked for the grave once and found it—barely marked and apart from the other graves. I do not know whether Esther or Danny ever visited it, but if they had, I don't think they would have talked about it. They both put on a brave front and went on with life.

Solace from a Kind Man

After the funeral Danny went back to Charlie Brennan's place, where he had been working. Charlie Brennan greeted Danny warmly and told him their two-year-old daughter kept asking for "Danny" while he was away, that it was good Danny was back, because otherwise, he said, "we might have lost her." That exaggeration was perhaps the greatest gift Charlie could have given Danny at the time. How many times I heard Danny tell the story of the little girl looking for him while he was away—without ever mentioning the reason he'd been away. How much it helped him to get back to the Brennan calm and kindness!

In the summer of 1932 Tommy announced that he would no longer be working on his mother's farm. He and Amelia Wilkowski were getting married and had found work as a couple for a Mr. Cormack of St. Paul. They planned to buy their own farm. Esther sent a message to Danny that she and his two brothers needed help on the farm. Charlie Brennan again showed what a decent man he was when he told Danny, "We need you here, but your mother needs you more."

Danny was just turning 19 when he assumed responsibility for running the farm. There was much to do, but in his characteristic way, he jumped into action. The uninsulated big frame house was actually colder than a well-chinked log house, so Danny used his axe and saw to amass a generous supply of wood.

From his father and neighbours, Danny had learned the rhythm of farming in four seasons. He knew how to work the soil and fertilize it so the crops he planted, as early as the spring allowed, would be lush and ready for harvest before frost. In the early summer he seized every opportunity to put up hay so the horses and cattle would have plenty to eat during the long winters. He cared about animals' welfare, giving them clean straw for bedding. When he could, he gave the horses their beloved oats and regularly used a curry comb to groom them. The horses rewarded him with welcoming whinnies when they saw him and willingness to work hard, obeying his every command.

Danny Runs the Farm

One story from Danny's early days on the farm illustrates his concern for the welfare of all animals, not just his own. One wintry day, as he was driving his own team of horses on a narrow road, he encountered a man whipping his horses as they attempted to pull a sleigh heavily loaded with logs. The horses were struggling to do what their driver wanted, but they were stumbling and slipping on ice under their feet. Danny told the man his load of logs was too heavy for the horses, but the man at first ignored him. As Danny repeated that the load was too heavy, the man shook his head and said, "No speak English." Raising his fist, Danny indicated that the man had either to remove some of the logs or deal with him. Suddenly the man understood what Danny had been saying. He took the securing chains off the logs and, with Danny's help, removed as many logs as necessary to give the horses a manageable load.

Danny's Concern for Animals

**A Pleasant
Place to Visit**

As time went on, Mama and Esther became friends. Mama, Vivi, and I enjoyed occasional visits to the prettily decorated house. Food was plentiful there, as Danny brought in venison, wild ducks, and geese for meat, and Esther, along with Reg and Allan, produced a surplus of garden vegetables. Like all their neighbours, they picked wild raspberries, blueberries, and saskatoons, some of which Esther preserved. Even during the

Flat Lake, 1936. Danny in front of the sleigh he used for hauling wood.

Flat Lake, 1937. L–R: Danny and Reg enjoying some horseplay.

Depression, Esther was able to buy flour, sugar, baking powder, and a few spices. Using butter and milk from their cows, she made puddings, bread, cinnamon buns, cakes, pies, and cookies. It was indeed a treat to visit there.

Danny worked on the Flat Lake farm for nearly eight years, during which his younger brothers, Reg and Mac, were getting an education and growing up. The Flat Lake School was three miles away, so in cold weather Danny sometimes hitched up the horses and gave the boys a sleigh ride to and/or from school. In very cold weather the school was closed. As Reg and Mac grew older, they helped more and more with the farm chores. The farm prospered to the extent that, even during the Depression, Danny and his mother were able to share in the purchase of a Model A car.

By the fall of 1939, life on the Flat Lake farm was coming to an end for the Smiths. After harvest that year, Danny left the farm in the hands of his brothers, Reg and Mac, aged 21 and 19, respectively. He took a Greyhound bus to Windsor, Ontario, the city which connected by bridge to Detroit, Michigan, where I was working. He and I were married the following spring, on March 1, 1940, in Windsor, in the manse of the United Church minister. On our month-long honeymoon we travelled by bus through the United States and visited with Danny's eldest brother, Charles, aka Bill Davis, and his wife, Florence in Minneapolis.

Smith Saga at Flat Lake Ends

Meanwhile things had changed at Flat Lake. On October 12, 1939, Reg married his fiancée, Velva Ross (not related to me), and the couple settled temporarily on the Flat Lake farm. World War II had started, and Mac enlisted with the Canadian army. Esther had decided to ride on the winds of change rather than be blown around by them. She moved into a two-bedroom log house on a farm a mile north of Glendon. She hired a carpenter to build a small house for her in Glendon and encouraged Reg and his bride to buy the farm north of Glendon. The saga of the Smiths in Flat Lake had come to an end.

Above, left: *Allan MacDonald in soldier's uniform, about 1941. Allan, who had been known as "Mac," chose to go by his first name after he enlisted.*

Above, right: *Flat Lake, winter, about 1941. Reg and Allan Smith. Allan, age 21, is going to war. Reg, as a farmer, will help to feed the Allies, but his thoughts will be with his brother. Their mother, Esther, probably took the photo.*

Left: Yorkshire, about 1946. The war has ended, and Allan visits his childhood home.

Left: Yorkshire, about 1946. L–R: Margaret Metcalfe, Allan Smith, Joan Metcalfe. Allan visits his sister and niece Joan.

Above: *Leighton Reservoir in Yorkshire. Here Reg Metcalfe was Superintendent of Waterworks for the City of Leeds. He was also Estates Manager. The lovely vista is probably much the same as it was when the Smiths left for Canada.*

Right, top; *Around Leeds, Yorkshire, about 1946. L–R: One of Allan's soldier friends biking with Allan's eldest sister, Ettie. Photo by Allan.*

Right, bottom: *The Metcalfe home at Leighton.*

Glendon, 1995. Tommy and Danny, two of the boys in kilts in the photo at the beginning of this chapter, as senior citizens.

Now that they are retired (somewhat), Tommy and Danny have more time to enjoy their old-time camaraderie. Although they have thrived in Canada, they fondly recall ties to the "old country," but only Tommy still has an English accent. Only Allan and Danny have been back to visit Yorkshire.

Charles's Reunion with Son Allan

As we prepared to send this memoir to our publisher, Jean and her brother Rick discovered a forgotten letter to Danny and me from Allan Smith's wife, Charlotte. It reveals that one family member was concerned about Charles's whereabouts and welfare. That person was Margaret Metcalfe. The letter also reveals what caring people Charlotte and Allan were. Charlotte's letter is quoted below.

Sept 29, 1955

China Creek PO BC

Dear Cathie and Danny

Here I am at last and I have some news for you. You might get as big a surprise as we did but I promised to let you know and then it's up to you. Well, Margaret wrote to us a couple of months ago and asked us about your Dad, Danny, and we wrote and told her we knew nothing about him but if she sent us his last address if he is still in this country, we would try and trace him. Well she sent it and it was Penticton, so we got the Salvation Army to trace him and he is still living in Penticton but working at Williams Lake. So we wrote there and we got an answer back saying he would be in Penticton last weekend and would be happy to see us. So we went down and saw him. He is really grand for his age and he told us to tell you he would really like to see you and us to give you his address. It is Mr. C. Smith 696 Ellis Street, Penticton, BC. I hope you will excuse this short note but I have to write to Reg and Tommy.

Love from us all,

Charlotte and Allan

At the time Charlotte wrote, 1955, Danny and I thought we were too busy to travel to BC to see Charles. Danny was expanding his farm operation and I was getting an education so as to become a teacher. We were both involved in raising our youngest son, Richard, who was only two years old. Our lives were hectic, but we should have found time to get in touch with Danny's lonely old father. Fortunately Charlotte and Allan acted differently, and eventually Charles retired to the West Coast where he took on the role of grandfather to Allan and Charlotte's children (See photo in Chapter 15.)

CHAPTER 8

Help with Work and Help in Crises

Celebrating horses. Maple Ridge, BC, 1966. Ed White riding his sister Lynne's horse, a handsome palomino called Flash. Ray White bought the horse for Lynne, but he also loved his evening visits with Flash at the horse's boarding place.

Before I leave pioneer days, I want to acknowledge helpers—those who contributed to Mama and Papa's successful venture into farming and helped in other ways.

Oxen and Horses—Silver Bell, Dan, King, Bird, Flash

I begin with the indispensable beasts of burden—horses and oxen, without which few people would have been able to "prove up" their homesteads. Horses were the preferred beasts of burden, but we must give oxen their due. With their powerful bodies they were able to pull out the most stubborn stumps and plow through the toughest sod. But oxen were not as versatile as horses and usually did not bond with their handlers the way horses did. Papa made some use of oxen, but like most pioneers, he preferred horses.

Horses are strong and intelligent creatures, willing to work in partnership with humans. To get the crops planted, they pulled plows, discs, and harrows. To get crops harvested, they pulled binders. To take a lone man, woman or child to town, to school, or to a country dance, a horse would accept the human being on its back, with or without a saddle, and walk or trot to the destination. If speed was needed, the horse could switch to a top-speed gallop and give the rider the thrill of almost flying. For a slightly slower, more relaxed ride, the horse might slip into a rhythmic canter. To get a family to a destination, a horse or team of horses would pull a wagon or buggy over bare ground or a sleigh over snow and ice. No wonder homesteaders valued and loved their horses.

Horses, however, are not all the same. Homesteaders had to be careful when they bought an unknown horse from a horse trader. Looking back on the four horses Papa brought from BC, I hope he got a bargain price for the four of them. Only Silver Bell, Vivi's pony, seemed without a serious defect. Dan was a kicking horse; he would lash out if he got startled or frightened. King was an old darling, but he had been foundered. At some time, his hoofs had not been properly cared for, so there was some inflammation and pain that caused him to go lame when a rider was on his back. Bird at some time had been in a runaway, a traumatic experience which can leave some horses ready to bolt at the least surprise. Once when the men were bringing in the horses at dinner time, she got startled, apparently by the wind. In her panic she ran seven miles until, exhausted, she stopped. Despite his horses' defects, Papa loved his horses and was able to manage them without any great calamity.

Horses and their masters often form bonds of affection which may cause the master to feel sorrow when a horse succumbs to old age. I believe horses also feel sorrow. Papa's horse Bird gave birth to a pair of twin colts, but they were born dead. Poor Bird must have had a strong motherly instinct. For quite a while after her loss, she would return to the spot where the colts had been born and whinny a few times and sniff the ground. Then she would have to give up and leave. Apparently she was grieving her loss.

Maybe like Robbie Burns's field mouse, animals do not guess and fear the future. In 1929, about seven in the evening, a terrible lightning storm came. A neighbour's four horses were leaning against a wire fence that got struck by lightning. All four horses were killed. The neighbour, Frank Sisco, had to deal not only with sadness and financial loss but also the worry that the future could bring him more trouble.

As farmers bought tractors, their horses were no longer needed. But the horses still needed to be fed. Sadly, many farmers could not afford the luxury of keeping the animals who had served them so well. No one wanted to buy them, so many horses ended up in slaughter houses, becoming glue and pet food.

Hired Men

I also acknowledge the hired men and women we had over the years, capable and diligent workers who contributed much to us both out in the fields and in the house. Some of these people went on to have farms and homes of their own. Some did not fare so well.

There was smiling Louis Fedorus, whom I remember most for what he did in his spare time—playing the violin while Mama played the piano. Of course, most of the time Louis was working in the fields or brushing trees in the woods.

There was Carlson Tollefson, who greeted us with smiles, worked hard at brushing, and went on to success in his own business venture at Franchere Beach—boat rentals and fishing equipment.

Next came Bill Ronayne, an Irishman. He had disappointed his parents when he refused to continue at Cambridge, as his father and brother had done, choosing instead to roam in Canada's backwoods and work for Papa.

There was Bill Kirkpatrick, another Irishman. He came to Canada with a group of Irish people who settled at St. Brides. Most of the people in his group were not prepared for the frigid Canadian winter and suffered from the cold. When he came to work for Papa, Bill finally had a warm place to sleep. From him we kids learned how to play whist. He would groan in despair when one of us would jubilantly "plunk" a bare king out for the opposition to jump on with an ace. We loved his reactions. I remember Bill, at the invitation of our teacher, Miss Ryan, singing at the Flat Lake School Christmas Concert. He rendered most beautifully the lovely song "Little Town in the Auld County Down."

I cannot leave out the sad story of William Whysk. He was a very competent worker, but he had gotten into trouble with the law for stealing. When he got out of jail, people were reluctant to hire him. Papa took a chance on him, and Bill seemed to be on the right road. He never stole anything from us; however, when other job opportunities came, Bill chose brighter lights. It was not long before we saw in a newspaper that a William Whysk had been arrested for stealing a car. We knew it was our Bill Whysk when Papa got a letter from prison. In it, Bill appealed to Papa to help him get out of jail, but Papa wrote back that he was regretfully not ready to give him a second chance. Not long after that we saw that William Whysk had hanged himself in jail. I will always remember Bill with gratitude. It was he who taught me to play "O My Darling Clementine" on the violin, and that is how I learned to play that instrument. Every one of our hired men had something good about him.

Occasionally Danny Smith worked for us. I remember Papa saying that Jim Fraser told him that if he wanted a fence to be built straight, the man to hire was Danny, who was about 15 years old at the time. After Danny, at age 19, took over running his mother's farm, he was too busy to work for anyone else for a few years—until his brother Reg, five years younger, had finished school and was able to handle most of the farm work.

Another hired man at Rife was Torkel Hallaland from Norway, brother to Kristine Haland, who farmed with her husband Chris Haland at Rife. Torkel played Norwegian tunes on his accordion, especially Norwegian waltzes. At dances I used to snag him to waltz with when the orchestra played a Norwegian waltz.

Matt Leslie was a valuable worker too, but after he and Donnie clashed (see Chapter 9), the situation became strained for a while. In the end, Matt remained a valued friend of the family.

Lester Story was the hired man who worked for Papa the longest—more than ten years. His help was much appreciated when Danny had to go to Edmonton for surgery on his back and I was left for several weeks with three small children.

Hired Women

Rosie Grant, Katie Kriaski, and Annie Whysk, sister of Bill Whysk, were the three main women who came occasionally to help Mama with preparing meals and housekeeping at especially busy times, such as harvesting.

Orphaned Children

After Vivi and I were married, Mama and Papa opened their home to three orphans who needed a home and who were willing and able to help with tasks around the house or outside. They also attended Rife School until they completed grade eight or turned 15.

Wallace Gray was about 14 when he came to Mama and Papa's household. Besides helping with chores, he

Celebrating hired helpers. Armstrong house, Christmas Day, 1944. L–R: Lester Story, Donnie Ross, Papa (William Ross). Lester was our reliable hired man for about ten years.

entertained Vivi's and my children, who all loved him. When he came of age, he joined the Canadian army and was sent to fight in Korea. When some of our children wrote to him, he wrote kind letters back. Then one day Mama got a letter informing her, as "next of kin," that Wallace Gray was missing in action and presumed dead. Mama and her grandchildren mourned his passing.

Norma McLaughlan and Isabel Sherman were about 12 when they came to live with Mama and Papa. Both girls soon developed a warm relationship with Mama and cheerfully helped her with some of the housework and gardening. Norma became an actual part of the family when she married our cousin Kenny MacLean, son of Florence and Alex MacLean. Norma and Kenny had three children, Roger, Morris, and Patty, but their marriage did not last. They both died in unhappy situations at relatively young ages. When Mama and Papa moved to BC in 1946, Isabel moved with them. She found her first job there in a cannery and went on to other better-paying jobs. She eventually married a dentist.

Cattle Buyer

Another person who had a role to play in Mama and Papa's success in farming was a cattle buyer, Tony Spence. Born in Scotland, Tony came for many years to bargain over the price of any cattle Papa had for sale. Tony was very shrewd, but then so was Papa. Tony always appeared just at dinner time. Mama always had a pie shell on hand and would find a lemon or two in the cupboard. Magically a lovely lemon pie would appear. Mama was shrewd too.

Ministers of the Church

Pangs of loneliness were part of the homesteader's lot, but worse than that was the terrible grief that had to be endured when a child in the family died. I know that at such times many people are helped by their religion or by talking with a spiritual guide. I saw the need for such solace at the first two funerals I attended, both at the Rife United Church. One was the service for a fine little fellow just under a year old. It was extremely sad to see his young mother, Ida Aylesworth, trying to stifle her sobs and her husband, Leland, trying to bury his grief in his handkerchief. The other funeral was for baby Septimus Fox. A heartrending sight was when his mother, Mrs. Stanley Fox, raised the tiny waxen hand to her lips for a final kiss. In both cases, I hope the minister managed to provide some comfort to the grieving parents.

Of course family members usually help provide solace too. Mrs. Fox had successfully piloted her six older boys to manhood, and I believe they supported their mother in her grief at losing her last baby. I also believe the six older Fox sons found ways to support each other and their mother when their father, Stanley Fox, went to Ontario to find work, sent money back, but never came back himself. Thinking of the heavy burden Mrs. Fox carried makes me think how fortunate we are when our lives go along comfortably, without the loss of any loved ones except through old age.

Relatives

In pioneer days, any death in wintertime meant hardship for the neighbourly helpers who took responsibility for digging the grave. I remember the funeral for an old man who died in January. A grave had to be dug by hand into the hard-as-rock frozen earth. Fires had to be lit on the grave site to enable the diggers to get down to unfrozen earth. On the day of the funeral, the noon temperature was 36 Fahrenheit degrees below zero. People shivered as they stood around the grave for the minister's final words and while the coffin was lowered. Men were expected to bare their heads by removing their headgear. How dreary and cold the burial was! I admired the way the minister did his best to help the bereaved people accept that death could be a time for rejoicing.

Neighbours

On the drive home, often in open sleighs, people did what they could with blankets over their coats and toques to avoid frostbite. If no one had been left at home to stoke the fire, a family would come home to a cold house. The first job would be to get a fire going; the next would be to make a meal. If they could, neighbours would bring dishes of food to a bereaved family. If it was needed, they would bring dry wood to help keep the house warm. Pioneers understood the need to help each other.

In pioneer days the most vital specialized help came from doctors. Without medical help, a broken bone could be crippling or fatal, a baby could be stillborn, a mother could die in childbirth. Fortunately there were excellent doctors in the area: Dr. Decosse was ten miles away in St. Paul and Drs. Miller and Ross 20 miles away in Elk Point.

Doctors

When a medical crisis arose, a pioneer had a difficult choice—try to "tough it out" or get help from a doctor. The latter choice could involve four hours of torturous travel over rough dirt roads by horse and buggy or less if a person had access to a car. Our friend Stanley MacKenzie was riding his horse several miles from home when his horse stumbled and fell. The big body of the horse landed on Stanley, breaking his leg. Stanley managed to crawl back on his horse and endure the ride home (and the loyal horse stood and waited to carry his master home.) Stanley was fortunate in having a car and someone on hand to drive him to see a doctor in St. Paul. Another friend, Cecil Wakefield had a similar experience, except he had no car to get him to a doctor. He had to endure the ordeal of the buggy ride. Our two friends survived and lived long lives, thanks to help from their doctors.

Long-Time Friends

Thinking about helpers and friendship reminds me of a sentence I copied from the *Family Herald*: "No matter how worthy the new friends are, they cannot seem to quite come up to the old friends." I noticed how my parents seemed to have especially strong bonds with the people they had met early on in their homesteading days. Later, when they were preoccupied with families of their own, they seemed less inclined to form close friendships. They lost their closest friends when Lucy Fraser died of consumption and eventually her husband, Jim Fraser, moved away, as did Stan and Nellie MacKenzie. Although she made new friends, Mama always seemed wistful when she talked about her old friends. Danny and I made dozens of valued friends over the years. Among them, I believe the most precious were our oldest ones—Jock and Rose Ross, with whom we travelled, and Lloyd and Frances Hill, who wrote such great letters and visited as often as they could. (Of course Ray White was a treasured old friend, but I count him as family.)

Papa had a special long-term friend, Frank Sisco. The two men had worked together in BC and moved to Alberta about the same time. After Frank moved away, Papa heard little of him for several years. However, when Papa heard that Frank was sick in a hospital in Edmonton, he was determined to see him. Seeing Papa walk into the hospital room, Frank was so touched that he wept. I suspect Papa wept too, but he did not tell us that. Obviously their friendship was important to them both.

As I write, I appreciate, perhaps more than ever, how our parents helped **Parents** to prepare us for life. Papa definitely succeeded in his role as provider for our family. Thanks to him we had the means for a comfortable life— well sheltered, clothed, and fed. Within the family, Mama had the central role. With her loving ways and shrewd insights, she prepared me and my siblings for life as adults. She taught us to accept and handle reality, to support each other and to develop our talents. She took us to church to help build our faith. She taught us values for everyday living—honesty, fairness, responsibility, kindness, and courage. By her example, she showed us how to be strong in times of hardship and how to forgive. She also showed us how to enjoy life, to see the beauty in things around us, to socialize, and to laugh.

CHAPTER 9

Growing Up and Getting Married

A composite wedding photo was created for our 50th wedding anniversary. The photo of Danny was taken in Haney, BC, about 1947. The photo of me was taken in Detroit about 1939.

Meeting Danny

In the summer of 1928, our first summer at Rife, Papa, Donnie, and a hired man worked long days getting hay cut, dried, raked, loaded on to hayracks, and then unloaded into a barn loft or made into haystacks conveniently near the farmyard. There was urgency about making hay while the sun shone, before rain came or heavy dew fell in the evening. Papa felt he needed another hired man, and he had heard that the newly arrived Smith family had three big boys. He drove over to Flat Lake and brought back Danny Smith.

On very long work days in the hayfield, Mama would take a mid-afternoon lunch of sandwiches, sweets, and coffee out to the workers. I was nine years old when I saw Danny in the hayfield using a pitchfork to load hay onto a hayrack. I was used to watching hired men work, so I realized how smoothly and quickly Danny worked. When he stopped work and came to the place where Mama had arranged a picnic lunch on a blanket, I went over to where Danny was sitting. I asked him his name, and he answered saying he'd tell me if I told him my name. I was fascinated by his English accent and questioned him about it. He was not shy and neither was I. While he worked for us he got room and board, coming in for meals and sleeping in the boys' bedroom with Donnie and Alex and the hired man. When he was on hand, I made sure to wear a pretty dress and have my hair nicely combed as I went about putting food on the table. Danny was needed to help with haying for only about a week, but by the time he left, I knew how it felt to have a crush on someone.

Below: Flat Lake, 1928. Danny Smith, age 14 or 15. This is how Danny looked when I first met him.

I didn't see Danny again until the summer of 1930, when Papa felt he needed more help in the hayfield. By then I had matured to the point that Mama and Papa had begun keeping an eye on me when a young man was on hand. Perhaps knowing I was under surveillance inhibited me. Now I did not feel so at ease chatting with Danny about my doll or how many raspberries I had picked. But Danny listened to me and told me some ways that Canada was different from the "old country." After a week or two, haying was finished and Papa was getting the buggy ready to take Danny home. I went out to say goodbye to him and was thrilled when he said, "You're a pretty one, Cathie." I knew he liked me, but I didn't know when I would see him again.

Arrival of Aunt Florence and Family

Life went on uneventfully until 1931. On a Sunday in August we were sitting around the table Mama had set with a white tablecloth, eating the wholesome supper she had made. Suddenly we heard a knock, and Papa got up to open the door. We heard him exclaim, "Florence" and craned our necks to see a short woman with grey bushy hair and a bunch of tiger lilies in her hands. We saw him stoop down to welcome his sister with a kiss on the cheek. Aunt Florence and her husband, Alex MacLean, and friends had left the drought-stricken Youngstown area in southern Alberta and were hoping to move to the greener pastures they saw all around Rife.

Right: Rife, Armstrong house, about 1932. Back row, L–R: Papa with his sister Florence MacLean. Front: Kenny MacLean. In the photo Papa and Florence are taking Kenneth with them on a trip to PEI to visit Grandma Ross (Mary MacKinnon) and brother Malcolm and his wife, Bessie.

A few days later, on a hot day, I looked out my bedroom window and there, watering his horses, was a tall, handsome fellow. I went out to greet him, and found him very sociable. He told me he was friends with Alex and Florence MacLean and had come from Youngstown. He said he called his horses Saygo and Hugo and that his name was Ray White. I later learned that in 1925, when Ray was 21, he had come to Youngstown from Brighton, England. Some years earlier, his father, who had owned a mill, died, after which his mother kept a green grocery store. Ray had wanted adventure, so he said goodbye to his mother; sister, Nell; and brother, Fred, and set sail for Canada. (Fred eventually followed Ray to Canada, settling in Guelph, Ontario.)

Arrival of Ray White

Ray had lived with the MacLeans during the winter of 1931, and when they decided to move to Rife, he chose to move with them. He packed up his belongings, arranged to load his horses, cattle, a few pigs, and farm implements into box cars, and travelled with them by train to Glendon. Like other such travellers, he supplied food and water to his animals during the trip. The morning I met him, Ray had ridden on horseback from Glendon to arrange for pasture for his livestock. When he and helpers herded his cattle and horses to Rife, Alex and I were shocked to see how thin the animals were. The MacLeans' cattle were in the same shape. How good it must have felt to be in a land of plenty, with lots of green grass and clean water for the animals.

Rife as a Land of Plenty

Vivi was about 18 years old at the time, and she immediately caught Ray's eye. Soon Ray was a frequent visitor at our place. He would sing while Vivi played the piano. He had a strong baritone voice, an excellent ear, and a super memory for lyrics. He seemed to know every popular song of the day from "Abdul Abulbul Amir" to "The Strawberry Roan."

Vivi Charms Ray

Papa helped the MacLeans find a quarter with a cabin on it, owned by Maurice Destrube. The property happened to be the quarter across the road from the Armstrong house. The cabin had been moved from the site of the Red Cross hospital, where it had been the kitchen part of the complex. The MacLeans, with their growing sons, Ross and Kenny, farmed the rented property until 1940. That year they bought a half

Red Cross Kitchen Becomes a Home

section and built a neat two-storey frame house on it. As it happened, they vacated the Red Cross kitchen just on time for Danny and me to move into it. But my story took a few twists and turns before Danny and I arrived there.

Ray Builds a Log Home

Ray White settled on a half section a little to the north of the MacLeans. He named one quarter "the quack grass quarter," a name which is still used locally. Ray's property had a little stream running through it to Moose Lake. The original homesteader had chosen an area near the stream to build a barn. The site was lovely, and at that time Ray was not much concerned that it was two miles from Rife School—a long way to walk for a child starting school. He set to work building a substantial log house on a small hill near the stream and barn. With the help of George Nordstrom he hewed logs (using an axe to make logs square rather than round) and dove-tailed the corners (using an axe to shape the ends of logs so they interlock at the corners). The house had a large room used as dining room and living room, a small kitchen, and a bedroom. It had large windows and a porch with a roof over it, a pleasant place to sit on a warm evening.

Vivi and Ray Become Engaged

As Ray was building the house he dreamed that he would one day bring Vivi to it as his bride. Vivi said she wanted to complete high school and train to become a teacher. Ray told her he would wait for her, and they became engaged.

Vivi Becomes a Teacher

In the fall of 1932 Vivi enrolled in Normal School in Edmonton, where she received standard teacher training. In the fall of 1933 she started teaching at Moose Lake School, where she taught more than three years, until the 1936 Christmas holidays.

Wedding of Vivi and Ray

On December 30, 1936, Vivi and Ray were married by a minister in a ceremony at the Armstrong house. After a reception there for 70 people and a dance at Rife School, the married couple escaped to the pretty log house Ray had built and began their life together.

Life for Vivi and Ray in the log house by the stream was as idyllic as anyone could wish. Vivi kept their house clean and tidy and used her sewing skills to add finishing touches such as curtains and cushions. Ray was established as a successful farmer with productive milk cows, pigs that rapidly reproduced, and sufficient farm implements to plant and harvest crops. His beloved work horses, Bubbles and Tillie, were the envy of neighbours for their stamina and the way they helped get the work done.

Looking back over Ray and Vivi's nearly 53 years of married life, I believe their marriage was an especially happy one. Some shadow inevitably falls into life, and Vivi tended to notice the shadows more than Ray did. Ray's irrepressible optimism enabled him to focus mainly on the sunshine. His cheery ways were uplifting to people around him—friends, family and eventually customers. Vivi especially benefitted from his positive attitude. Not long before Vivi and Ray's 50th wedding anniversary, Ray wrote a letter to Danny and me telling us about Vivi's health problems, concluding, "She is feeling some better and [I] hope to get her as good as she was first time I saw her August, 1931." Later, when Vivi had recovered good health by dint of her own determination to control her food and drink intake, a smiling Ray said to me, "She has brought springtime back into my heart." For Vivi, the only disadvantage to Ray's sunny ways was that she sadly missed him during the 17 years she lived after he died.

Left: Ross farm at Rife, summer 1965, after Mack and Diane's wedding. L–R: me, Olive Ross, Donnie Ross, Vivi White, Ray White. After nearly 30 years, Ray and Vivi are still having fun. Probably Danny took the photo.

Eight Glitches

"True love will find a way" is a saying which is only sometimes true. I have friends who feel they missed out on their one true love. I had Vivi and Ray's example of true love sailing smoothly along, without, at least as far as I knew, any glitches. In contrast, my romance with Danny was long and intermittent, with glitches galore. Looking back I see at least eight glitches—setbacks that could have meant the end of our romance and even our friendship.

Ray Brings Danny to Our House

In the fall of 1933, after the harvest was over and fall work done, Danny temporarily left the farm chores at Flat Lake in the capable hands of his 15-year-old brother, Reg, along with their younger brother, Mac, and their mother. He went to work for a few months at the Jones place, where he had room and board. The Jones place being near Ray's place, Danny and Ray saw enough of each other to discover how much they had in common. Tall, handsome, and gregarious, they made friends easily. They were both successful farmers, Ray on his own property, Danny running his mother's farm. They both took pride in their work, took good care of their livestock, and prized their horses. They both danced well and loved to laugh and sing. Not surprisingly, they added fun to any gathering.

For some time we Rosses had been hearing Ray's smooth baritone while Vivi played the piano. When Ray brought Danny to join in the singing with his deep bass, we were thrilled as they sang their various songs. We especially liked "On the Road to Mandalay," where "the dawn comes up like thunder out of China 'cross the bay."

From the time I was 12, I was lucky enough to be going with Ray and Vivi to dances. One summer day, after I turned 14, Ray had Danny with him in his "democrat" (buggy) when he came to pick up Vivi and me for a dance. I felt proud to have 19-year-old Danny, a renowned dancer, as my partner for the dance. The dance, at Hoselaw, about eight miles away, was especially lively, and we were on our feet dancing to the beat until well into the morning. When we had set out for the dance, I sat with Ray and Vivi on the seat of the democrat and Danny stood behind us. When we climbed back into the democrat for the drive home, Danny and I sat on the floor behind the seat where Ray and Vivi were sitting. By the time Ray's horses had delivered Vivi and me to our home, the sky in the northeast was bright.

When Vivi and I got up around noon the next day, Papa was fuming about my behaviour. In the dawn light he had looked out the window and seen me sitting on the floor of the democrat with Danny. Papa forbade me to go to dances with Ray and Vivi if Danny was with them. That was the first setback to romance with Danny.

Dances were held only about six times per year, and snow was on the ground when the next dance was held. It was again at Hoselaw, organized by Mama and Papa's friends, Amy and Bill Fraser. For some reason Ray and Vivi did not go to that dance, so I went along with Papa and Mama. To my delight, Danny was there, and I danced a lot of dances with him. Amy Fraser invited Papa, Mama, and me to come to their place for Sunday dinner the day after the dance. (Amy had a lot of energy.)

The following day, when Papa drove his cutter (sleigh) into the Fraser yard, I was surprised to see Danny there. I was beyond surprised—even thunderstruck—to hear my father shouting, "Double cross! Double cross!" These words were addressed to Amy, who looked shocked and embarrassed. Papa did not elucidate, but Danny quickly surmised that Papa's rage must have something to do with him. Danny said calmly, "I won't stay where I'm not wanted," turned around and started walking out of the yard toward the highway. Papa was not satisfied that Danny had absented himself from the dinner. He insisted that Mama and I get back in the cutter and go home. Mama tried to persuade him that not having dinner with Amy and Bill would be too rude, but Papa insisted.

On the way home, I felt distressed and tried to guess what the double cross was that so enraged Papa. To this day I can only guess that Papa had confided to Amy that he wanted to put a stop to any relationship between Danny and me, probably because I was only 14 and Danny was 20. Amy's double cross may have been inviting Danny to the dinner. On the way home, our horses trotted by Danny walking in the snow at the side of the road. Mama commented, "Danny looks kind of noble." I never forgot her words. After the double-cross incident, Danny did not come to the Armstrong house for perhaps two years. He and Ray, however, became and stayed close friends. I continued going to dances with Ray and Vivi, where I noticed Danny was never lacking female companionship. He "went with" several women, including two teachers and a pretty party girl who worked as a housemaid. He usually danced one or two dances with me and chatted in a brotherly way.

Grain Truck Transportation

One year a friend, Cedric Fraser, son of Amy and Bill, developed a new mode of transportation to dances farther away, such as at Glendon. He had a grain truck, which he fixed up to carry a dozen or so people in relative comfort. The box of this grain truck was quite spacious, and Cedric rigged it up with a tarpaulin stretched over a frame so as create a peaked roof over the truck box. Around the sides and front of the box were benches where people could sit. As I recall, we had a lantern in the middle of the floor to provide light and heat on winter trips. I expect we compensated Cedric for the transportation, a mode that enabled people to enjoy trips to and from the dance almost as much as the dance.

Lloyd Hill

A third Englishman, Lloyd Hill, lived close to Ray. Born in 1904, Lloyd was an adventurer from London. His father was a lawyer, but the family name was probably best known for manufacturing pipe organs. When Lloyd was six years old, his life took a turn toward melancholy: his mother died. When he was 12 years old he received another blow: his eldest brother, Michael, who had acted as father to him, was killed in 1916 at the Battle of the Somme. In contrast with the sadness of his life in London, Lloyd found his happiest times were summer holidays he spent in the country with his mother's sister. At age 18 he embarked for Canada, looking for outdoor work and a place to homestead.

One might wonder how someone raised in a city such as London would know enough about taking care of livestock and growing crops to be able to manage on a farm. As it happened, Lloyd's family, the Hills, knew another prominent London family, the Destrubes. After working for a year or so in Manitoba, Lloyd came to Rife to work for Maurice Destrube and to learn how to farm. (Maurice had similarly learned about agriculture from his cousins in Missouri before he ventured into farming.) Lloyd could not have had a better instructor and role model than Maurice. By 1925, when he was only 21, Lloyd had filed on his own homestead. He soon became expert with an axe, able to hew and dove-tail logs for the attractive log house he built for himself. He also became a successful farmer.

Lloyd was more sombre than Danny and Ray, but he found time to attend some of the dances in the area. Having been educated in England, where dancing was part of the curriculum, all three men were good dancers. Lloyd, however, stayed free of entanglements with women and looked as though he might remain a life-long bachelor—as many men did in those days.

At a dance in Glendon, in collusion with the town's postmistress, Rowena Munroe, I introduced a new friend of mine to Lloyd Hill. Rowena knew her post office assistant, Frances Hillary, had her eye on Lloyd and she suggested that I invite Frances to come home with me after the dance. Rowena may have guessed that the flickering lantern light in Cedric's rigged up grain truck provided an exiting atmosphere for romance. Within a year Frances became Lloyd's wife and joined the Rife community. By then Frances and I were close friends, as were Danny and Lloyd. We four remained friends for life, keeping in touch through visits and letter writing. (A more detailed telling of Lloyd and Frances's story—their romance, their challenges, and their incredible success in business in BC—is beyond the scope of this memoir. Their story will be told in another publication.)

Frances (Hillary) Hill

I wasn't pining away by myself at dances. When I was 15 Papa got a new hired man, Matt Leslie, and I got a boyfriend. Matt was a tall, well-educated, outgoing man who could dance well and call square dances. He owned a quarter section with a small log house on it, where he lived, about two miles from the Armstrong place. He was a Catholic, but that fact did not concern Mama, Papa, or me. At 30 he was twice as old as I, but that fact did not seem to concern us either. In Papa's eyes, Matt was all a girl could ask for in that he hailed from Prince Edward Island. To me, Matt seemed youthful enough and he was a good dancer. I was pleased to have him as my boyfriend. Danny's and my involvements with other partners could have kiboshed our interest in each other, so I consider those years glitch number three. As it happened, my siblings were less than enthusiastic about my older boyfriend, and they had some influence over future events.

Glitch 3: Other Romantic Interests

Attending church with one's boyfriend or girlfriend was the most positively sanctioned courtship activity possible. Matt's being Catholic, however, meant that he rarely attended church with me. Some of my most pleasant memories are of Sunday evenings when the household was rounded up to go to church. The minister would come out from St. Paul to hold a church service in the United Church, less than half a mile from our house. He would come usually by horse and cart or horseback, but eventually one of these men came by car. Church was held about 7:30 in the evening, and I don't recall rain ever falling during a church service. The ministers

Church as a Site for Courtship

were young men from New Brunswick or Nova Scotia. They always had a well-prepared sermon for the handful of people who came. I feel we owe eastern Canada a sincere thank you for the young students who came so cheerfully to do their work. I liked going to church; however, looking back, I wonder whether the fact that the ministers were all single males gave church attendance a special non-spiritual appeal for me.

Boarding School for Me

In 1935, when I was 16, Vivi persuaded me, Mama, and Papa that I should pursue a high school education by going to a United Church boarding school at Radway. The school was co-educational—that is, there were boys there. At some point Vivi revealed that she was less concerned with my education than with preventing me from getting too serious about Matt, whom she considered too old for me. The young fellows at Radway, however, seemed to me too juvenile compared with the men I danced with around Rife.

The school year ended in June, and I came home by train. When I got off at the train station in Glendon, Papa and Matt were there to meet me. I also glimpsed Danny among the crowd meeting the train, but I never found out whether he was there to meet me or someone else. It seemed that Vivi's attempt to break up my involvement with Matt was foiled.

Donnie and Matt's Fight

As it happened, however, my gentle, peaceful brother, Donnie, caused a change in my involvement with Matt. By 1936 Donnie was nearly 20 years old and used to being Papa's lieutenant. He apparently told Matt to handle a particular task, but Matt refused to take orders from a boy so much his junior. Donnie did not back down, and, to everyone's surprise, the dispute erupted into fisticuffs. Neither man suffered much physical damage, but the incident put a damper on my relationship with Matt.

Ray and Vivi's Wedding

A big event in 1936 was Ray and Vivi's wedding, on December 30. Mama, knowing what good friends Ray and Danny were, invited Danny to the wedding. After the wedding ceremony and reception for 70 people at the Armstrong house, the wedding party and guests drove or walked up the hill to Rife School for the wedding dance. Perhaps just as Mama planned, my partner at the dance turned out to be Danny. While I was dancing with him, Danny said to me, "I'm a free man now." He told me he had just returned from a trip to BC where he had broken off with the pretty party girl.

Near the end of the dance, Danny asked me if I would be his partner at the next dance, which was scheduled for February 27 at Hoselaw. I felt I had no choice but to refuse Danny's offer. I had committed by letter to going to that dance with Raymond J., who owned a lumber mill northwest of Rife. As it happened, Raymond wrote to me that he could not come to the dance because he was too busy with mill work, so I went to the dance without a partner. Danny was not there, but Matt was.

Matt drove me home in his sleigh, a drive I well remember. The brilliant full moon seemed to travel along with us, making the snow sparkle all around and the night seem like day. Matt told me he missed me and would like to have a serious relationship with me. I replied that I liked him but the fact that most of my family was opposed to him as my partner would make it hard to carry on a relationship. Maybe I was subconsciously clearing the way to see more of Danny. Matt got over his disappointment, remained a family friend, married happily and occasionally came with his wife to visit Mama and Papa.

Even though no phones had been installed in our countryside, news made the rounds surprisingly quickly in those days. People simply dropped in to each other's home to pass on news. I told Mama I had broken off with Matt, and Mama told Vivi, who told Ray, who told Danny. I wasn't aware that my news had been so quickly spread, and I was caught off guard a few days later.

Shortly after the February dance, before the spring sun started to soften the ice, my brothers arranged a skating party on Green Slough. They put out the word to the neighbouring Armagosts; our cousins, Ross and Kenny MacLean; and anyone else who wished to come. After the skate, people would be invited to come into the nearby Armstrong house for hot chocolate or coffee and some of Mama's sugar cookies. Because I knew Danny had never skated and did not own a pair of skates, I was somewhat surprised to see him show up at Green Slough. He said cheerfully that he had come to eat some of Mama's cookies and watch me do some fancy skating. I was even more surprised when Matt arrived on the patch of ice my brothers had

**Glitch 4:
A Previous
Commitment**

**Glitch 5:
Skating Party
Fiasco**

cleared. He laced up his skates and asked me to come for a skate with him. Thinking a skate with him would be all right, I went with him, hand in hand. After a few rounds of skating, I sat down on a snow bank beside Danny. In an attempt to be friendly and include him in some way in the action, I asked him to tighten the laces on my skates. His reply still seems a bit churlish to me: he said, "Tighten them yourself." I guess sitting like a lump on the snow bank and then kneeling on the ice in front of me to work on my skates did not fit his image of himself. He left and I got up to skate with less enjoyment than before. I felt rebuffed and angry.

Much later, when I knew more about empathy, about putting myself in someone else's shoes, I realized how unpleasant it would be for Danny to have his rival flying around the ice with me while he sat on the bank. He must have felt misled by news that I had broken up with Matt.

Glitch 6: Revenge Backfires

A few Sundays later, when I went to church, there was Danny's car at the church, as it fairly often was. Danny's mother, Ettie, was there too, sitting in a pew. She smiled at me in her usual friendly way, reinforcing my impression that she favoured me as a partner for Danny. A common practice after church was for people, including Danny and Ettie, to drop in at the Armstrong place for coffee and some of Mama's baking. After church, as I started to walk down the hill toward home, a car pulled up beside me and Danny called out, "Would you like a ride?" I said curtly, "No thanks." I guess I thought by being coy I would teach Danny to appreciate the honour of tightening my skate laces. I expected he and his mother would continue on to our house where I would then be friendly and magnanimous, as befits a teenage princess. But no! Danny turned his car around and went in the opposite direction. I now realize that offering me a ride was Danny's way of apologizing for refusing to tie my skates. My response to his offer of a ride was peevish.

Glitch 7: Gossip about Me

Some weeks later, at our next church service, Danny was not there. It was springtime, and someone else offered me a car ride down the hill from church to home. It was a person devout and pure of heart. It was a person who walked with angels and, in our family, ranked as a philosopher king. It was the young United Church minister. The first time he offered me a ride, which I accepted, he amazed me by pulling his car to the side of the road opposite the church and parking. Parking! As I recall, he didn't talk about his sermon or tell me he'd been admiring me. He reached for my hand and I soon realized that a man of God could be much the same as a decent but bold farm boy. After a few minutes he started his car and drove me home. I was left wondering what it was all about.

After the next church service, I again accepted the minister's offer of a ride home. It went much the same as the first ride home—with two exceptions. One difference was that while I was sitting with the minister in his parked car, keeping him from getting too forward, he told me he was going home to New Brunswick. The other difference was that, in the darkening twilight, unbeknownst to either the minister or me, two interested observers had walked silently and maybe stealthily past the car. The two observers were a family friend, Jock Ross, and Danny (!). They apparently had gone somewhere on foot and were walking down the hill and on to the Browning house, where Jock was working and living.

With the Rife/Hoselaw Speedy Communication System working in high gear, by evening the next day, everyone within a ten-mile radius of the church knew that Cathie Ross and the United Church minister had been seen sitting together—in a parked car—in the dark. Wanting to find out the significance of the parked car incident, Danny talked to Ray about it. Ray told Vivi, who told Mama, who told Papa. The story might have stopped there, but Jock enjoyed telling a few people, who told a few more and so on. Gossip was threatening my future with Danny.

"What does it all mean?" Papa wanted to know about my parking with the minister. I could only reply, "I really don't know."

About two weeks later, Danny drove his mother to the Armstrong house to visit Mama. Ettie had news: Mrs. Nelson of Flat Lake had received an invitation to the wedding, in New Brunswick, of Reverend Nameless Here and his bride. I was surprised but in no way heartbroken by the news. I just hoped that, after my little adventure with the minister, Danny would be interested in having me as his partner for the coming Canada Day dance. Which he was.

A few days before the dance, Danny told me he had questioned Papa directly: if he, Danny, started coming around to see me, would Papa object? Papa said he would not object. In February 1938, Danny gave me a beautiful turquoise engagement ring, which of course I still have.

Danny Secures Papa's Consent

Glitch 8: Allure of Detroit

The eighth glitch on my way to matrimony resulted from my going on a Greyhound bus trip with Mama to her home territory in Ontario. Before we left, Aunt Alice archly predicted, "Danny has had lots of girlfriends. He will have another one in no time." I liked Aunt Alice, but as she spoke this time, the image of a cawing crow came into my head. The trip was tedious, but when we arrived in Petrolia we knew the trip was worthwhile for both of us. Mama's sister Ethel greeted us, and I have never forgotten the joy that she packed into the single word, "Helen." The trip went well—so well that for me it lasted nearly one and a half years.

Webster's Corners, BC, about 1947. L–R: Aunt Jessie, Aunt Alice, and myself in front of our acreage home.

After we visited with Aunt Ethel in Petrolia, Mama and I went to see Aunt Jessie, who worked as a domestic in Detroit and loved her work. She had a comfortable room in her employer's house and a bank account. She offered to help me find work in Detroit so I could, for the first time in my life, earn some money. She, Mama, and I visited an Employment Office, and within a day I was employed as a maid in the home of Judge and Mrs. Nicol.

The Great Depression was ongoing, and jobs in Alberta were scarce, so I felt lucky to land a plum job in the Nicols' home. I lived there in comfortable quarters, with electric lights and running water. My duties as maid were not heavy, certainly lighter than my work in the Armstrong house. Mrs. Nicol planned the menus and gave me her recipes, which I prepared. I enjoyed using many ingredients that were new to me and preparing interesting meals, usually just for the three of us. I served the meals, cleared the table and did some light housekeeping. The Nicols treated me with kindness and consideration, even inviting me to go with them to attend a concert sponsored by Henry Ford at a major Detroit venue. I truly loved my job.

One day a week the laundress, Lucille, came to the Nicols' home to do the laundry, and on that day I prepared food for her too. Lucille was the first black woman I had ever met, and we soon became good friends. We enjoyed eating lunch together in the kitchen, listening to each other's stories about our lives, laughing a lot. Like me, Lucille considered herself lucky to be working for the Nicols, and I revelled in my friend's high spirits and humour.

Besides friends, I also had family in Detroit. On my day off, Sunday, I usually went to visit Aunt Jessie, who often planned outings for us, using public transportation to see the sights of the city. Sometimes we went to movies. Sometimes we visited Aunt Edith's daughter, my cousin Lulu, who also lived in Detroit with her husband and family.

I was also becoming a woman of means in Detroit. I was earning eight US dollars a week, which, thanks to the exchange rate, turned into considerably more money in Canada. Aunt Jessie advised me to set up a Canadian bank account in Windsor, just one bridge away. With room and board at the Nicols' home, I had few expenses. By the time I left Detroit, my bank deposits along with interest had turned into 800 Canadian dollars. At a time when a loaf of bread cost eight cents, I could buy a lot of bread.

A new set of experiences for me came when the Nicols went on a six-week trip to Scotland. They sent me to work for their friend, Miss Hayes, a retired teacher. Miss Hayes's father had been a banker, so she had more than an ordinary teacher's wealth and influence. She was on the Board of Governors for a prominent university. I enjoyed the luxurious surroundings of her home, and she and I became friends. When she saw me reading *Jane Eyre,* she asked me about my family and my interests. She asked me why I hadn't become a teacher like Vivi. I replied, not quite honestly, that my family was short of money. A more honest answer would have been that I did not have enough ambition. Miss Hayes tried to persuade me to stay on working for her after the Nicols came home. She offered enticements such as going with her by Pullman to New York. One day she asked me, "If I sent you to university, what one would you like to attend?" The fact that I was not yearning to go to university became obvious. She asked me if I ever had a boyfriend. I said yes, I had a boyfriend, to whom I was engaged and to whom I wrote a letter every week. She raised her eyebrows and said, "Catherine, get yourself a man—any old stick of a man."

Being certain Danny would exceed her criteria for a husband, I considered showing Miss Hayes this photo of him. But concerned that the photo would make her feel more lonely, I did not show him off.

When the Nicols returned, I went back to work for them. They greeted me warmly, and I realized I was feeling very much at home in Detroit. In my mind I contrasted the luxury and excitement of my life in Detroit with the hardship of life on the frontier in Alberta. Warm running water, bathtubs, flush toilets, electric lights, gas stoves, telephones, and concerts contrasted with buckets of water carried from a well, a galvanized tub on the kitchen floor, a back house, Aladdin lamps, wood stoves, the Rife/Hoselaw Speedy Communication System (specializing in gossip), and church—and dances. I could not forget the dances, but I felt more free, more in charge of my life than ever before.

Offering Danny His Freedom

In the fall of 1939, in one of my letters to Danny I wrote about the satisfaction and opportunities of my life in Detroit. I concluded by writing that if he wished, he could make himself a free man by breaking our engagement. He wrote back that he would be on the next bus to Windsor.

Being Proud of My Fiancé

I was glad Danny hadn't seized the opportunity to break up with me. I was thrilled when my tall, handsome fiancé met me in Detroit, and I was proud to introduce him to Aunt Jessie, Lulu, and the Nicols.

Flat Lake, 1938. Danny in a photo he sent to me in Detroit. On the back he had written, "This is the pup we found & part of the new barn I built."

A Wedding and a Honeymoon

Danny soon found a job in an auto body shop in Windsor. A few months later, when he told his boss he would be getting married and going back to Alberta, his boss offered to double his pay to entice him to stay. Danny thanked him but said he wanted to be his own boss on a farm. The Nicols did not want me to leave either, and Judge Nicol offered to get Danny a good job so we could stay in Detroit and live in a suite in their house. Danny and I both thanked the Nicols and explained that we were going to buy a farm in Alberta.

We set March 1 as our wedding day and obtained a marriage certificate.

Certificate of Marriage

This is to Certify that, on the *first* day of *March* — A.D. 19*40*, at *Windsor* in the Province of Ontario, I solemnized the Marriage of *Daniel Smith* and *Catherine Anna Ross* — under Marriage License No. K 39904 issued on the *26th* day of *February* A.D. 19*40*.

Witnesses: *Herbert Wills* *Lulu G. Phillips*

Henry Mick M.A. B.D. S.T.D.
618 *Ouellette ave., Windsor Ont.*
United Church 765 5
(Denomination) (Registration Certificate Number)

Windsor, February 1940. Our certificate of marriage.

Danny's boss kindly offered Danny his car for our wedding. I finished work on a Thursday and we were married on Friday at the minister's manse in Windsor. Aunt Jessie and Lulu were our witnesses. We returned the car with many thanks and the next day set out by bus on our month-long honeymoon through the United States. We visited with Danny's brother Charles and wife, Florence, in Minneapolis before travelling on to our destination—Rife.

Smith Siblings' Success in Marriage

Moving briefly into the present, where 50% of marriages are broken, I want to note the matrimonial success of Charles and Esther's offspring. The following four photos, taken at a reunion in Glendon in the home of Elaine and Peter Doonanco, show the four Alberta brothers with their wives in 1979, all happily married until death did them part. The three other surviving Smith siblings, Ettie, Margaret, and Charles (Bill Davis), had similarly successful marriages. With their parents' marriage being broken the Smith siblings' record is impressive.

Left: Tommy and Amelia
(Wilkowski) Smith

*Married in August 1931
Parted when Amelia died in
March 1993
Tommy died in April 2000*

Right: *Reg and Velva (Ross) Smith*

Married in October 1939
Parted when Reg died in 1995
Velva died in July 2013

Reg's dark complexion is partly the result of the different light used for the photo. (Notice how golden the curtain and wall appear in the photo of Tommy and Amelia compared with how grey they appear in the opposite photo.) Reg had also suffered an injury to his face a day earlier.

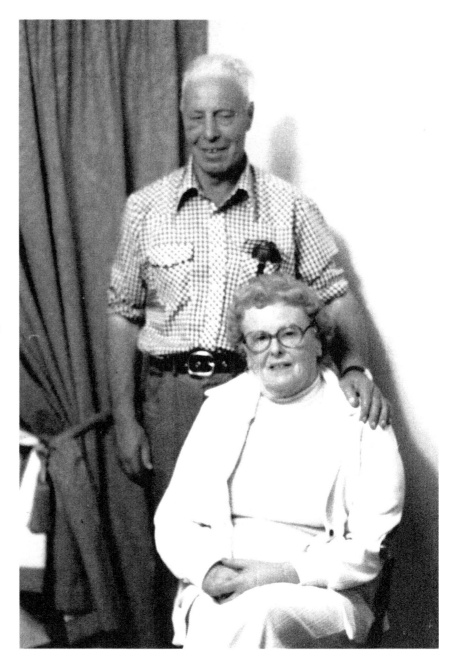

Left: Danny and Catherine (Ross) Smith

Married on March 1, 1940
Parted when Danny died on
*   October 25, 2006*
Cathie living (only living
*   biological member of her*
*   generation of the William*
*   Ross family and only*
*   living member of Danny's*
*   generation of the Charles*
*   Smith family)*

Right: Allan and Charlotte (Harper) Smith

Married March 20, 1949
Parted when Charlotte died
    in 2007
Allan died in March 2010

Opposite: Jones place, 1944. After years of suffering from a back injury, Danny was at last scheduled for surgery in Edmonton. He was dressed for the trip, and I wanted a photo of him with our family before he left. Dr. Armstrong removed two slipped discs from Danny's spine and the pain was gone.

CHAPTER 10

Our Six Years of Farming at Rife

Jobless and Homeless

When Danny and I returned to Rife after our honeymoon, we realized we were jobless and essentially homeless. Reg and his bride, Velva Ross (no relation to me), were living in the family home at Flat Lake, taking care of chores there. We did not want to intrude on them. Furthermore, Danny's mother, Esther, was shutting down the farm operation there. The Great Depression had afflicted the country during most of the eight years that Danny, with help in the later years from Reg and Mac, had been running the Flat Lake farm. The farm had prospered in that food was always plentiful and machinery and livestock had been accumulated, but the land did not belong to the Smiths. Danny and I knew that if we were going to farm, we had to find a way to buy land and set up our own operation.

Esther's Astute Decisions

I believe one of Esther's main goals was to see herself and all four of her Alberta sons reasonably secure financially. At the time, her decision to abandon the Flat Lake property was probably astute. In those days, a farm's distance from a railroad was a major consideration. Towns with a railway going through them had towering elevators, where farmers sold their grain, and noisy stockyards, where they either sold their livestock or loaded it onto stock cars to go by train to a city packing plant. To transport products to a railway station, most farmers used a horse and wagon—a difficult and time-consuming job over roads that were usually either muddy or rutted. The Flat Lake property had the drawback of being far from a railroad.

In contrast, the town of Glendon had a railroad running through it, with a grain elevator and stockyard. When Esther had a chance to rent a two-bedroom log house on a farm about a mile north of Glendon, she seized it. She was living in the rented house with her youngest son, Mac (later known as Allan) when Danny and I came back from the east. She saw the potential of the farm on which her rented house was situated and thought it would be an ideal place for Reg and Velva to settle. She hired a carpenter to build a small house for her in Glendon. She organized a sale of surplus items from the Flat Lake property, including the car she and Danny had bought and which he agreed to give her for the sale.

As soon as Esther's new house was ready, Reg and Velva moved into the log house on the farm north of Glendon. Machinery and livestock from Flat Lake were moved there, with the understanding that these valuables would be shared with Danny when he had a place for them, which he soon did.

In retrospect, I admire how effectively Esther managed the situation. I think she would be pleased to know that her three Alberta sons prospered in farming, despite the changes that were driving many people away from it. In Truman, Tommy and Amelia ran a productive farm for many years. Without a son to take up farming, they chose to sell their farm and retire comfortably in Glendon. Reg and Velva farmed successfully on the Glendon farm, which was greatly expanded when their two sons, Mervin and Allan (widely known as "Jeep"), joined in the farming. Danny had several occupations besides farming, some of which I mention below, along with my own eventual career. Despite getting out of farming for a few years, Danny loved that occupation most. He returned to it, worked very hard to make up for lost time, and succeeded. Like Reg, he had the pleasure of seeing two sons, Mack and Sid, greatly expand the farm operation.

In April 1940, Danny and I were lucky to immediately find a place to live and start farming. Aunt Florence and Uncle Alex MacLean were about to vacate the Red Cross kitchen cabin, which they had rented for about nine years. They were moving into their newly built house on their recently bought farm in Hoselaw area. Our friend Jock Ross had bought the property with the Red Cross kitchen cabin on it from Maurice Destrube, and Jock readily agreed to rent the house and property to us. After staying with Mama and Papa in the Armstrong house for only a day or two, we moved into the Red Cross kitchen home. An advantage for me was that the cabin was just across the road from the Armstrong place. Like typical newlyweds, we were thrilled to have our own home. Our first guests were Ray and Vivi and their six-month-old baby, William Raymond Edgar White, born while I was in Detroit. Edgar, as he was called, was a bright and sturdy little fellow, the star of the Ross family. I believe I served a venison roast for dinner that day. (Deer were plentiful, and Danny was keen to hunt them for meat.)

As soon as we were settled in our home, Danny sprang into ways to earn a living. He met with his brother Reg and came to an agreement on what stock and machinery from Flat Lake would go to whom. Within a week we had three milk cows and a few days later a pig, which soon produced a litter of piglets. Danny also got his five horses—Jude, Major, Queen, Molly, and Dixie—which he had bought before he went to Windsor. With these horses and his skill at driving them in tandem, he won a contract to pull a grader to maintain a section of roads in the Bonnyville municipality.

In Retrospect

Settling into a Home and Farming

Our Daughter Is Born

In May that year, 1940, Danny also busied himself planting a garden. I attempted to help, but I was feeling so indolent and sleepy that the work seemed strangely challenging Mama asked whether there might be a baby on the way. And so there was. Ray liked to tell the story of the cold night in mid-December when he and Vivi were in bed and heard the jingle of harness chains and squeaking of sleigh runners on snow and then Danny's voice calling out, "I've got a baby daughter." Christmas of 1940 was a merry one in the Armstrong house with toddler Edgar and newborn Catherine Jean, whom we called Jean.

Tommy's Daughter Joan Boards with Us

Taking care of a baby made life a little more hectic, but I was pleased with my situation. Then one day in March 1941, when baby Jean was just over three months old, Danny went to see his brother Tommy, in Truman. When he arrived home, he had his seven-year-old niece, Joan, with him. (Contacting me by phone was impossible in those days.) No school was available in the Truman area, so to get an education, children had to leave home and stay with friends or relatives. The situation was not ideal for the children or for their parents. Children were homesick and parents missed them. In the previous school year, Joan had stayed with her grandmother, Esther, to attend grade one in Glendon, but she had missed so much school that she had not completed the grade. At our place, Joan had some distraction from homesickness in that she was fascinated by Jean and loved to amuse her. Joan attended nearby Rife School, where she succeeded in completing grade one before summer holidays. In September Joan was back with us to take grade two at Rife School, where our friend Rose Procyk was the teacher. Even though her schooling was disrupted by a move and a birth in our family, Joan successfully completed grade two in that school year.

Purchase of the Jones Place

After we had lived in the Red Cross kitchen home for a year and a half, Danny heard the Jones place was for sale. Having worked on that farm, he knew the house and land well. I agreed when he suggested we should immediately make an offer to buy the property. We had machinery and livestock. We had my $800 from Detroit and about that much from Danny's work in Windsor and for the Bonnyville municipality, and some money from the sale of cream from our cows. Papa offered us a loan of $900, so we were able to put a substantial down payment on the Jones house and land.

Rife, 1941. Joan Smith and baby Jean Smith. Joan completed grades one and two while living with us. She loved to help take care of the baby, and the baby loved her attention.

While we were busily planning our move into the Jones place, Vivi and Ray welcomed baby Helen Diane, born February 1942. Big brother Edgar declared the new baby "quite cute." A week after we moved into the Jones place, on April 30, 1942, our first son, Daniel MacKinnon (Mack), was born. A year later, Papa was surprised when we handed him a cheque for the full amount of his loan. He said, "So soon! All of it!" Not much later we paid off the mortgage.

Diane White and Our Son MacKinnon Are Born

Farming went well for us that first year on the Jones place. The land was fertile and ready for growing crops, and Danny had the machinery and horses to do the work. Crops of wheat, oats (for the horses), and barley had tall stalks with heavy heads full of plump kernels. Danny's close friend, Jock Ross, owned the threshing machine that harvested most of the grain in the Rife area. What a thrill it was to put our place on Jock's schedule for threshing!

On the Threshing Schedule

But Danny had lots of work to do before the threshing machine came. When the grain was finally yellow enough, thankfully before a frost came, he hitched his horses to the binder and rode on it around the fields, cutting the grain, binding it with twine into bundles and dropping the bundles one by one onto the ground. Next came the hard physical job of stooking the bundles. Stooking involved propping six bundles up, cut end in the stubble on the ground and heads together, to form stooks. Stooks were tent-like structures that allowed the grain to dry and become ready for threshing. How exciting it was when Jock's tractor pulling the threshing machine chugged and rattled into our yard!

Along with it came a crew of five men: my brothers, Donnie and Alex; their hired man, Lester Story; a transient worker, and Jock. The crew and Danny drove teams of horses hitched to hayracks to pick up stooks in the field. Using their three-tined pitchforks, they pitched bundles onto the conveyor belt, carrying them into the voracious mouth of the machine. Out came our precious grain and useful straw.

In the house I was kept busy roasting big cuts of beef or pork or two or three plump chickens, along with pots of vegetables—turnips, beets, carrots, peas, spinach, and mashed potatoes. Early in the day I made desserts—cake or pies. I also took care of five-month-old Mack and toddler Jean. The work was a challenge, but I was young and it was an exciting time.

Left: *Jones house, about 1944.*
L–R: Jean and Mack.

Rife, about 1944. Jean in buggy with reins of horses.

Along with harvest time came the opening of school. Fortunately, a school had opened at Sandy Rapids, so Joan was able to live at home and spend time with her frisky year-old baby sister, Frances. School, however, was five miles away from Tommy and Amelia's home. It was arranged that Joan, who by then was eight years old, would travel to school with her cousin Edmund Grant, who was starting grade one. The two would travel by horse and two-wheeled cart over bare ground and by horse and sleigh in snow.

Joan laughingly tells about the day after a heavy snowfall when their old horse, Maggie, plodded through the deep snow most of the way to school then suddenly stopped. She refused to go any further, and nothing the children did or said made her take one more one step. Realizing they could not sit in the cold sleigh for long, the two kids got out and started

Joan Goes to School in Sandy Rapids

walking to school, breaking a trail as they went. Maggie, apparently inspired by their efforts, plodded along behind them all the way to school. A neighbour was on hand as usual to take care of the horse until school was over.

Getting an education in a remote area was always a challenge and sometimes an adventure. The next year the Sandy Rapids school had no teacher, so Joan had to stay with Grandma Smith (Esther) in her small house. She had a good year, completing grade four in Glendon and having her grandmother put on a birthday party for her. To this day, Joan remembers that party and treasures a small glass piggy bank that was one of her gifts.

My Worst Fright

In April 1943, I had the and the worst fright of my life. It happened when Mack was nearly one year old. I had an appointment for a final checkup before a new baby (Sidney) was due to arrive, about mid-June. We had arranged for Eddy Corbett, who ran the Rife store, to take me and little Mack in his new car. I was sitting in the front passenger seat, and baby Mack was happily bouncing around on my knee. Suddenly he was gone. The car door had flown open, and he was taken by the wind. You can imagine how I rushed back as best I could, about two telephone pole spaces, to where I could see a little blue coat. When I got to the baby and picked him up, he was crying a bit, but no damage had been done. I still shudder when I think of that experience. (I later heard that type of door, hinged to open in the opposite direction of modern car doors, was soon dropped by car makers. The wind rushing by a moving car with such doors was likely to force the doors open rather than hold them shut.)

Birth of Kenneth Sidney

Our second son, Kenneth Sidney, arrived on June 11, 1943. At nine pounds, three ounces, he was my biggest baby. He was also the most active, quick to learn how to sit, crawl, walk, and stand up in his high chair (not that I approved of such standing). When he was three, he demonstrated how to throw a big beet through a glass window. I was busy indeed with our three lively children.

Right: *Jones place, 1943. Sidney at five months.*

Jones place, 1944. Smith family gathering. L–R: Danny's and my kids, Jean, Mack, and Sid; Reg and Velva's kids, Elaine and Mervin; Reg. A sign of change is Reg and Velva's car beside a horse-drawn wagon. In the background is the blacksmith shop and forge, where Danny shoed horses.

One summer day we had a very lively gathering at the Jones place. Reg and Velva loaded up their car and drove their children, Mervin and Elaine, along with Grandma Smith to visit us. Getting all the children to sit for a photo involved some drama and produced some entertaining expressions.

Purchase of Destrube Piano

Another memorable day for me was when Danny suggested we buy a piano that Maurice Destrube had for sale, a beautiful instrument that had belonged to his sister-in-law, Suzanne Destrube. The piano was delivered to us at the Jones house in 1945, and we immediately started having singsongs around it. Ray and Vivi were our regulars, and our friends Jock and Rose (Procyk) Ross sometimes joined in too. The piano became an essential part of our lives, coming with us whenever we moved to a new home—until, that is, we moved into Bonny Lodge.

Attending the Anglican Church

A regular event in our life was going to the Anglican Church. After the circus of getting everyone dressed for church, I was happy to relax and play hymns on the church organ. Danny saw that the kids behaved well beside him in a pew.

Danny's Back Surgery

During much of our early years of farming in Rife, Danny had an on-going problem with a back injury. The injury happened just before Jean was born. Danny was attempting to make travel more comfortable for me by setting up a sleigh for winter travel. While he was removing a heavy hayrack, he slipped

Jones place, Easter 1946. Ready for church: me with (L–R) Jean, Sidney, MacKinnon. (My hat got knocked crooked in the circus to get dressed.)

on ice, wrenching his back. He was often in excruciating pain until, in 1944, a Dr. Armstrong in Edmonton removed two slipped discs from his spine. The doctor warned Danny not to do any heavy lifting, so it seemed that farming was no longer a viable occupation for us. However, Danny recuperated quickly and, despite my concern, soon resumed farming, even brushing and breaking a new field.

By the summer of 1946, change was in the air. Lloyd and Frances Hill had moved with their family of four girls—Evelyn, Claire, Patsy, and Dorothy—to Vancouver Island. Jock and Rose Ross and their baby son, Robert, also moved, joining the Hills for a short while in Comox, BC. Lloyd and Frances were planning to buy a store, which they did. Ray White was also contemplating a new occupation—storekeeper, as his mother had been after his father's death. Mama and Papa were eager to go to "the coast," where winters were much milder. Danny and I were keen to enter into a partnership with Ray and Vivi in a BC store we had seen advertised. In August our three men, Papa, Ray, and Danny, piled into Danny's car and travelled to BC to check out the store. When they returned, Ray and Danny had bought the Maple Ridge General Store, and Papa had bought an acreage in Webster's Corners.

Heading to British Columbia

Above: Maple Ridge General Store, 1946.

We all looked forward to the venture into business and the warmer coastal climate, but we had mixed emotions as we prepared to leave our farms. Danny and Ray each found buyers for their farms—Mike Ruddell for ours and Nick Wakaruk for Ray and Vivi's. (Our two older sons, Mack and Sid, later bought Ray's property.)

Because they were leaving their farm and house in the hands of Donnie and Alex, Mama and Papa had fewer preparations and fewer qualms.

Sale of Our Farm and Possessions

There was a lot of work to be done before November, when we were to take possession of the store. Danny consulted with a professional auctioneer, a Mr. Krevenki, who advised him about holding a sale. After we listed everything to be sold, Mr. Krevenki prepared a sale bill, which was posted in Bonnyville, St. Paul, and Glendon and published in the town newspapers. Over at their place Ray and Vivi were making similar arrangements.

Jones place, October 1946. Sale bill for the auction of our possessions.

The day of our sale, October 22, 1946, was chilly, but a good crowd of interested buyers came. Mr. Krevenki briskly sold our livestock, farm implements, Danny's blacksmith forge, and our household items. Danny and I had agreed that my piano was not for sale, so it was safely in its crate, ready for the trip to BC. While Danny met with customers, demonstrating and answering questions, Ray neatly recorded items sold, prices, and in some cases purchasers. At the bottom of each page Ray totalled the money collected on that page.

It was impossible not to feel some sadness about leaving our homes and our community. The money collected was important, but when Danny paraded his team of Major and Queen, who trotted around so perfectly in step, his eyes got misty. Happily, Mike Ruddell, the new owner of our farm, bought the horses, so they stayed in their familiar surroundings. Our family watched sadly when our collie dog, Lassie, rode away with Aunt Florence and Uncle Alex. We hoped she would be happy.

Ray and Vivi held their sale a week later, where Danny handled the paperwork. Vivi's piano had been sold privately to the Eastbourne Hall Committee.

As soon as our and Ray and Vivi's sales were over, we turned our thoughts to the future and our venture into commerce in British Columbia.

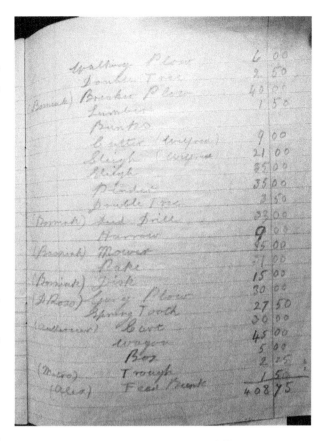

Right, top: Jones place, October 22, 1946. Ray White's record of Danny's sales.
Right, bottom: Jones place, 1946. Get-together before goodbye: L–R: Danny, me, Velva, Reg.

CHAPTER 11

Three Years in British Columbia, at Maple Ridge and Webster's Corners

In early November 1946, the move was under way. Danny, Ray, and Papa travelled in Danny's car to BC to take possession of the properties they had bought. Ray and Danny took over as equal partners in the store, and Papa moved into the comfortable house in Webster's Corners.

Taking Possession in BC

A few days later, Mama, Vivi, and I travelled with our kids—my three and Vivi's two—by train from Glendon to Edmonton. Vivi was nearly seven months pregnant, but she managed babies and baggage very well. She and I were both glad to have Mama with us to alertly lend a hand when needed. Mama was expert at settling the kids down with stories, even if she had to resort to the one she'd often told me and my siblings—about the horse-eating wolves in Russia. When they heard that frightening story, children tended to become silent and stay close to their adults. We stayed one night at the Edmonton YWCA and then boarded a train to New Westminster.

Women and Kids Go by Train

When we arrived, our men were standing on the platform to meet us. Four-year-old Mack gave us all a scare when he yelled, "Dad!" and leapt from the slow-moving train. Fortunately Danny caught him in mid-air.

Opposite: *Webster's Corners, Golden Ears Mountains in the background, 1948. L–R: Mack, Sid, and Jean with toys bought with money from Aunt Catherine, who had recently visited.*

Glorying in Our BC Homes

We excitedly went to see our new homes. Papa took Mama in his new coup, with a rumble seat, to their Webster's Corners home. We settled into our living quarters at the store, Whites in the suite above the store and Smiths in the suite at the back of the store. I revelled in having our own home where bright lights came on at the flip of a switch and warm steam rose as hot water gushed from a tap into the big white tub.

Birth of Madelyn Ann White

In mid-February we happily welcomed baby Madelyn Ann "Lynne" White when Vivi and Ray brought her home from the hospital. We developed a routine: Edgar and Jean walked themselves to and from school; Mack, Sid, and Diane played at home. Vivi had time to spend with her new baby.

Solutions to a Problem

Ray and Danny's partnership was harmonious. But we had a problem: the store was not generating enough income for our two families, each with five people. We needed another source of income. In the spring Danny started full-time work at Essendale, an institute for people with mental disabilities or dementia, and Ray continued to run the store. Danny and I had to come up with new living arrangements.

Mama and Papa were finding life in Webster's Corners not as interesting as life on the farm in Rife, so Papa came up with a plan. He offered to trade the Webster's Corners property for Danny's share in the store. He said he would be a silent partner, not active but deriving a small percentage of the profit from the store in return for his investment. Ray and Danny both gladly accepted the offer. Danny and I were delighted to take over the acreage, with its two-storey house, two barns, a hayfield, and an orchard. A lovely shallow stream flowed across the back of the acreage. Mama and Papa moved back to the Armstrong house and resumed a more active life.

Grandma Smith Arrives

Shortly before we moved to Webster's Corners, Danny's mother also moved to BC. She sold her small house in Glendon and bought a small but pleasant house in Hammond, a little town only three or four miles away from the Maple Ridge store. When she came to visit us in Maple Ridge, she also visited with Ray and Vivi, delighting their kids and ours with her entertaining poems and songs, so much so that Edgar firmly claimed her as his grandmother, too. One summer Jean managed to overcome her tendency to homesickness and stayed with Grandma Smith for a few days.

Allan Awaits His Scottish Bride

Also about this time, a rather gloomy brother Allan came back from his time in the army to live with his mother. He was waiting for his Scottish wife, Charlotte, and their little son, Allan, to come to Canada. When he was finally united with his family, his spirits picked up marvellously. When Charlotte died many years later, Allan commented, "I loved her every day." I enjoyed Charlotte's company, and so did Esther.

Opposite: *Webster's Corners, 1947. Papa and Mama in front of their home, car in background.*

Left: *Hammond, BC, about 1948. Allan Smith is reunited with his Scottish bride, Charlotte Harper, and their son, Allan Smith.*

Reg Visits Us at Webster's Corners

About 1948 Reg came to visit his mother and of course also visited Danny and me. We were glad to see him, and Danny was pleased to hear how well Reg was doing on his farm. I think talking with Reg renewed Danny's excitement about farming.

A Good Life in BC

By this time financial worries were over for everybody. Ray

and Vivi had enough income from the store to provide for their family and hire a clerk or two. They kept their store until they retired, steadily building up business and making many friends in the community. But Ray always had a yen for country life. When Lynne was old enough to want a horse to ride, he enthusiastically bought her a

Above: Webster's Corners about 1948. Reg, Esther, Danny. Reg came to visit his mother and brother.

Left: Webster's Corner's, about 1949. House with Danny's new Ford in front.

Opposite: Webster's Corners, 1994. Our old house has been remodelled. Photo by Ross White.

beautiful palomino horse named "Flash" and found a place to board it. In the evenings, how he enjoyed spending time with that beloved horse! On retiring, Vivi and Ray moved to a more rural and drier part of BC, Osoyoos, where Ray connected with the land in a small garden.

Maple Ridge, about 1975. Lynne (White) Sutherland and her first son, Dwayne, on her palomino, Flash. Maple Ridge still had many rural areas.

Danny and I were happy to live on the Webster's Corners acreage, with its mild climate and view of the mountains. Danny made the acreage into a productive hobby farm with a Jersey cow for milk, chickens for eggs, and pigs for meat. We kept a garden and harvested fruit and berries from the orchard. In his limited spare time, Danny used a scythe to put up hay for the cow. Friends at Essendale often gave him five-gallon buckets of food scraps to take home for the pigs.

Our children were also happy at Webster's Corners. Jean, a shy child, had found being in three different schools for grade one unsettling, but she was at ease in grades two and three. Mack felt at home with his grade one teacher, Miss Mack. Without a brother at home, Sid was lonely. He wanted to tag along with Jean and Mack to school. Surprisingly, when I spoke to Miss Mack, she gave permission for Sid to occasionally crowd into a desk with Mack and observe activities. He soon became a regular but not very legitimate attendee.

At home the kids loved playing outside, climbing what they called their "monkey tree" and splashing around with the neighbours' kids in the shallow creek that ran at the back of our property and theirs. By April 30, Mack's birthday, they considered the water warm enough to jump into.

Danny Chooses Farming

We might have stayed at Webster's Corners until Danny retired, but two things happened. At Essendale, Danny agreed to take some tests, not really knowing the purpose of them. The outcome was that he was selected for training as a psychiatric nurse. While he was mulling over the questions of whether he wanted to go to school for the training and whether he wanted to spend his life doing psychiatric nursing in a government institution, the second thing happened: he slipped on a bar of soap and fell, breaking a kneecap. In springtime, on leave from work, with one leg in a cast, and partially immobilized, he became restless. He found himself yearning to go back to farming full time—in business for himself, close to the land, seeing the miracles of spring births and autumn harvest.

Emotional Farewells

In September of 1949 we sold our acreage on a credit arrangement, packed up our belongings, including the piano, and headed back to Rife. Ray agreed to receive the purchaser's cheques each month and send them on to us. (The credit arrangement gave us income for a number of years but not a large sum to start up a farm.)

The day we left, Danny drove our Pontiac over to the Whites' store to say goodbye. Tears were shed on both sides. I knew I would miss Vivi and her family. On the other hand, in Alberta we would be close to Mama and Papa. I liked the mild climate and the rural nature of Webster's Corners (which is now part of Maple Ridge). It was a place where a person could easily have a hobby farm and own a riding horse. Danny, however, was keen to plunge into farming on a bigger scale. Acting on the White kids' suggestion, the cousins all memorialized our departure by ceremoniously nailing pop bottle caps onto the big maple beside the store. We all said we would keep in touch, and we still do.

CHAPTER 12

Back to Farming in Alberta— 53 Years at Rife and Bonnyville

Browning house, fall, 1979.

A Warm Welcome from Mama and Papa

When we arrived at Rife two or three days later, we had a warm welcome. While we were in BC, my brother Donnie had married Olive Munroe, from Apple Hill, Ontario. The newlyweds were living in the Armstrong house. Mama, Papa, and Alex had moved into the neighbouring five-bedroom Browning house. Mama had beds made up for all of us in the house, and she and Papa invited us to live with them until we found a home of our own.

Back to Square One of Farming

We had no firm plan for how we would get back into farming, but we were fortunate in how things worked out. Using our prized 1948 Silverstreak Pontiac as a down payment, we bought the Browning house and 60 acres around it from my brother Donnie. In place of the car, Danny bought a Model M John Deere tractor. He also bought two quarters of "quack grass" land, six milk cows, and three pigs. From salvaged logs he quickly built a log barn for the milk cows. On one side of the barn he rigged up exterior covered mangers that opened to the cows' stalls so he could conveniently and hygienically feed hay to the cows. Through special effort he also bought back his favourite horses, Major and Queen. The log building that had been the residence of one of the Rife teachers became a maternity ward for the pigs. After our three-year sojourn in BC, we were back on square one of farming, but we had a better house and a brand new tractor.

Soon after we arrived in Rife, we walked with our three children up the road to register them in Rife School, the same one-room, eight-grade school I had attended. Their teacher that first year was a pleasant woman

Right: The Browning house two or more decades after we bought it. The sign was a much appreciated gift from Mack and Diane. On it they used Scottish spelling for both our names.

I knew well—Clara Zamzul, married daughter of our neighbours, Chris and Kristine Haland. The following year their teacher was John Sawchuk. With consolidation of schools, the rest of their public school education was in Glendon.

On January 27, 1950, only a few months after we'd moved into the Browning house with Mama and Papa, we almost lost the house. Had it not been for Danny's courage, resourcefulness, and strength, the house and everything in it would have burned. That cold afternoon I was upstairs lying reading on the bed in the west bedroom. Mama was in the kitchen and Papa was in the living room on the main floor. Papa had a roaring fire going in the basement furnace. I thought I heard a crackling noise, and sure enough I had. Under the north eve was a closet through which a chimney passed. I hurriedly jerked open the closet door and saw flames flickering a foot or two high around the brick chimney. Danny had driven Major and Queen to "the jack pines" to get a load of wood, so he was not on hand. I dashed downstairs, out the front door and up the little hill to tell Wade Armagost that our house was on fire. Papa went out and stood on the road shouting, "Fire! Fire! I panted out my news to Wade and his wife, "Mrs. Wade" and then ran with Wade back to my burning house.

Wade saw there was nothing he could do to stop the fire, so he suggested we get as much as we could out of the house. Meanwhile, Mrs. Wade dashed onto the road, where she could see Danny about half a mile away, on his way home with his load of wood.

Danny saw Mrs. Wade out on the road desperately waving her apron, so he urged his team to a gallop. When he got to the top of Wade's hill, he saw instantly the flames that were already leaping above the roof of our house. In seconds, his team was at our gate. He shouted "Whoa" to them, threw the reins on the road, and grabbed his double-bladed axe. He ran to the porch and somehow got onto its roof. From there he scrambled up the steep north pitch of the roof, which was covered with snow except where the fire had broken through. With his axe he furiously pushed snow onto the flames shooting up from the roof, smothering and quenching them.

Looking through smoke and steam into the hole in the roof, Danny could see fire spreading below. A tongue of fire had moved several feet

*Above: Rife,
January 27, 1950.
Danny saves the
Browning house from
burning down. Sketch
by Blair.*

on the floor of the attic and was licking the boards of the ceiling of the master bedroom. Again using his axe, Danny pushed snow as fast as he could through the big hole in the roof and managed to douse the flames in the attic.

By then, however, fire had already burned a hole through the ceiling of the master bedroom, and embers had fallen down into the bedroom below. Danny dropped down off the roof of the porch and ran up the stairs inside the house. There he found embers and growing flames on the floor of the master bedroom and beat them out with the flat side of his axe. Meanwhile, Wade, Mama, and I were frantically getting our treasures out of the house and out onto the snowy lawn. We didn't notice that flames and smoke had stopped rising from the house until Papa shouted to us, "It's beat!"

Later Papa said, "There isn't one man in a hundred—no, a thousand—who could have put that fire out." I hope we also acknowledged Mrs. Wade's quick thinking and effective use of her apron to signal an emergency. Fighting the fire was a momentous task, but it probably took only ten minutes or so of frenzied action. The fire had burned unchecked perhaps ten minutes from the time I heard it until Danny attacked it, but by then it was already close to destroying our house. Before it was snuffed out, it made a hole in the roof about three and a half feet in diameter. It charred at least a dozen square feet of attic floor and burned a hole a foot in diameter through the ceiling of the master bedroom. Its falling embers burned a hole a foot and a half in diameter in the floor of the master bedroom.

When our kids came home from school, they smelled the smoke and looked in wonderment at the black-edged holes and wet ceiling and floor. They could not have imagined all their father had done to save their home. But what he did lives in my memory. I realized later how dangerous it was for Danny to be up on that roof, but I know I could never have stopped him from going up there. It was winter, and cold air was pouring down through the hole in the roof. Before nightfall, Danny had nailed down some boards and a piece of plywood as temporary patches over the holes in the roof, ceiling, and floor.

That evening our superb neighbours, Wade and Mrs. Wade, invited us all for supper at their house. We talked of little else than the fire. Danny could not remember how he made the seven-foot ascent onto the roof of the porch. We also marvelled that Major and Queen, well trained as they were, stood waiting on the road until the fire was over. Later that night, how thankful we adults were to be sleeping in our own beds! The next day our kids had a story to tell at school. And I had been invited to call Mrs. Wade by her actual name, Edna.

Aftermath of the Fire

In the spring, our insurance paid for a bricklayer to build two new chimneys and a carpenter to repair the house. Fortunately the large "Canon room" had its own chimney, so we set it up as a kitchen with a cook stove for me to use in preparing meals for the family and the construction workers. (As mentioned earlier, the "Canon room" was the addition where Canon Browning had lived.)

Repairs

Surviving Crop Failure

Nineteen fifty was a disastrous crop year, so money was tight that fall. After the extreme drought of that summer, Danny harvested only as much wheat as he had planted. But we never felt desperate.

We ate well, with garden vegetables watered from a well, milk from our cows, and wild saskatoon berries, raspberries, and blueberries, picked by our whole family. Thanks to our cows we also got small cream cheques every week. Fortunately, the family who had bought our Webster's Corners place on credit was faithfully making payments, delivering a cheque each month to Ray, who sent it on to us. That money meant we could pay the taxes on our property.

Fun with a Makeshift Truck

We had no surplus money for entertainment, and we were about seven miles away from our community's beach on Moose Lake. Playing at the beach was really all the entertainment our kids wanted in the hot days of that summer, but we no longer had a car to take them there. Danny rigged up a wooden box, which he fitted securely onto the back of our John Deere tractor, making it into a little truck. The kids were happy to sit on the floor of the box and ride to their beloved lake. I never rode in the box, preferring to have a day of rest and reading at home. Neighbours told me the little John Deere truck was an object of interest in the community.

Mama and Papa's Dream Home

In the spring of 1950, Mama, Papa, and Alex moved to the Perry place. A half-section of land with a small house on it, the property had been bought for Alex to farm when Donnie got married and took over the Armstrong place. Mama, Papa, and Alex lived in the Perry house while Mama and Papa's dream home was being built. Mama and Papa had designed the new house for themselves and Alex—if he remained single. They hired the superb carpenter, Vivian Scheldro, to build it. (Mr. Scheldro had built both the Rife and Hoselaw schools and Maurice and Pem Destrube's house.) He was a craftsman who aimed for perfect workmanship.

When Mama and Papa decided to move to Bonnyville in their declining years, they sold their sturdily built home to family friends, Bert and Audrey Layh. The Layhs hired a house mover for the formidable ask of moving the two-storey house to a site in Bonnyville. The house was later moved to an acreage, where it still stands.

In June 1951, Vivi and I and our sister-in-law, Olive, organized a banquet and dance at Eastbourne Hall to celebrate Mama and Papa's 40th wedding anniversary. It was a pleasant event, highlighted by Papa's gracious speech about the woman he married. It was also the first time in five years that my siblings and I were all together.

Celebration of a 40th Anniversary

Five Babies Complete Our Families

That fall, after the 40th-anniversary celebration, the first of a group of five younger grandchildren joined the extended Ross family. On November 13, 1951, Donnie's wife, Olive, had a lovely baby girl, Elsie Catherine Ross. In BC, in July of 1952 Ray and Vivi's family was completed with the birth of Phillip Ross White, called "Ross." Our family was completed on April 24, 1953, when Richard Alexander Smith was born. In May, 1954 Laurence Munroe Ross was born, a brother for Elsie Catherine and a cousin pal for our Richard. A relative remarked that finally there was a boy to keep the Ross name going. Donnie loved his sweet-natured baby boy but not the idea that being the carrier of the Ross name made a boy more valuable than Elsie. When Allan was born in October 1959, Donnie and Olive's family was complete.

His older siblings loved to play with Richard and make him laugh. Jean especially liked to carry the little fellow on long walks to pick berries. For years Danny enjoyed taking him, whom he called "Little Man," with him on various jobs and on trips to town.

Above, left: Rife, Armstrong house, spring, 1951. Elsie Catherine Ross.

Above, right: Rife, Browning place, winter, 1954. Cathie with toddler Richard. Danny and I were thrilled to have a baby boy, and so were our older kids.

Being well supplied with babysitters, I set out upon an adventure that occupied me for the next 20-some years. The whole time I received encouragement and support from Danny. From a newspaper article I learned that if I completed six grade 12 courses I could gain entrance to the Faculty of Education at the University of Alberta. By working at night after everyone else was in bed, I completed correspondence courses and prepared for diploma exams in English 30, Social Studies 30, Biology 30, Latin 30, and French 30. By taking the grade eight piano exam from the Western Board of Music, I obtained credit in Music 30. Next I attended four summer school sessions at the U of A, which gave me an Elementary School Teacher's Certificate. The professor who handed the certificate to me said, "This certificate is good anywhere in the world." I spent 18 happy years teaching grade one and music, first at Glendon and then at Bonnyville.

Building My Career

Glendon school, 1957. Staff photo of me as a grade one teacher.

Selling the Farm to Sons Mack and Sid

While I was working on my career, our family was growing up. Danny had been steadily expanding the farm, buying more land and pure-bred cattle. His dream was to see our two older sons, Mack and Sid, take over the farm. He encouraged them to attend the Agriculture Program at Vermilion, which they did. When "the boys" were only in their early twenties, Danny acted on his dream by offering to sell them most of our land, the Browning house, livestock, and farm machinery. Danny and I retained two quarters, which the boys also farmed. In return for the use of that land and as payment for Danny's work, the boys gave us 10% of the farm profits and allowed us to live rent free in the Browning house.

For the next 30-some years, Danny continued to put in full days on the farm and did the chores when the boys went on hunting trips to get deer, elk, and moose meat for the table. As the farm became bigger and more profitable, Danny insisted on reducing the percentage of profits he was paid. He was pleased with the boys' hard work and bold decisions to buy more land, bigger machinery, and top-quality stock, notably Charolais cattle.

Mack and Diane Marry

In July 1965, Mack and Diane Mercier, a teacher, were married, necessitating new living arrangements. We agreed that Mack and Diane would live in the Browning house, and Danny, Richard, and I would move to Bonnyville. I had been teaching in Bonnyville, renting an apartment there to live in during the week, and spending weekends on the farm. (I was not a good enough driver to commute.) I was ready to move into Bonnyville full time, and I felt lucky when we bought a small but comfortable house perfectly located for me, across the street from Duclos School, where I taught. Sid, who was not yet married, stayed on in the Browning house. Danny commuted to the farm, where he had his noon meal. Diane gave up teaching, preferring to focus on cooking, managing the household, gardening, and eventually raising a family. Mack and Diane's offspring are Danielle Jean, Denise Elaine, and Douglas Ian.

Opposite: *Fort Kent Catholic Church, July 3, 1965. Daniel MacKinnon Smith and Diane Ella Mercier were married. Reception banquet and dance were at the Tropicana.*

Lonely times for Rick

Living close to my workplace made life easier for me, but I did not realize that moving to Bonnyville could make life less enjoyable for Richard. He had to leave his brothers and interesting things and activities on the farm. He had to leave Glendon School, where he knew all his classmates and many others. Perhaps the biggest wrench was leaving his main playmates, Laurie and Elsie Ross, who lived near the Browning house and with whom he rode the school bus.

Right, top: Rife, beside Donnie and Olive's home, about 1961. L–R: Richard Smith, Laurie Ross, Elsie Ross. The cousins were great playmates.

Right, bottom: Rife, about 1960. Rick with steers, Sid in background. Rick enjoyed the animals and the excitement of the farm. Photo by Donnie's long-time hired hand, Peter Sherman.

After selling the farm to Mack and Sid, Danny had more free time. When the manager of the bank we used offered him an interesting part-time job, he accepted. He evaluated business plans of people wanting to borrow money from the bank to finance farming ventures—for example, purchase of land or machinery. An example is the case of a family with only two quarters of land wanting to include their son in farming, Danny advised the family to invest in dairy farming. He was gratified to see the family prosper as dairy farmers.

Danny's New Part-Time Job

In the spring of 1967 Danny noticed a bargain price on flights to England and realized he had a yearning to go back to his hometown, Masham, in Yorkshire, where he had gone to school and where his sister Margaret and her husband, now retired, were living. He also planned to look up some school friends. He talked to his friend, Jock Ross, who had a similar yearning to go back to the highlands of Scotland. We arranged a three-week trip to Britain in August with Jock and his wife, Rose. When our daughter, Jean, heard about our plans, she arranged to join the group.

A Trip to England

As soon as possible after our plane touched down in England, we excitedly began to explore wonderful, historic London. We found our way around the famous sites we'd read about, travelled down the Thames, and took a few tours during which we heard gruesome tales of long-ago crimes and wars. We saw the musical *Oliver* before it became a hit in North America. But all the while I knew Danny was wanting to get to Masham to see his sister Margaret.

We finally bought train passes and set out for Yorkshire. We had no idea that we would find Margaret and her husband Reg mourning the loss of their beautiful daughter Pauline. We had no idea that we would seem insensitive boors.

How we learned about the family's loss of this lovely young woman is a story in itself. When I knew we were actually going to England, I wrote to Margaret saying we hoped to visit her and Reg. I did not think to mention that the last letter we'd received from her was unreadable. Margaret wrote back, saying Reg had retired and they no longer lived in the big house at Haighton. She gave me their new address and phone number in Masham.

Sad News Delayed

Yorkshire, about 1963. Pauline Susan Metcalfe. The younger daughter of Reg and Margaret Metcalfe was training to be a nurse when she had to have brain surgery. The surgery was successful, but an aneurysm took her life on August 13, 1965.

We arrived in Masham in mid-afternoon, and as soon as we had found lodging, Danny was determined to find Margaret and Reg's home by exploring on foot. As it happened, Jock, Rose, and Jean decided to join us, so we were in a group of five when we found the Metcalfe home.

We had neglected to phone, so we arrived unheralded. I felt we were not getting a particularly warm welcome, and I wondered whether being in a group of five was problematic. We were invited to come in, which we did, sitting rather stiffly in the living room. Someone in our group admired a photo of Pauline that was on display and asked where she was. Margaret and Reg looked startled, and after a pause Margaret said, "She passed away." We were taken aback, and Danny and I both said we had not heard anything about her death. Margaret said, "I wrote a letter to you, telling you about it."

Masham, Yorkshire, mid 1960s. Danny and his sister Margaret Metcalfe enjoy looking at photos and reminiscing.

Danny and I immediately remembered the strange letter we had received. It had somehow fallen out of the Postal Service bag or the postman's hand into the snow outside the Rife Post Office. When the snow melted in the spring, the postmistress found the letter in her yard. The ink had washed away so completely that she couldn't read the address on it. Taking the British stamp as a clue, she showed the letter to Danny when he came for the mail. He opened the letter in the post office and found it looked like a water-colour painting of a blue sky. In a few places he could make out a letter or two, enough to make him think the letter had been written by his sister Margaret.

After we told the Metcalfes about the letter, the atmosphere warmed. Naturally we offered our belated condolences. We chatted a little, and Margaret invited us all to come for tea the next day.

The next day, we arrived at the Metcalfes' at the appointed time. The three men, Reg, Danny, and Jock, went for a walk to some place of interest, while Rose, Jean, and I visited with Margaret. Jean said we would be interested if Margaret felt like telling us about Pauline. I think Margaret welcomed the opportunity to tell us how beautiful Pauline was in every way. With tears streaming down her cheeks, she told about Pauline as a loving little girl and as a capable student preparing to do the work she loved. By becoming a nurse she wanted to contribute to the well-being of others.

Tea and Heartfelt Conversation

Then Margaret told about the headache that came to Pauline, so intense that Pauline's older sister, Joan, a highly experienced nurse, came to see about it. When Joan looked into Pauline's eyes, she said with urgency in her voice, "She needs medical attention immediately."

After surgery to remove a tumour on Pauline's brain, the doctor said the operation was successful. He warned, however, there was a risk of an aneurysm that could be fatal. Despite hopes and prayers, Pauline had an aneurysm and died on August 13, 1965. As Margaret talked, we all had tears in our eyes.

The men came back from their walk, and we sat down for tea and talk. Margaret had baked the coconut cones that Danny remembered from his childhood. David, the Metcalfes' elder son, showed us slides of beautiful flowers that he helped to grow at Swinton Castle. Danny and Margaret had some opportunity to reminisce. Margaret was a delightful host, like her mother—perceptive, witty, and quick to laugh. I was glad Danny had a warm and pleasant reunion with his sister—and found her coconut concs as delicious as he remembered.

Danny and I and Jean would have liked to spend more time in Yorkshire, but we had to move on to Scotland to visit Jock's relatives. We left Masham feeling great empathy for Margaret and Reg. We imagined the sadness and ache that they would probably feel for the rest of their lives. We hoped they would find consolation in knowing that Pauline's 20 years on earth were happy ones, blessed with a loving family, joyful times, and the beginning of a fulfilling career.

Scotland, Ireland, and France

We had pleasant times travelling across picturesque Britain by train, spending some time in Edinburgh then going north to Inverness to visit Jock's relatives. Quick trips to Belfast and Paris were great learning experiences. In Paris our hotel, the Bristol, served incredibly delicious food, starting with strong coffee and crusty bread delivered to our bedrooms in the morning. The sumptuous dinners went on for about three hours, ending with a huge tray of fruit—which I could not resist depleting as long as it was in front of me. Years later Jock and Rose were still marvelling at what they politely called my "hearty" appetite.

Sid and Shirley Marry

On July 4, 1968, our son Kenneth Sidney and Shirley Rhoda Witwicky, a teacher and social worker, were married by the Reverend Minister of the Bonnyville United Church. Danny and I were the only witnesses, and unfortunately we did not get a good photo of the bride and groom. Our photo shows them as they were six years later. For a while the newlyweds lived in a rented house in Bonnyville, and Sid commuted to the farm.

Soon, however, plans were under way to build a house for them on the farm. Mack and Sid, "the boys," started from scratch, cutting down trees to mill into lumber. Sid and Shirley modelled the house after the one they rented in Bonnyville, drawing their own plans. Working together, Danny, Mack, and Sid built the forms for the cement foundation, which was a full basement. Then they framed the house, put on the roof, installed the plumbing, wired the house for electricity, laid the floors, put up the drywall, and painted the whole house inside and out. I still marvel at how quickly and surely they did the work. I guess Mack and Sid learned

Browning house, Christmas, 1974. Shirley and Sid Smith. In July 4, 1968, Shirley Rhoda Witwicky and Kenneth Sidney Smith were married by the Reverend Minister of the Bonnyville United Church.

the basics of the trades in Vermilion. They may also have consulted with friends at times and read construction how-to books. In its 48 years the house has shown no flaws, not a single plumbing or wiring problem. Sid and Shirley, however, have kept busy adding features to their house. Most notable is a beautiful living room with a vaulted ceiling and attractive masonry, where a stylish wood stove throws out heat. Outside, Sid built wrap-around decking with attached high-backed seats. Downstairs Sid and Shirley finished the basement with cozy pine panelling. Shirley, who opted out of teaching and social work to be a full-time homemaker and mother, has for many years been an avid gardener, a singer, a musician, and a sometime painter of pictures. Her flower gardens are gorgeous in spring, summer, and fall. The couple's latest project, completed in 2015, is a gazebo or "yurt" with glass windows all around. Sid and Shirley have two daughters, Heather Dawn and Kim Janelle, who live nearby with their families.

Right; *Rife area, 2016.*
Sid and Shirley's house and
landscape. The house was
built entirely by the farmers in
1969.

__Below:__ Sid and Shirley's
"yurt." A pleasant retreat.

Rick and Janet Marry

In July 1971, in a beautiful teenage wedding, high school sweethearts, our son Richard (Rick) and Janet Lay were married. As newlyweds they moved into our basement bedroom and living room and shared our kitchen. To my delight, Janet, who was already a superb cook, did most of the cooking during the year they lived with us. In 1972 a frisky baby boy, Terry Lee Smith, was born to the young couple, who handled parenting with confidence and ease.

Ernie Lay's Gift to Rick

Janet's father, Ernie, hired Rick as a welding apprentice, but suddenly, at age 43, Ernie had a fatal heart attack. Losing him was hard for Ernie's whole family and for his new son-in-law. But Ernie had given Rick the start

Bonnyville, July 16, 1971. Rick and Janet (Lay) are married.

he needed. Rick completed his apprenticeship and had a very successful career in specialized welding, often creating original objects for use in the oilfields. Janet completed high school and business courses and now does accounting for her clientele.

Great-Grandparents Rick and Janet

In April 1979, baby LeeAnn Catherine Smith was born to Janet and Rick, who were by then living in Rife. Now both married, Terry and LeeAnn live with their spouses and families also in the Rife area, on a quarter of land that Danny and I gave to Rick's family. Rick and Janet are busy grandparents and great-grandparents. Terry's daughter, Samantha, made them great-grandparents by giving birth to Kaylee Mare. At the same time Samantha made me a great-great-grandmother. (See five-generation photo in Chapter 16.)

In Chapter 6 I showed you photos of the 2015 wedding of Samantha Smith and Brian Mare, parents of Kaylee. Now I want to go back 24 years to show you a photo of the missing link between the weddings of Rick and Janet and Samantha and Brian. That link is the couple Terry Smith and Marci Wishart, who married in 1991. Samantha was their first baby, born 1992, followed by Kyd Daniel in 1996 and Anson William in 2001.

Left: *Eastbourne Hall, September 7, 1991. Marcella Wishart and Terence Lee Smith were married. I recall Rick and Janet, Terry's parents, were misty-eyed as they walked down the aisle with their son. On June 13, 2015, it was Terry's turn to be misty-eyed when he walked his daughter, Samantha, to the arbour where the groom, Brian Mare, was waiting.*

Our Return to Country Living

Getting back to some chronological order, in 1973 work started on a new house for Mack and Diane. The same three men worked as they had on Sid and Shirley's house with one difference: rather than milling their own logs, they bought lumber from a lumber yard. Later Mack and Diane added a big sunken living room with a built-in fireplace made from stones that Mack split into flat slabs.

With our two sons living at Rife and capably managing the farm, Danny and I were able to travel more. Several years after our trip to England we travelled with Jock and Rose to Hawaii, another delightful experience. Another summer we four travelled by car across Canada, spending some time in Prince Edward Island, birthplace of Papa. I feel so fortunate to be able to look back on these travels with our good friends.

Left: Hawaii, about 1974. L–R: Jock Ross; Rose (Procyk) Ross, my friend and colleague at Glendon School; and Danny.

In 1975, after Mack, Diane, and family moved into their newly built home, Danny and I moved back to the now-vacant Browning house. I also retired that year and was glad to be back in the country, in the house we loved.

Joys of Retirement

I loved retirement. I finally had time to read new books, try my hand at quilting and song writing, and quite often see our grandchildren. My grandchildren seemed to appreciate the quilts I made for them, but my song "I Must Hurry to Fort McMurray" did not make the charts. However, the Glendon Historical Society included my song "A Salute to the Brave Pioneers," with words and music, in their superb community history, *So Soon Forgotten.*

I appreciate the way the book presents my song with a sketch by Sid's wife, Shirley, and an appropriate photo. There was not room on the page for the third stanza of my "Salute" song, so I include it below:

> They cleared the wild upland, where trails there were none.
> They bared the brown patches of loam.
> The ox and the plow and the sweat of his brow
> Established the pioneer's home.

I also had time to become a founding member of Rife's Three-Woman Band. Our band entertained at community events and the Lodge where I now live. We had no thought of making money; we simply enjoyed making music together.

Bonny Lodge, Bonnyville, 1983. Rife's Three-Woman Band. L–R: Victoria Armagost, me, Mae MacLean.

Mr. and Mrs. Reahm 1935, lived on Chicken Hill farm.

A Salute to the Brave Pioneers
by Catherine A. Smith

A young couple stood by a rude cabin door,
In the light of the Alberta sun.
And watched the wee baby who played on the
    floor,
And thought of the baby to come.

They'd taken the trail of the "True Pioneer",
To follow a dream they loved best.
"Forsaking all others", and things they held dear,
To carve out a home in the West.

Music to "Salute To The Brave Pioneers", composed by Cathrine Smith.

127

After we moved back to the farm, friends from Bonnyville enthusiastically came to our house for celebrations. As a house-warming gift they gave us a handsome wood holder for our newly built fireplace.

Browning house 1975. A thoughtful gift.

My favourite times were family gatherings. A memorable occasion developed spontaneously after Laurie "Louie" and Donna Ross's joyous wedding and dance in Rocky Mountain House. Danny and I invited all the BC Whites—Ray and Vivi, Ed and Terri and family, and Diane (White) and Ken Brown—to carry on to our house the next day. We were delighted when they all accepted our invitation, and we cheerfully got up early the next day to get back to Rife to make arrangements for beds and food for everyone. We had a wonderful time. We older people were reminded of pioneer times when hospitality was the rule. Fortunately we have a photo of most of the guests.

Browning house, 1975. Ross descendants' gathering. Back row, L–R: Richard; Diane Brown; Ray White; Danny; Ken Brown; Edgar White; Julia Ross, Alex Ross. Middle row: Diane; me, holding Douglas; Vivi, holding Denise; Janet; Terri White; David White; Scott White. Front row: Danielle; Terry; Kelli, Ed and Terri White's adopted daughter.

Jean and Don Marry

Our first-born child was last to marry. In 1973 Jean met Don Mottershead when they both were graduate students at the University of Alberta. In 1977 they were married in Edmonton, and Don went on to complete his PhD. Jean finished her Master's degree then opted for motherhood, having two sons, Jeffrey Daniel Frederick Mottershead, born in 1979, and Blair Donald Smith Mottershead, born in 1980. After being a full-time mother for five years, Jean resumed work at NorQuest College, teaching and managing a program until she retired in 2008, 50 years after she had started teaching. All members of the Mottershead family, including one grandson, Devlin, live in BC, Don and Jean on the lush, green island of Quadra.

Danny and I drove into Edmonton to attend Jean and Don's wedding. It took place early in the evening of October 7, after Jean had put in a day at work. The only guests were Danny and I, Don's mother, Hilde Stewart, and Don and Jean's friends, Robin and Rachelle Smith (not relatives). The ceremony was in the home of marriage commissioner George Debonnaire, an Englishman who instantly recognized Danny as a fellow countryman. He pointed out that he had modified the marriage vows to eliminate obedience on the part of the wife. After the ceremony we went to Christopher's, which served an excellent prime rib dinner. After dinner we all went to the condominium that Don and Jean owned to have a piece of the wedding cake that Hilde had bought.

Right: Edmonton, October 7, 1977. Catherine Jean Smith and Donald Harold Mottershead give each other wedding rings.

Danny and I were home before midnight. We knew Ray and Vivi would be arriving at our place the next day, followed by the newlyweds. A family gathering was always a happy time for me.

Above, left: Me, Jean, and Danny.
Above, right: Edmonton, October 7, 1977. The marriage commissioner, who took the group photo, got only half of Rachelle's face and only my hand (on Danny's arm). L–R: Rachelle and Robin Smith, Hilde Kruse Stewart, Jean and Don Mottershead, Danny, and my hand.

Sid and Shirley held a celebration of our 35th anniversary at their home, a short walk away from the Browning house. Many family members and friends attended. Shirley made a beautiful tiered cake, which Danny and I cut. Danny's brothers Tommy and Reg were there and we managed to get a photo of the three Alberta Smith brothers together.

Our 35th Anniversary

Left: Rife, 1985. Our 35th anniversary. L–R: Reg, Danny, Tommy.

Smaller Family Gatherings

Top left: *Browning house, about 1995. Sisters, Vivi and me. The redness of my nose indicates that we have had one of our sessions of cathartic laughter—eyes tearing, noses wrinkled, gums bared, shoulders shaking.*

Top right: *Janet, Terri White, and Lynne Sutherland show they are pretty good at laughing too.*

Above: *Browning house about 1995, a typical dinner party scene. L–R around the table: Janet, me, Vivi White, Bob Sutherland, Lynne Sutherland, LeeAnn, Rick, Danny (top of head).*

For 27 years after I retired, from 1975 to 2002, we lived happily in the Browning house. We had many family gatherings, but gradually these became smaller and less frequent. Younger families held parties in their own homes with their friends and their children's friends. I had less work and commotion, but I missed the times when we had our whole family together for Christmas.

Christmases over the Years

I include a few pages of photos from past Christmases at the Browning house and in Edmonton. They document the additions of grandchildren until we were blessed with nine.

With Grandma and Grandpa Ross

Browning house, 1959. Christmas. Sitting on sofa L–R: Jean, Grandma and Grandpa Ross (Mama and Papa). On floor: Elsie Ross, Richard (Rick), Lawrence (Laurie) Ross. These three children were about ten years younger than Mama and Papa's first set of grandchildren.

With Farm Families

Top: *Mack (with Christmas bowtie).*

Bottom: *Kids at their own table. L–R: Danielle, Terry, Heather, Denise, Kim.*

Top: L–R: Denise, Danielle, Kim, Jean, Heather, Shirley.

Bottom: Sid playing with Douglas, age 14 months.

With Farm Families (continued)

Top: *Rick trying on several gifts.*

Centre: *Danielle, Denise.*

Bottom: *L–R: Rick, Kim, Diane.*

With Little Newcomers

Browning house, 1979. Danny and Jeff, focusing on the fire in the fireplace.

With Little Newcomers (continued)

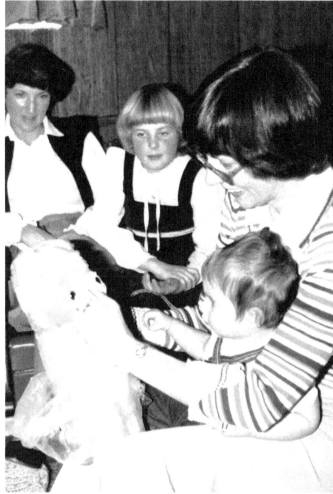

Opposite: In 1979 two little newcomers took in their first Christmas.

Top left: Janet with LeeAnn, age 8 months.

Top right: L–R: Shirley, Kim, Jean Mottershead holding Jeff Mottershead, age 11 months.

Bottom left: L–R: Sid, Muffy, Danny. During her long and privileged life, Muffy charmed and entertained everyone.

Bottom right: Shirley, Kim, and Heather.

With Youngest Grandchild

Left, top: Edmonton, 1980. Early Christmas with our youngest grandchild, two-week-old Blair Donald Smith Mottershead, and his brother. L–R: Danny, me, and Mottersheads, Jeff, Jean, Baby Blair, Don.

Left, centre: Browning house, Christmas 1981. L–R: Diane; Blair Mottershead, age 1; Douglas, age 8.

Left, bottom: Edmonton, 1982. Christmas with grandsons. Jeff, age 3, on the left; Blair, age 2, with Danny and me.

Farm Family Award

A highlight for the farming members of our family came in 1976 when the Edmonton Exhibition Association sponsored a competition for a "Farm Family Award." The Bonnyville Chamber of Commerce selected "The Dan Smith Farm" for the award in their zone. We were invited to Edmonton to receive the award plaque and to enjoy a day of celebration.

Edmonton, summer 1976. Official Farm Family photo. Back row, L–R: Sid, Al "Boomer" Adair, a police officer, Lieutenant Governor Steinhauer. Middle row, L–R: Shirley, Danny, me, Diane, Mack, holding Douglas. Front row, L–R: Kim, Heather, Denise, Danielle.

Danny and I, along with Mack and Sid, their wives and children, joined 25 other farm families from other municipalities for registration and a coffee party. From there we were taken by Edmonton Transit bus for a tour of City Hall and greetings from Mayor Terry Cavanaugh. Next we went to the Legislature for a tour and greetings from the Lieutenant Governor, Ralph Steinhauer, and Minister of Recreation, Parks, and Wildlife, Al "Boomer" Adair. Both men made thoughtful speeches about the importance and future of farming and chatted informally with us. They joined us when we went to The Old Timers' Cabin for dinner. The Cabin, situated on Scona

Hill and overlooking the river valley, was a perfect place to dine and gaze out the big windows and feel that life was good. After lunch each family had a photo taken with the dignitaries. From there we were free to use our complimentary tickets for admission to the Edmonton Exhibition. This time was undoubtedly the most exciting part of the day for our young grandchildren. There was something for everyone that memorable day.

Our Anniversary Dinner Circle

For perhaps ten years we also participated in an informal group that celebrated wedding anniversaries with dinners in each other's home. There were four couples in the group: Danny and me, Bert and Audrey Layh, Harvey and Nellie Vezeau, and Bud and Pauline Marchand. We all enjoyed the company and the cooking, but now only Pauline and I remain on this earth, both in Bonny Lodge.

Left: *Bonnyville, 1978. A party to celebrate our anniversary at the home of Pauline and Bud Marchand.*

Just Touring Around

Danny and I enjoyed travelling, often just the two of us touring around Alberta and BC in the summer. We also made a practice of weekly jaunts to restaurants for supper, sometimes going as far as Meadow Lake, Saskatchewan.

Fiftieth Wedding Anniversary

Our most memorable evening was the 1990 celebration of our 50th wedding anniversary. The event included a banquet and a dance, with the Norman Ward band from Glendon supplying music. All our children and grandchildren played important roles in the celebration. The highlight for me was the program they put on. Jean had written a little play called "The West, a Nest, and You." It was about Danny's and my engagement, our separation while I worked in Detroit, and our marriage in Windsor. Rick made a plywood "fliver" to represent the car Danny's boss loaned him for the wedding day. Jeff Mottershead played the role of Papa, Blair Mottershead the role of Danny, and LeeAnn Smith the role of me—all very charming and entertaining. The "fliver" appeared again in one of the humorous anecdotes, an exposure of my lack of skill at driving a car. Janet played a recording of a waltz to signify our love of dancing. Besides acting as emcees, Jean and Shirley harmonized in singing the chorus of "The West, a Nest, and You." Mack's daughters, Danielle and Denise, sang "The Rose," and LeeAnn sang "Grampa."

Top: Don Mottershead with our grandson Blair at 50th anniversary.

Bottom: Eastbourne Hall, 1990. Smith cousins at our 50th-anniversary celebration. Back row, L–R: Rick, Mack, Sid, Jeep. Front row: Frances, Jean, Elaine, Joan.

Mack and Diane arranged for a professional photographer to take a formal portrait of all of us. They also surprised us with a composite photo to represent us as newlyweds. (The photo of Danny was taken about ten years after we married.) Don Mottershead videotaped the program, and that video tape enabled me and Danny to occasionally enjoy reliving our most memorable anniversary.

Opposite: Eastbourne Hall, April 1990. Our 50th wedding anniversary. Top row, L–R: Diane, Terry, Danielle, Denise. Middle row: Janet, Kim, Rick, Mack, Don Mottershead, Sid, Shirley. Front row: Jeff Mottershead, Heather, Doug, me, Danny, Jean, Blair Mottershead, LeeAnn.

Danny's 80th Birthday with English Relatives

To celebrate Danny's 80th birthday, August 7, 1993, I arranged for an open house at the Browning house. Shirley brought a beautiful cake decorated with purple pansies, Danny's favourite flower. We were delighted when Danny's nephew from England, Peter Metcalfe (son of Margaret), and his wife, Joan, arrived at the party. They were house guests of Elaine and Peter Doonanco, who brought them. Unfortunately we did not take any photos that day, but I include a photo of Peter and some family members at garden party the Metcalfes hosted two years later for the Mottersheads.

Top: Saltburn, England, 1995. A garden party for visiting Alberta relatives at the home of Peter and Joan Metcalfe. L–R: Peter Metcalfe; daughter, Lesley; sons Roger and Richard.

Bottom: Canada cake in Yorkshire—just one of the sumptuous desserts the Metcalfes had on the dessert table.

My 80th Birthday

Top: *Rife District, Rick and Janet's home, my 80th birthday party, June 26, 1999. Back row, L–R: Don and Blair Mottershead, possibly Tom Charawich. Front row: me; Kyd; Samantha; Mack holding granddaughters Mikayla Weeks and Arcana.*

Above, left: *People relaxing at my birthday party. L–R: Ross MacLean, Danny, Rick, Jeep.*

Above, right: *Lineup of cousins at birthday party. L–R: Jean Mottershead, Rick, Mack, Sid, Louie Ross, Ed White, Allan Ross.*

Continuing to Work in Old Age

Time passed pleasantly and quickly on the farm. Danny had more difficulty in getting around, but each year he produced bountiful crops of vegetables and raspberries in his garden. I was kept busy cooking the organic produce, giving some away, and preserving some.

Top: Browning place, about 2000. Danny grooming his garden.

Bottom two photos: Rife District grain field, 2001. Danny, age 88, climbs up into the small combine and harvests a crop for the last time.

Our 60th Anniversary

In the spring of 2000 we celebrated our 60th wedding anniversary by holding an open house at the Browning house. I think that was the last time we entertained there. We managed to get our four offspring together for a photo and a few of our grandchildren and great-grandchildren.

Browning house, 2000, our 60th wedding anniversary. Standing, L–R: Sid, Jean, Mack, Rick. Seated, L–R: Danny and me.

More anniversary photos.
Top: *L–R: Arcana, Doug's daughter; Grandpa Danny; Samantha and Kyd, Terry's daughter and son; Grandma Cathie; Mikayla Weeks, Danielle's daughter.*
Bottom: *Standing L–R: Tom Charawich, Denise (Smith) Charawich, Mack, Diane, Denaige (Shanks) Smith, Doug. Seated, L–R: Arcana, Grandpa Danny, Grandma Cathie, Mikayla Weeks.*

CHAPTER 13

Danny's Life Ends Four Years after Moving to Bonny Lodge

In the fall of 2002, a year after he had last driven a combine, Danny busily but painfully winterized our house for the coming cold months. In November word came from Bonny Lodge that our names had come to the top of the waiting list for a two-room suite. We decided to take the suite. Moving from the home we loved was somewhat of a wrench, but our sons and their wives helped tremendously. We brought some of our own furniture and soon felt at home.

Danny and I lived comfortably at "the lodge" for three and a half years. We relished the meals, and I, more than Danny, enjoyed socializing. Before supper, I often played songs on the piano for the people coming into the dining room. I enjoyed meeting new people, but Danny was more interested in visits from our kids. He delighted in seeing his family, especially the little ones, at his 92nd birthday party in 2005.

Left: *Browning house, 2002. This is the house we left when we moved to Bonny Lodge.*

Bonny Lodge, August 2005. Danny's 92nd birthday and a party organized by Diane and Janet. Back row, L–R: Terry, Rick, Samantha, Marci, Janet, LeeAnn Vachon, Vern Vachon, Danielle Smith-Weeks, Denise (Smith) Charawich, Diane, Jeff Weeks, Mack. Middle row, L–R: Danny, me, Jean (Smith) Mottershead. Front row, L–R: Anson, Kyd, Mikayla Weeks, Jayden Weeks. Missing are Sid and Shirley and family, Tom Charawich, and Jean's husband and family.

In summer we enjoyed going outside into the pleasant yard and gently rocking on the swing.

Swing at the lodge, July 2004. Danny, me.

Forced Move to Smoky Lake

On March 1, 2006, ironically our wedding anniversary, the administrator decided that Danny must move into Extendi Care, just across the street from the lodge. Unfortunately there was no room there, so he was sent to Smoky Lake Extendi Care.

The following days were the hardest time of my life. Mack came to pick up Danny and me, and Jean came from Edmonton to meet us in Smoky Lake Extendi Care. Mack and I felt we had no choice but to lead Danny to believe that we were just going for a visit there.

We four spent some time in a room at Smoky Lake while a staff member interviewed Danny. When the woman left, Danny said, "This place isn't doing anything for me. Let's go home." Jean then explained that the administration in Bonnyville said he had to move out of Bonny Lodge. He thought perhaps the rent had not been paid and said he would look after it. Mack joined in the attempt to convince him he could not go back to Bonnyville. Jean said his room had been given away, the furniture moved out. Surprised, he said, "Already?" With only a little more discussion,

Danny accepted as fact that our home had been taken away from us. In his typical way he attempted to adjust to facts and look after me. Seeing only a single bed in the room, he asked where I would sleep. Kindly, the Smoky Lake caretakers moved another cot into the room. Danny calmed down, not knowing that I could sleep there one night only. Before that day ended, Danny said he did not like the "two-faced" way he had been treated. Mack, Jean, and I did not like it either.

Jean found that I could get a temporary room at the Smoky Lake Lodge across the street from where Danny was. The next day I moved into that lodge. While Danny was in Smoky Lake Extendi Care, Jean came to help me take Danny outside in his wheelchair and otherwise entertain him. He wanted to see where I was sleeping, so we took him to my room in the Smoky Lake Lodge. I had my guitar there and strummed it a little. Danny joined in briefly as we sang "Home on the Range."

Disappointment in Bonnyville

After nine days in Smoky Lake, a room opened up in Bonnyville Extendi Care. Jean came to see us off, and it was a fairly cheerful time. Danny thought that going back to Bonnyville would mean that he and I would be together again. The situation was decidedly not cheerful when we got to Bonnyville Extendi Care and Danny realized he was still going to be sleeping by himself at night. Mack, Danny, and I had a very stressful time that afternoon. I went back to Bonny Lodge that evening feeling very sad. When I started to play the piano before supper that evening, I was cheered up by a great round of applause. I felt I was at home, but my heart was aching.

Resignation

Right after breakfast the next day I went to spend time with Danny, bringing toasted raisin bread, which he liked. I left for my lunch at the Lodge and came back to spend time with him in the afternoon, and left again for supper and the night. That was the pattern of our days, which Danny soon accepted as the best he could hope for. Now and then he still schemed about improving the situation, once asking Jean, "What's the salvation?"

That summer we spent a lot of time outside on the grass among the evergreen trees of the Extendi Care's fenced grounds. Danny's face became tanned as it used to be. He commented once that this was as pleasant a place as anyone would want.

In September a flu struck Extendi Care, and a quarantine was ordered. I was not allowed to visit for two weeks. When I finally got a chance to see Danny, he wasn't sure who I was. He said, "I know you're important to me, but I can't think of your name." Mack heard him and said, "She's 'Sweetheart.'" That was what Danny had called me for years, and he seemed satisfied that was my name. He said several times that there had been a terrible flu and that he hadn't wanted other people to get it. Someone must have helped him understand why I wasn't visiting during the quarantine. Staff were very kind at Extendi Care.

Only a few weeks before Danny died we had a visit from two very kind people—my nephew Ross White and his partner, Pat Williams. They arranged for a photo, which turned out to be the last one of Danny. Although Danny does not look well in it, I like the photo. It shows that he was outdoors, where he loved to be, and he was surrounded by caring people.

Bonnyville Extendi Care, summer 2006. Around the wheelchair, L–R: Pat Williams, Ross White, me. In the wheelchair: Danny, age 93, still lucid and physically strong but only occasionally happy. Photo probably by Mack using Ross's camera.

Danny's Departure

On the day Danny died, October 25, 2006, I was at Extendi Care early to give him a kiss and sit beside him. For about a week he had not eaten any food. Jean came and sat with me and we chatted quietly, noticing his soft but somewhat laboured breathing. Suddenly he made a little cry, and his face turned pale. Saying, "I think Dad is going," Jean went to get a nurse. The nurse came with her stethoscope and said, "Yes, he's going. You can take his hand." One after another, staff at the Lodge came to the room, giving me hugs and condolences. Doctor Lamoureux came to sign a death certificate. Jean said to him, "Dad wanted to go, and he succeeded." The doctor nodded agreement.

Knowing that Richard and Janet were away on holiday and Mack and Diane were in Edmonton that day, Jean called Sid to give him the news and ask him to come. Sid soon met us at the undertaker's premises, and we three—Sid, Jean, and I—worked out details for a memorial service on October 29, 2006. After we'd made our plans, we went out to the Two Brothers Steakhouse, where Danny and I had often gone for supper before we lived in the Lodge. Sid said he felt like having a bottle of beer, and Jean and I agreed we felt like splitting a bottle between us. The beer was exactly what we needed to relieve tension. Sid raised his glass and said, "Here's to Dad." Jean and I raised our glasses to toast Danny, too. I was glad we were toasting him in a way he would understand and approve. I was sad, but I was also happy that Danny was at peace. I looked forward to going to Eastbourne Hall to celebrate his life.

Celebration of Danny's Life

I look back on Danny's memorial service with great satisfaction—even joy. With photos, flowers, and candles, family members and friends made Eastbourne Hall into a lovely place for a celebration of life. It was so heartening to see all the seats in the hall filling up—about a 150 people there to show their respect for my 93-year-old Danny Boy. Especially gratifying to me was seeing all four of Ray and Vivi's children there, and all of Reg's and Tommy's children there, except a niece, Frances, who was ill. Four people had travelled from BC, and Ross White came from Montreal. Other special guests were my grandson Jeff's parents-in-law, Charles and Rosita Cheung, who came from Edmonton.

The celebration of Danny's life was all I could have wished for. Jean officiated, and her son Jeff delivered the eulogy. After welcoming everyone, Jean quoted a Chinese saying, "Under heaven there is no feast that does not end." She said her father had considered his life a feast, but the time had come when he was ready to leave this feast. Jeff gave a brief biography of Danny's life and concluded with a list of his grandfather's principles for living. He said these principles made him realize why his grandfather was loved and respected. Other people spoke affectionately about Danny. Frank Sandmeyer said he used to think Danny was the strongest man in the world, that he was like a machine when he handled bales. He also remembered that Danny often had Richard with him and called him "Little Man." The music was just what Danny would have liked—"The Old Rugged Cross" and other songs sung or recorded, including "Danny Boy."

The hospitality provided by the community seemed magical. Hall Committee members made sandwiches and coffee. Marci, my grandson Terry's wife, arranged catering with two kinds of soup, especially welcome on a snowy fall day. Neighbours brought fruit and sweets. Remembering how family and friends gathered to celebrate Danny's life always warms my heart.

Eastbourne Hall, October 29, 2006. Danny's memorial. My kids with me. Back row, L–R: Mack, Sid, Jean, Rick. Front: me.

Top: Danny's memorial. White kids with me. Back row, L–R: Edgar White, Ross White. Front row, L–R: Diane Brown, me, Lynne Sutherland.

Bottom: Danny's memorial. My granddaughter Heather and kids. Standing: me. Below: Dylan Hebert, Heather (Smith) Hebert, Halle Hebert. I enjoyed seeing grandchildren and great-grandchildren at the memorial.

Danny Remembers Ray

The fact that all of Ray and Vivi's children came from afar to attend Danny's memorial service gives me great satisfaction. At this point in my story, I will reveal a wish Danny expressed a few months before he died—a wish that shows the bond of friendship between himself and Ray. That wish was to be buried beside Ray. I still have Danny's ashes with me, but in the fullness of time, I want his ashes and mine to be buried beside Ray's and Vivi's ashes. The appropriate plot has been purchased.

CHAPTER 14

Celebrating Life despite Aging, Upheaval, and Partings

Adjusting to Being a Widow

After Danny died, of course I had some sad moments. Often I would think of something to tell him or ask him and suddenly realize he was no longer here on earth. But I had more moments when I was glad he would not have to face a winter in a wheelchair, looking out at snow, unable to have even the small pleasure of my taking him outside, parking him beside the pine trees, under the blue sky and summer sun.

In Bonny Lodge, my life went on comfortably. I realized my secure situation as a widow was what Danny had the foresight to plan for me when he agreed to move into the lodge four years earlier.

Heart Attack Sparks a Reunion

A few weeks after Danny died my calm was shaken by news that Mack was in hospital after a heart attack. He urgently required open heart surgery in Edmonton. Thankfully, he survived, recovered well, and resumed life as a retiree. After Mack had his brush with death, he realized his generation was next in line to die, and he wanted to celebrate life while he could. To that end, he and Diane organized a Smith reunion. They sent out invitations to a lovely event at Moose Lake/Eastbourne in July 2007.

The day of the reunion was bright and sunny, and a good number of people came out to maintain family ties and to enjoy the sparkling lake, blue sky, whispering poplar leaves, and delicious food.

For many of us, the most memorable part of the reunion came when cousin Joan brought out a photo taken 60 years earlier. Danny, I, and the kids had travelled by car from Webster's Corners to visit relatives in Alberta. A highlight of our trip was a get-together at Truman for Tommy, Danny, and Reg and their families. I believe Tommy took this gem of a photo: children from all three families lined up against our Pontiac, with Joan, the eldest, looking more adult than child, good-naturedly agreeing to stand with the children.

Someone suggested that, since all the cousins in the photo lineup were present at the reunion, they should lineup again for another photo. Though they were 60 years older, they all lined up with alacrity beside a red Caravan. They all insisted that Rick, born in 1953, should be in the photo too.

Photos previous page—top: *Truman, Alberta, Tommy and Amelia's farm, fall, 1947, lineup of Smith cousins. L–R: Elaine, Jean, Frances, Jeep, Mervin, Mack, Sid, Joan. Photo by Tommy Smith.*
Bottom: *Moose Lake, Eastbourne Ball Diamond Grounds, 2007. The same Smith cousins, with an addition, at the family reunion. L–R: Rick, Elaine (Smith) Doonanco, Jean (Smith) Mottershead, Frances (Smith) Kuori, Jeep (Allan), Mervin, Mack, Sid, Joan (Smith) Doonanco-Gray.*

Mack and Diane had a big beef roast on the BBQ, and others brought tasty savoury dishes and sweets. Joan brought a huge chocolate cake to mark the birthdays of several of her family members. My sister-in-law Velva and I were the only two remaining Smiths of our generation, and we both received plenty of courteous attention.

Velva told the charming story of how Jeep got his nickname. When he was 3 years old, Allan was entranced by an army Jeep going back and forth on a construction job near his home. After his mother told him he was just like that Jeep—always moving, doing something useful—he announced that his name was now Jeep. And so it has been ever since.

The reunion was an occasion to look back at our forebears, contemplate our own mortality, and think deep thoughts about what makes life worthwhile. I was 88 years old at the time, but I found myself learning new things about life as I chatted with the admirable people there. I feel we all left the reunion with stronger ties to our extended family.

About a year after the reunion, Jeep sent out to cousins packages of photos complete with comments on post-it notes. The collection included 8½ × 12-inch copies of the two lineups of cousins. Jeep's thoughtful gifts are much appreciated.

Departures after a Long, Full Life

By the time I finish this memoir, I will have seen 97 years' worth of arrivals and partings in the Ross and Smith families. Happily, most of the partings have come according to nature's pattern—that is, after a normal lifespan. As far as I know, these people were all loved, their lives eulogized and celebrated. I will say a few words about some of these dear departed ones, beginning with my parents, siblings, and brother-in-law, Ray White.

William Ross

In November 1963, William Ross, Papa, died at age 83 in Bonnyville Hospital after several years of heart problems. His funeral service was in Rife United Church, and he was buried in the cemetery there.

Helen Ross

On September 28, 1968, Helen (McClure) Ross, Mama, died at age 86 in Maple Ridge Hospital in BC. Her usual residence was Bonny Lodge, but she was visiting Vivi and Ray when she was admitted to hospital and died. When the sad news came, I cried because I felt I had lost my main conversationalist. As I mourned, my daughter-in-law Diane helped me accept the loss by pointing out that Mama would only have slid farther into frailty if she lived longer. Vivi and some members of her family travelled from BC for Mama's funeral in Rife United Church and burial in the cemetery there.

Ray White

In 1989, Ray White died at age 82 in Oliver Hospital, with Vivi and Diane by his side. Danny and I attended his funeral service, where their youngest son, Ross, delivered a beautiful eulogy. Later Vivi, along with Donnie and Alex, placed Ray's ashes in a grave in the Rife United Church Cemetery.

Donald Ross

In July 1994, my brother Donald Ross died of cancer in Bonnyville Hospital at age 76. He had been in hospital on life support for several weeks when he asked to be allowed to die without artificial prolongation of his life. Danny and I visited him in hospital as he awaited his death. We brought some fresh BC cherries, which he eagerly ate, remarking that "our mother" loved cherries too. At that moment, I felt closer to my brother than I had in years. Donnie told Danny he would like a drink of whiskey, so Danny went out and bought a bottle. They shared a drink; we hugged Donnie and left. A day or two later my brother left this earth, described by his doctor as "a wonderful man." His funeral service was in Rife United Church. Son-in-law Jim Cunningham delivered a lively eulogy that portrayed Donnie very well. Donnie's tombstone is inscribed with the words "The End of the Trail" and includes Olive Ross's name.

Vivian (Ross) White

On April 10, 2006, after several years of physical frailty, my sister Vivian (Ross) White died in Osoyoos at age 93. For a few years I had been missing her witticisms and wisdom, and our sisterly snickering sessions. I was busy with Danny's situation and could not attend Vivi's memorial service held in Haney, BC. Jean attended it and gave me an account of it and the reception at Bob and Lynne's home. Ray and Vivi's son Ross delivered an eloquent eulogy, and bagpipes celebrated her Celtic ancestry and her life. A few months later, at the Rife United Church Cemetery, Ross and Rife relatives gathered to speak of Vivi, as her ashes were placed beside Ray's in their grave. Jean told us that Vivi had never taken her wedding ring off her finger. Ross, with his siblings' support, had a tombstone for Vivi and Ray engraved with Robbie Burns's words, "I will luve thee still, my dear, Till a' the seas gang dry."

In 2012, my twin brother, Alex Ross, died in Oliver at age 93. A few years earlier he had made a surprise trip by bus to Bonnyville. When he arrived, not long before midnight, he called Janet to pick him up, correctly judging her to be kind and generous. He stayed a few days with me at Bonny Lodge, where he especially enjoyed the food. He also stayed a few days with his nephews "Louie" and Allan. On his return trip he rested at Jean's house for a few hours before he set out again. It was his last trip to Alberta. For several years Edgar White took responsibility for seeing that Alex was comfortably situated in a care home in Oliver. In July 2009, my daughter-in-law Diane accompanied me on a Greyhound bus trip to visit Alex in his lodge in Oliver, BC. That was the last time I saw him. He died three months later.

Alexander Ross

Left: Oliver, BC, 2009. My last visit with Alex.

A few months after Alex died, Ross White, along with relatives from Rife and Bonnyville, gathered at the United Church Cemetery for a brief ceremony to remember Alex and put his ashes in a designated grave. Ross White, who shared Alex's love of music, spoke fondly about him. The inscription on Alex's tombstone is "The Lord Is My Shepherd."

Tombstones of My Siblings

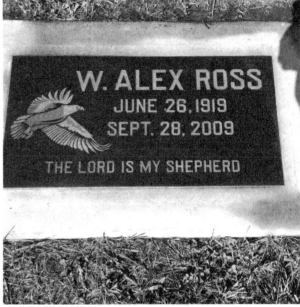

Departures in the Smith Family

In this section I write a few words about the Smiths and their spouses.

In 1954, my mother-in-law, Esther (Greening) Smith, by then Esther Sonnichson, died at 75 years of age. The circumstances were unusual, and I will elaborate in the next section of this chapter. Danny and I and all of Danny's brothers, Charles (Bill), Tommy, Reg, and Allan, attended the funeral. It was the first time the brothers were all together since they were in England.

Esther (Greening) Smith

On March 31, 1993, Amelia (Wilkowski) Smith, Tommy's wife, died of a stroke at the age of 86. Elaine Doonanco wrote and delivered a factual and warm eulogy. Amelia's ashes were placed in St. Paul's Union Cemetery. Tommy lived by himself for the next eight years, but he said, "I don't like going home to an empty house."

Amelia (Wilkowski) Smith

On August 8, 1995, after years of illness, Reg Smith died at 77 years of age. A large crowd of friends and family came to his funeral in Glendon. Peter Doonanco delivered the eulogy, which was written by Elaine, Reg's daughter. Danny remarked that he especially liked the eulogy—sincere and factual. The funeral procession travelled around Reg's farm before taking the coffin to Glendon Community Cemetery.

Reginald Smith

On April 3, 2001, a week before he would have turned 90, Tommy Smith died of old age in St. Paul Hospital. His funeral service, in St. Paul, was attended by a sizable crowd of friends and family. His ashes were placed beside Amelia's in the Union Cemetery.

Thomas Smith

Daniel Smith

On October 25, 2006, Danny Smith died at age 93. (See Chapter 13.)

Charlotte (Harper) Smith

In June 8, 2007, Charlotte (Harper) Smith, Allan's wife, died at age 83 in Chilliwack, BC. Allan commented that he had loved her every day.

Allan MacDonald Smith

On March 2, 2010, Allan (Mac) Smith died at age 90 in a Chilliwack care home. He was the last member of that generation of the Charles Smith family, so no sibling was there for his funeral.

Far left: Danny Smith.

Left: Allan (Mac) Smith.

Unusually Sad Departures

In this section I commemorate the lives of people who died young or in unusual circumstances.

Jack Smith

When Allan "Jeep" Smith provided me with a photo of Jack, he wrote an apt caption: "Uncle Jack Smith at Flat Lake. Guessing around 1930. An uncle we should have known but something went wrong. Sure has the Smith look." Handsome, athletic, charming, and scholarly, Jack seemed to have everything to live for—except the will to live. From what Danny told me, I think Jack's depression came from within him as much as from outside circumstances. Possibly he felt forever thwarted when the family emigrated and he could not attend grammar school. Nowadays depression such as his might be successfully treated. I believe his mother tried to help him, coddling him when he complained of not feeling well. In the end, though, he left home and in the chill of a cold March night cancelled all his promise.

When she was eulogized at her 1955 funeral in Haney, BC, Esther was called "Mrs. E. Sonnichson" (see newspaper clipping on the next page). About three years after she moved to Hammond, BC, Esther married Sonnich Sonnichson. The couple travelled to Alberta to visit Esther's sons, Tommy, Danny, and Reg, and their families. That was the last time I saw Esther alive. She was still slim and beautiful, excited about the trip, keen to hold our baby son, Richard, and chat with me and everyone else.

Esther (Greening) Smith Sonnichson

Left; Esther (Greening) Smith (Sonnichson), with her new husband, Sonnich Sonnichson. Esther seemed happy at the beginning of her marriage to her second husband, but the couple soon separated. Esther died in 1955.

Not many months after the trip, Esther and her new husband separated but did not divorce. The newspaper clipping (see next page) describes her as a "well known" resident of Maple Ridge and lists some of the roles she had held in the community. I was surprised by how quickly this capable and irrepressible woman had risen to prominence in the Maple Ridge community.

I was not surprised, though, that until the end of her life Esther had maintained her passion for singing. On the night she died, Esther was dressed up to go to a Robbie Burns Night, where she had been requested to sing. In her coffin she was dressed in the outfit she had died in—a stylish black dress, trimmed with lace. She was wearing her triple strand of pearls and a pretty rose corsage. When people who were waiting for her to sing went to see why she had not arrived, they found her lying on her sofa, dead. Police were called. They told Charlotte there had been an accident: the gas stove had been left turned on.

Funeral Services Jan. 28 For Mrs. E. Sonnichson

Funeral services were held from St. George's Church, Haney, on January 28. for Esther Sonnichson, a well known resident of Maple Ridge district who passed away suddenly on January 24 at her home, Menzies street, Haney.

Mrs. Sonnichson was in her 75th year. She was born in England, and has lived in Canada for twenty-six years. Coming to this district from Alberta she lived in Hammond and for the past four years in Haney.

She was an executive member of the Maple Ridge Old Age Pensioners Association, a former director of Haney Women's Institute, past member of Hammond Women's Institute, and was a member of Mizpah Chapter OES.

She is survived by her husband, five sons, Bill Davies, Los Angeles; Dan, Reg, and Tom Smith, all of Alberta; Allen, Trail, B.C.; two daughters, Mrs. R. Metcalf and Mrs. R. Spence.

Rev. A. L. Davies officiated at the service at St. George's Church where Mrs. Sonnichson was a member. Interment was made in Maple Ridge Cemetery. Garden

Mr. and Mrs. Danny Smith of Rife. Tom Smith of Truman and Reg Smith of Glendon travelled by plane last week to Haney, B.C., to attend the funeral of their mother. Mrs. Esther Smith, on Jan. 28. The funeral was held in the Anglican Church. Another son. Charles. went by plane from Los Angeles, and Allen Smith from Trail, B.C.. also attended the funeral. The five brothers met for the first time in 35 years.

I noticed something the police perhaps did not notice. On the table, a song book that I had often seen Esther use was opened to a sacred song, "Looking This Way." I quote the lyrics below so you can consider the song and its possible significance in Esther's passing away.

Looking This Way
Words and melody by J.W. Van de Venter

Over the river, faces I see,
Fair as the morning, looking for me:
Free from their sorrow, grief and despair,
Waiting and watching patiently there.

Chorus
Looking this way, yes, looking this way;
Loved ones are waiting, looking this way;
Fair as the morning, bright as the day,
Dear ones in glory looking this way.

Father and mother, safe in the vale,
Watch for the boatman, wait for the sail,
Bearing the loved ones over the tide
Into the harbour near to their side.

Brother and sister, gone to that clime,
Watch for the others, coming sometime.
Safe with the angels, whiter than snow,
Watching for dear ones waiting below.

Sweet little darling, light of the home,
Looking for someone, beckoning come,
Bright as a sunbeam, pure as the dew,
Anxiously calling, mother, for you.

Jesus the Saviour, bright morning star,
Looking for lost ones, straying afar
Hear the glad message, why will you roam?
Jesus is calling, "Sinner, come home."

When she failed to turn off the gas, did Esther sense her mother, Jack, baby Joe, and others looking her way? Whatever she felt, she departed from this world before old age could ravage her body and crack her voice.

Pauline Metcalfe

Yorkshire, 1954. Pauline and her mother.

Back in England, all was going well with the family of Danny's sister Margaret and her husband Reg Metcalfe until 1965, when sadly the youngest family member, Pauline, died. (See Chapter 12 for communication gone awry in connection with Pauline's death.) We invited Peter Metcalfe to write about the lives of his sister and brother, and we are delighted to give you what he wrote, starting with a brief description of family life at Leighton.

The following three paragraphs were written by Peter.

Our family life as children being brought up high in the Yorkshire dales was in many ways privileged, but it could have been lonely were it not for close relationships among our siblings. Joan,

13 years older than me, was absent working as a nurse for much of my childhood. I have memories of the excitement felt when she was coming home but acknowlcdgc that to some extent this may have stemmed from her kindness in usually bringing us gifts. She also took me on holiday for a week at Scarborough when I was about 12 years of age. It is such kindness on her part that encourages me to now do everything possible to help her with her difficulties [with dementia] in later life.

Pauline Metcalfe: There was an age gap of five years between Pauline and me, but we grew up as children together. She was intelligent, very sociable and grew into a very attractive young lady. We spent a lot of time together as children, but after I left home to join the Police Cadets at the age of 15 years, our time together was somewhat restricted. This was even more the case when I joined the RAF and spent two of my three years stationed in Cyprus. When I returned home and joined the Police Service, Pauline and I saw much more of each other. She was a bridesmaid at our wedding and was a frequent visitor to our home when she had days off. She had a very close friend, Mavis, who was an orphan, and she too stayed with us along with Pauline when we lived in Richmond, Yorkshire. Pauline's tragic death was a devastating shock for the whole family as it occurred a mere 14 days after she was taken ill. It was hard to come to terms with the fact that such a young, vibrant, intelligent and attractive young lady could be taken from us. (Pauline died August 13, 1965, of an aneurysm after surgery to remove a tumour from her brain.)

Left: Yorkshire, Metcalfe home at Leighton Reservoir, about 1952. When Peter learned that Danny and I had included one of Jean's dolls in a parcel we sent, he searched for and found a photo of Pauline with her dolls. The doll we sent is at Pauline's knee, and Peter is smiling in the background.

David Metcalfe: Since they were at home as I grew up, David and Pauline were much more a part of my daily life than our sister, Joan. We three younger ones were very close and would work, play, and socialize together daily. David's life was blighted by ill health and very poor eyesight, but that did not prevent him from becoming a very knowledgeable gardener and later head chef. As a child I would play cricket and table tennis with him but was regularly cautioned not to bowl or hit the ball too fast as he could not see it. We also spent many happy hours making models from wood, and I recall that despite his disabilities he made some fantastic model buses, cars and carts. It is a great sadness that I do not have an example of his work. After Joan and I married, David was a regular visitor and stayed with us on many occasions. We also took him on holiday with us and our young family. David, it has to be said, had the capacity to be grumpy and was not slow to display that Yorkshire characteristic of saying exactly what he thought. Despite all this, he was a good friend of mine, was best man at our marriage and was much loved by our children. [David died in 1997 at the age of 66.]

Probably Leighton, about 1939. David.

Charles Smith

For years Danny and I had heard nothing about his father. All we knew was that his father, Charles, had attempted to communicate by letter with him, but Danny's mother had destroyed the letter before Danny could see it. After about 20 years had passed, Danny was excited to hear some intriguing news from a neighbour: a man travelling on the train running between Edmonton and Cold Lake, had asked about his sons, Tommy, Danny, and Reg Smith. The neighbour was able to tell the man that all three were married, had families, and were successful farmers.

We did not hear whether Charles had inquired about his youngest son, Allan MacDonald, whom Esther considered to be his father's favourite son. In 1955 we received news that Charlotte and Allan, acting on his sister Margaret's suggestion, were in touch with Charles. We failed to act on that news, but we do know that, during the last years of his life, Charles lived with or near Allan and Charlotte in Chilliwack, BC. The

arrangement apparently worked well for all concerned. Charles was always a hard worker, so I expect he would have had money to pay for room and board and for his eventual funeral. (Some people think he was a blaster in the Alberta coal mines, in which case he would have been well paid.) I wish we had taken the time to visit him.

Allan and Charlotte had a close relationship with Esther, so Charles must have heard news from them of his ex-wife. In a gesture of goodwill, possibly with help from Charlotte, he bought a pretty dress and sent it to Esther as a gift, which she accepted. He also sent a wreath for her funeral. Thus the story of Charles and Esther Smith finished with a touch of grace.

Left: *Probably in BC, in mid to late 1960s. Charles Smith. With his sleeves rolled up (just as Danny usually had), an elderly Charles looks sturdy and strong.*

Aunt Alice Longley McClure

Earlier, when I introduced Aunt Alice in a photo, I commented that if she knew what sadness and struggles lay ahead of her, she might not look so calm and secure. However, she travelled her difficult road with amazing equanimity.

Aunt Alice and Uncle Len worked very hard to gather money for Muriel, Len's daughter, to train as a nurse. Naturally they were distressed when Muriel took the money and disappeared. That, however, was only the beginning of Aunt Alice's difficulties.

Aunt Alice's father, Charles Longley, began to suffer from dementia and had to be moved into the McClure's one-bedroom log cabin on Chicken Hill. Aunt Alice took care of him there, coping with his incapacity and incontinence. How her heart must have sunk when, after a few years, she realized her husband, Uncle Len, was showing signs of dementia too! Before long she was taking care of two incontinent men, bringing in pails of water to heat on the stove so she could use her scrub board to launder their clothes and bed sheets.

When Mama and Papa visited her, they found her tired but coping, resolved to see the situation through to the end. Danny and I went to see her too, but with three little ones with us, I could not offer much help. Danny, however, noted that her woodpile was low and learned Aunt Alice had been rationing wood, which meant having a cold house at times. After that, Danny and my brother Donnie made sure she did not run out of the essential fuel. Finally, two funerals ended Alice's ordeal.

Aunt Alice sold her small property and moved to Vancouver, where winters were warmer. I do not think she considered a teaching job at her age, but she needed to work. Deciding in her positive, practical way, that she had valuable experience caring for people with dementia, she advertised herself as a practical nurse and immediately found employment. Ray and Vivi, living in Maple Ridge, were close enough to visit Aunt Alice in the various homes where she lived and worked in the 1950s and '60s. They routinely invited her for Thanksgiving and Christmas dinners, she arriving by bus and Ray driving her home.

Chicken Hill about 1929. L–R: Aunt Alice McClure, Muriel McClure, Uncle Len McClure.

Eventually Aunt Alice retired and came back to Alberta to live in Bonny Lodge, where Mama was living and where I now live. After a few months, Muriel, Alice's stepdaughter, came. Saying she wanted to take care of her mother in her home, she took Aunt Alice away. A few weeks later, Aunt Alice was dead. According to people who talked with Muriel, there had been an unfortunate accident: Aunt Alice died in a bathtub, unable to either turn off the hot water or get out of the tub.

When Aunt Alice's will was read, a lawyer informed Ray and Vivi that Alice had left them $10,000. Weeks later, a lawyer representing Muriel sent them a threatening letter saying the money belonged to Muriel. Ray and Vivi did not contest the matter. Aunt Alice's will was thwarted, but her intentions were revealed and appreciated.

I think Aunt Alice was satisfied with her life, pleased with her marriage and her careers in teaching and practical nursing. She accepted and coped with whatever miseries cropped up in her life—until the end. I can only hope that nightmarish end was brief.

Webster's Corners, BC, about 1947. Alice McClure remained calm, cheerful, and resolute in caring for her father and husband during their last years of life in a small log cabin.

David White

After David (Dave) White was killed by an avalanche, professional foresters and friends were profuse in their praise of him. The words "love" and "passion" kept coming up in their comments to the journalist who interviewed them. Dave was killed doing something he loved—skiing with a friend in the back country of the Purcell Mountains of BC.

Son of Edgar and Terri White, grandson of Vivi and Ray White, Dave was only 34 when he died, February 24, 2001. After touring in Europe, and earning a degree in forestry from the University of British Columbia, Dave worked as a forester in the Columbia Valley. For a dozen years or so he lived in the beautiful mountain town of Invermere, his last several years with his partner, Kate Inglis. (See Chapter 15 for a photo of David with Kate.)

Outdoorsman lived for the valley

by Pablo Richard Fernández
ECHO REPORTER

It was a competition Dave White and Grant Neville had between themselves. At last count White was up five to four.

White and Neville were best friends and not too long ago they competed to see how many times each of them could have their pictures in *The Valley Echo*.

According to friends, only White, 34, could be so in-tune with the little things in life.

It was the little things he loved and he found them when he moved to the Columbia Valley. He already loved the outdoors and he quickly learned to love the valley, said those who were close to him.

"This guy had so much passion for being a part of Invermere. Invermere is what made him who he is. He had such a passion for this place he would never leave," said a close friend. That theory was put to the test when a girlfriend of five years tired of the community and chose to leave. Torn between the love for a girl and his love for the valley, White chose to stay in Invermere.

This was his paradise, this was his place, this was his heaven, his friends said.

It was White's passion for everything he did that attracted people to him. It was that passion that was extinguished when an avalanche cost White his life while ski touring west of Radium Hot Springs last weekend.

For White's friend Kirk Mauthner, the tragedy was foretold by a Canadian Mountain Holidays helicopter that flew over his house.

He had "a very positive and healthy outlook on life," said Mauthner.

"I never met him down," he recalled.

The two met thanks to their common interest in ski touring when White, an incremental forester with the Invermere Forest District (IFD), moved to the valley from Vancouver.

ECHO FILE PHOTO
Dave White loved paddling, mountain biking and skiing in the valley.

When they were being interviewed, colleagues and friends seemed to jockey for chances to praise Dave. Here are a few of their remarks:

- This guy had so much passion for being a part of Invermere. This was his paradise…his place…his heaven.
- He was a terrific travelling companion for me…. He was strong, capable, intuitive, and resourceful. He could put up with a lot and cared about the well-being of the group…had innate leadership qualities….
- He will be remembered for his generosity and his contributions to the valley in a variety of ways…. He was a keen hockey player, mountain biker, kayaker and an accomplished professional forester.
- He was never one to boast. He was always laughing. You could tell he loved life.
- This world is going to miss that guy. We need people like him who will follow through with what they believe in. The journalist ended his article saying, "Dave White died…never leaving behind the valley he loved, only all those who loved him."

I was not able to attend David's memorial, held on February 29, 2001, but my daughter, Jean, and her son Blair were there. My sister Vivi was also there. Jean described the service, which was in a large inter-denominational building, filled to capacity. A huge crowd gathered outside, and when they found there was no room for them, they went to the place designated for the reception afterward, the Lakeside Pub.

Dave's brother, Scott, emceed and began with these simple words: "I used to say, 'I have a brother.' Now I must say, 'I used to have a brother.'" He turned away from the audience for a few seconds, then added," I could never see enough of my brother." Strumming his guitar, he sang a song Dave had made up. Nine men got up and took the microphone to talk fondly, sadly, sometimes humorously about Dave.

Dave's father, Edgar, came to the podium and said firmly, "I have never been as proud of my son as I am tonight." He introduced the closing song, a favourite of his father, Ray White. The song, "Springtime in the Rockies," brought tears to many eyes and sobs from Kate. (Fifteen years later, Kate focuses on her career as a pilot, Captain for WestJet, and has never married. She stays in touch with Dave's parents, Edgar and Terri White.)

Opposite: *Invermere, BC, 2001. This article of David White is from* The Valley Echo *newspaper. Reprinted with permission.*

Many people in Invermere and the Columbia Valley obviously wanted some last connection with Dave. At the Lakeside Pub that night, places were reserved for Dave's partner, brother, parents, and grandmother (Vivi), but throngs of people had to be turned away.

Months later, Terri, Dave's mother, told me about a photo Dave had pinned up in his office. It was of three elderly women—his grandmother, Vivi, and two great aunts—Olive Ross and me. I was touched by my hitherto unknown attention from Dave. (See photo at the end of Chapter 6.)

In the spring of 2001, Lynne and Bob Sutherland planted a tree in memory of their nephew, Dave. The tree grows outside the Forestry building in Invermere. A sign below it reads, "He touched our lives."

Grace (Erickson) Smith

Grace was the beloved wife of Allan "Jeep" Smith, younger son of Reg and Velva Smith. Grace brought to the marriage her two children, Daryl and Donna Knapp, from a previous marriage. With Jeep as stepfather, the new family was a harmonious one. Grace contributed much to make their home a lovely place to live. Besides working at a job in town, Grace planted trees to enhance the landscaping, grew a garden for fresh food, and made delicious meals. She was renowned for her cooking, so attendees at her funeral were pleased to receive a scroll of her favourite recipes tied up with a ribbon.

At a young age, Grace was diagnosed with Alzheimer's in its early stages. She and Jeep did their best to manage the illness, and, for a number of years, they succeeded in keeping her at home and participating in community events. Finally, when it became unsafe to leave her alone at home while Jeep was involved in farm work, Grace was moved to Vilna Extended Care. However, when Grace showed she much preferred to be at home, Jeep hired a personal care attendant to take care of her at home. Grace lived at home as happily as possible under the circumstances until pneumonia caused her to be hospitalized. On February 15, 2013, she died in hospital at the age of 71. She was mourned by the community, her extended family, and especially by her devoted husband.

Glendon district home, about 2000. Grace (Erickson) Smith, wife of Allan "Jeep."

When we first entered Raelyn's name in Chapter 15 of this memoir, Jean and I felt joyful. The family of Tommy and Amelia Smith was thriving: on May 26, 2016, a healthy baby girl had been born, making their daughter Frances a great-grandmother. Tragically, Raelyn's precious life was cut short. We celebrate her short life by providing a photo and a copy of her obituary, published in the *Edmonton Journal* on August 15, 2016. The obituary was written by Raelyn's grandmother Robin Kuori.

Raelyn Robin Amelia Supernant

Raelyn Supernant, May 26, 2016–August 8, 2016

On August 8, 2016, a beautiful little angel was sent to heaven. Raelyn Robin Amelia Supernant died at the Stollery Children's Hospital, in Edmonton, Alberta. Raelyn is loved and will be dearly missed by her mother, Carley Supernant; grandmother, Robin Kuori; great-grandmother Frances Kuori; great Uncle Dean and Auntie Desire Kuori; and Auntie Reese Kuori. Raelyn was with us for a short 2 months when she passed away, leaving us only with memories, which we will cherish forever. Please donate to the Stollery Children's Hospital in Raelyn's name.

CHAPTER 15

Descendants

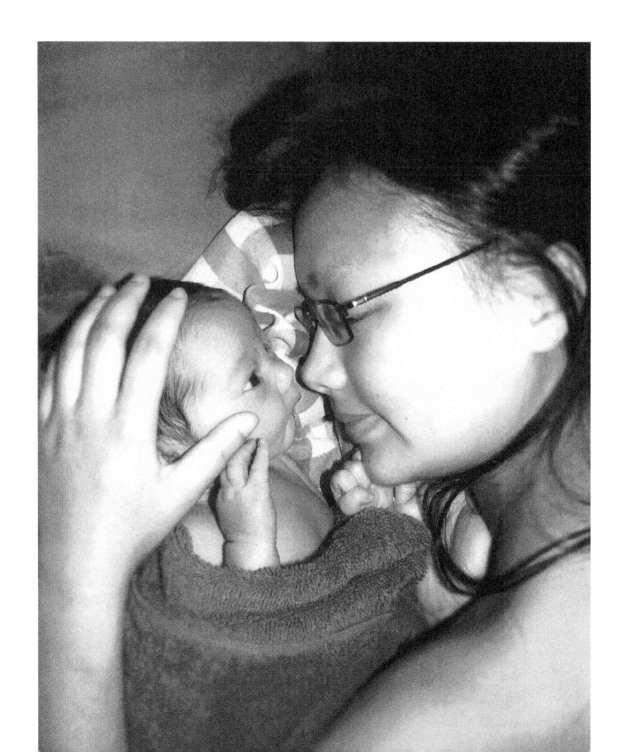

This photo shows the wonder of the moment when a mother and her newborn baby come face to face for the first time. Luckily the thrilled dad was on hand with a camera to capture the moment. We hope the photo has a universal appeal for all parents who look at it.

For the purpose of this chapter, two couples, William and Helen Ross and Charles and Esther Smith, born in the 1800s, are considered generation one. Their children, born in the early 1900s, are considered generation two, my generation. These people are central to this memoir. They are presented here in the order of their birth, with their own family groupings also in the order of their birth. For example, this generation of Rosses consists of Vivian, Donald, Alex (who did not have descendants), and me, Cathie. The men who married into the Ross family—Ray White and Danny Smith—are included with the Rosses. We have at least one photo for each member of this generation. We have many photos of generation three, our children, born from the 1920s until nearly 1960. We have received fewer photos for generations four and five. (Possibly there are unprinted photos trapped on computers.) As far as I know, my great-great-granddaughter, Kaylee Mare is the first sixth-generation child, and of course I have photos of her.

In the listing of family groups an asterisk indicates my generation of Rosses and Smiths.

Opposite: *Vancouver, July 24, 2008. L–R: Devlin Bodhi Cheung Mottershead, Iva Wai-Yun Cheung. Photo by Jeff Mottershead.*

*Vivian and Raymond White Family

Above: *Lions Den, Pitt Meadows, December 30, 1986. Vivi and Ray's 50th wedding anniversary.*
Opposite: *White family reunion, Maple Ridge, about 2000. Back and middle rows, L–R: David White, Heather Sutherland, Ray Sutherland, Rita Brown, Chris Brown, Craig Brown, Terri White, Ken Brown, Dwayne Sutherland, Greg Sutherland, Bob Sutherland, Scott White. Front row, L–R: Diane Brown, Ed White, Vivi White, Ross White, Lynne Sutherland.*

Vivian Ross (Mar 1, 1913–2006) m. Raymond White[1] (Dec 18, 1904–1989)

Edgar White[2] (Aug 1939) m. Terri Barrie
    Scott Raymond Louis White[3] (Feb 6, 1964) m. Ann Elizabeth Eede
        Elsa White (Oct 15, 2005)
    David Edgar White (Jun 22, 1966–Feb 24, 2001)
    Kelli Jennifer White (Aug 13, 1972)

Helen Diane White[4] (Feb 1942) m. Ken Brown
    Christopher James Brown (Jul 12, 1966) m. Rita Caulien
        Claire Brown (Nov 25, 1994)
        Adam Brown (Aug 18, 1996)
    Craig Allen Brown (May 5, 1969) m. Tammy Boljuncic
        Tristan Brown (Aug 9, 2000)
        Kate Brown (May 6, 2002)

Madelyn "Lynne" Anne White[5] (Feb 1947) m. Bob Sutherland[6]
   Dwayne Howard Sutherland (Oct 7, 1966)
   Raymond Grant Sutherland (Mar 6, 1974) m. Heather Marie Jones
      Duncan James Sutherland (Dec 10, 2004)
      Dean Mitchell Sutherland (Mar 1, 2008)
   Gregory James Sutherland[7] (Jul 25, 1978) and Carolyn Marie Marsh
      Vivian Rochelle Sutherland (July 27, 2016)

Phillip Ross White[8] (Jul 1952) and Patricia Lynn Williams (Apr 1958)
   Pat's daughter Melissa James (Jun 18, 1978) m. Peter Kosa (Oct 1978)
      Wyatt Hunter Kosa (May 16, 2012)
   Pat's daughter Sarah Lee James, (May 29, 1980)

[1] Ray's parents were Edgar White and Annie (King) White; Ray's brother, Fred, later immigrated to Canada, lived in Guelph, Ontario. Ray's sister, Nell, in England, kept in touch, sending gifts at Christmas.

[2] Retired Vice President of Bank of Montreal (Corporate Controller); plays in top league slow-pitch ball & Huntsman International; noted for donating blood 100 times

[3] Multi-faceted bassist, band leader, composer, Cirque du Soleil music director, music therapist; lives in Berlin; performs, teaches in Europe, Canada, worldwide

[4] Trained at Royal Columbia Hospital, specialized in operating room work; retired

[5] Ran on NDP slate for Vancouver School Board, 1990

[6] Awarded Queen's Diamond Jubilee medal for work with veterans, 2012; donated bone marrow, 1993

[7] PhD candidate in Education, Simon Fraser University

[8] Autism research with Pat W.; iPad and autism, Ari-Art; blogger; bassist in band

Above: *Maple Ridge about 1982. Cousins. Back row, L–R: Kelli White, David White, Chris Brown, Dwayne Sutherland, Craig Brown. Front row: Scott White, Greg Sutherland, Ray Sutherland.*

Opposite, top: *Vancouver airport, about 2013. Ed and Terri White family. Back row, L–R: Ed White, Ann Eede, Kelli White, Ronnie Douglas. Front row, L–R: Terri White, Elsa White.*

Opposite, bottom: *Invermere, late 1990s or 2000. David White and his partner, Kate Inglis. (David was killed in an avalanche February 24, 2001.)*

Ed and Terri White Family

Diane and Ken Brown Family

Opposite, top: *Haney, 2006. Ken and Diane Brown family (Brown surnames). Back row, L–R: Chris, Diane, Craig, Ken. Front row: Rita, Adam, Claire, Kate (in front), Tristan. The occasion was Vivi's funeral.*

Opposite, bottom left: *Maple Ridge, 2006. Diane and Ken Brown.*

Opposite, bottom right: *BC, 2010. Craig and Tammy Brown.*

Top left: *Sechelt, 2015. L–R: granddaughter Kate, Diane.*

Top right: *Sechelt, 2015. L–R: Craig with son Tristan.*

Above: *Vancouver, 2015. Chris and Rita Brown family. L–R: Chris, Adam, Claire, Rita. The occasion was Adam's graduation.*

Lynne and Bob Sutherland Family

Opposite, top left: *Coquitlam, about 1982. Bob and Lynne Sutherland family. L–R, standing: Dwayne, Bob. Sitting: Greg, Lynne, Ray.*

Opposite, top right: *2016. Dean Sutherland, age 8.*

Opposite, bottom left: *Coquitlam, November 11, 2008, Bob and Duncan, age 4, salute the honour guard. Photo by Ward Perrin. Reprinted with permission.*

Opposite, bottom right: *Coquitlam, July 2016. Lynne Sutherland holding granddaughter Vivian Rochelle Sutherland.*

Above: *Heather and Ray Sutherland's wedding, about 2002.*

Left: *Greg Sutherland, proud father of baby Vivian.*

Ross White and Pat Williams Family

Above: *Osoyoos, August 2007. L–R: Ross White, Alex Ross, Pat Williams, Melissa James, Peter Kosa.*

Below, left: *Montreal, 2009. Phillip Ross White and Patricia Lynn Williams.*

Below, right: *Montreal, 2015. L–R: Wyatt Hunter Kosa with Grandpa Ross White.*

*Donald and Olive Ross Family

Farmhouse at Rife, about 1994. Olive (Munroe) Ross and Donnie Ross.

Donald Ross (Oct 4, 1917–Jul 1994) m. Olive Munroe[1] (1920)

Elsie Catherine Ross[2] (Nov 13, 1951) m. James Murray Cunningham[3]
  Ian David Ross Cunningham (Aug 3, 1990)

[1] Olive's parents were William Munroe (1873–1955) and Ida (Cochrane) Munroe (1886–1959). Her sisters are Alma Munroe (1921), Edith Munroe (1925), and Lorna Munroe (1931).

[2] Associate editor of *Daily Oil Bulletin*; 15 years reporter and copy editor for *Calgary Herald*

[3] Journalism professor at SAIT; @newsknine; former host of Alberta TV political talk show; former reporter for *Calgary Herald*

(continued overleaf)

Laurence Donald Munroe Ross (May 7, 1954) m. Donna Jean Black
    Scott Laurence Ross[4] (Nov 4, 1977) m. Brenda Marie Layton
       Mikayla Anne Michaud (Apr 14, 1996)
       Kaylie Marie Ross (May 15, 2005)
       Grady Tracy Ross (Jul 16, 2007)
    Nicole Dawn Ross (Jun 28, 1980) m. Norman Kendall Gillis
       Morgan Patricia Gillis (Nov 25, 2005)
       Lachlan Laurence Gillis (Jul 22, 2008)
    Jonathan Patrick Ross (Feb 8, 1985) m. Brittany Diane Guy
       Ben Donald Ross (May 20, 2016)

Allan Jamieson Ross (Oct 3, 1959) m. Shannon Dawn Schwan
    Colin Brendon Burns (Jul 1, 1989)

[4]Semi-professional hockey player—Alabama, Florida, Texas

Elsie Ross and Jim Cunningham Family

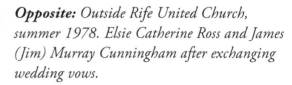

Opposite: *Outside Rife United Church, summer 1978. Elsie Catherine Ross and James (Jim) Murray Cunningham after exchanging wedding vows.*

Left: *Red Deer, about 1976. Elsie Ross at the beginning of her long career as a journalist. Photo courtesy of the* Red Deer Advocate. *Reprinted with permission.*

Below, left: *Calgary, about 2016. Ian Cunningham.*

Below, right: *Moose Lake, about 2008. L–R: Ed White, Jim Cunningham.*

Laurence and Donna Ross Family

Above: Rife District, about 1986. L–R: Nicole Ross, Scott Ross, Jonathan Ross, with LeeAnn Smith.

Left: Bonnyville, July 2004. Wedding of Scott and Brenda. L–R: Scott Ross, Brenda (Layton) Ross, Mikayla Michaud.

Top left: *Nicole Ross, high school graduation, 1998.*
Top right: *Admiring a gift quilt, 2008. Back: Norm and Nicole Gillis. Front: "Louie" Ross holding grandson, Lachlan. Photo by Donna Ross.*
Above: *Grandchildren Morgan and Lachlan Gillis, 2011.*

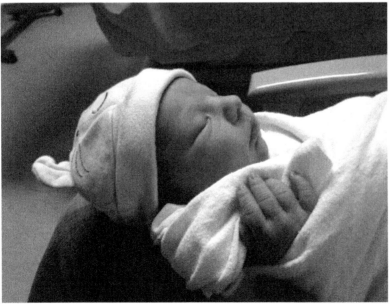

Above: July 17, 2015. Cold Lake, Laurie and Donna Ross family. Wedding of Jonathan and Brittany. Back row, L–R: Scott Ross, Brenda (Layton) Ross, Brittany (Guy) Ross, Jonathan Ross, Hazel Black, Donna (Black) Ross, Louie Ross, Nicole (Ross) Gillis, Norm Gillis. Front row, L–R: Kaylie Ross, Grady Ross, Lachlan Gillis, Morgan Gillis. Jonathan and family live in Edgerton.
Left: Red Deer Hospital, May 20, 2016. Jonathan and Brittany's son, Ben Donald Ross.

Allan and Shannon Ross Family

Above: *Rife District, December 31, 2015, Allan Jamieson Ross and Shannon Schwan have their wedding ceremony in their home.*

Left: *Shannon's son, Colin Burns, joins in celebrating the wedding.*

*Alex and Julia Ross

William Alexander Ross (Jun 26, 1919–2012) m. Julia (Strumecki) Ross (about 1915–1980)

Fort Kent Catholic Church after wedding, July 1965, of Mack Smith and Diane Mercier. Guests of Smith family. Alex Ross and his wife, Julia, shown here, had no descendants. Back row, L–R: Rick, Ann Erickson, Rowena Munroe, Julia (Strumecki) Ross, Alex Ross, Rose (Procyk) Ross. Second row: Margaret (Nordstrom) Fraser with daughter, Elsie Ross, Olive Ross, Donnie Ross, Helen Ross, me, Vivi (Ross) White, Valmai (Nordstrom) Harper.

*Cathie and Danny Smith Family

Maple Ridge, about 1947. Dan and Cathie Smith family. L–R: Jean, Danny, Sid, Cathie, Mack.
Inset: *Rick Smith, born 1953, school photo, about 1964.*

Catherine Ross (Jun 26, 1919) m. Daniel Smith (Aug 7, 1913 – Oct 25, 2006)

Catherine Jean Smith[1] (Dec 14, 1949) m. Donald Harold Mottershead[2]
   Jeffrey Daniel Frederick Mottershead[3] (Jan 20, 1979) m. Iva Cheung[4]
      Devlin Bodhi Cheung Mottershead (Jul 24, 2008)
   Blair Donald Smith Mottershead (Nov 30, 1980)

[1] MA Sociology, U of A; retired Program Coordinator, NorQuest College, Edmonton
[2] PhD Sociology, U of A; retired Chief Information Officer, Solicitor-General Dept., Alberta
[3] PhD Physics, UBC; research, Vancouver
[4] PhD candidate, SFU; MSc Physics; MPub; Certified Professional Editor

(continued overleaf)

Daniel MacKinnon Smith (Apr 30, 1942) m. Diane Mercier
  Danielle Jean Smith (Aug 9, 1970) m. Jeff Weeks
    Mikayla MacKinnon Weeks (Feb 17, 1996)
    Jayden Richard Daniel Weeks (Apr 10, 1999)
  Denise Elaine Smith (Aug 26, 1971) m. Thomas Loren Charawich[5]
  Douglas Ian Smith[6] (Oct 10, 1973) m. Melanie Denaige Shanks (divorced)
    Arcana Eryna Shanks (Sep 20, 1997)

Kenneth Sidney Smith (Jun 11, 1943) m. Shirley Rhoda Witwicky
  Heather Dawn Smith[7] (Mar 5, 1969) m. Shawn Hebert
    Halle Shea Hebert (Jul 31, 2002)
    Dylan Brady Hebert (Feb 28, 2005)
  Kim Janelle Smith (May 11, 1970) m. Ray Parenteau
    Amy Lauren Parenteau (Sep 15, 2003)
    Macie Addison Parenteau (Jan 4, 2007)

Richard Alexander Smith (Apr 24, 1953) m. Janet Lay
  Terence Lee Smith (Jan 14, 1972) m. Marcella Anne Wishart
    Samantha Catherine Smith (Feb 2, 1992) m. Brian Mare
      Kaylee Lorene Mare[8] (Aug 5, 2013)
    Kyd Daniel Smith (Feb 5, 1996)
    Anson William Smith (Apr 30, 2001)
  LeeAnn Catherine Smith[9] (Apr 27, 1979) m. Vern Vachon
    Brooklyn Ann Vachon (Nov 7, 2007)
    Jerzey Lee Vachon (Jan 17, 2010)

[5] Built and operates Starline Trucking and Services Ltd., Bonnyville
[6] Oilfield consultant; summertime owner/operator of charter fishing boat, Blew By You
[7] Inclusive Education Coordinator, Duclos School, Bonnyville, Alberta
[8] My first great-great-granddaughter
[9] Built, operated, and sold Evolution Beauty Salon

Jean and Don Mottershead Family

Above: *Edmonton, 1981. Family portrait. Jean (Smith) Mottershead, Don Mottershead, Blair Donald Mottershead, Jeffrey Daniel Mottershead.*

Left: *Rife, 1982. Jeff, Blair, and Don on a visit to the farm.*

Above, left: *Edmonton, 1984. L–R: Jeff and Blair Mottershead, ages 6 and 4.*
Above, right: *BC, about 1990. Blair, Jean, Jeff Mottershead. Photo by Don.*
Below: *Edmonton, April 26, 2002. Jeff and Iva's Wedding. L–R, back row: Don Mottershead, Blair Mottershead. Front row: Jean Mottershead, Hilde Stewart, Jeff Mottershead, Iva Cheung, Charles Cheung, Rosita Cheung.*

Top left: *Vancouver, 2012. Iva Cheung and Jeff Mottershead as Jeff receives PhD in physics. Photo by Jean.*
Top right: *Devlin Mottershead on a glacier.*
Above: *Campbell River, 2016. Devlin with Mottershead grandparents. L–R: Devlin, Don, Jean. Photo by Arlene Gort.*

Mack and Diane Smith Family

Left: Glendon, 1983. Mack and Diane Smith family. Standing: Mack, Diane; Sitting: L–R: Danielle, Douglas, Denise.
Above: September 1974. L–R: Danielle, age 4, Douglas, age 1, Denise, age 3.
Below, left: Danielle, U of A graduation, 1992.
Below, centre: Douglas, high school graduation, 1991.
Below, right: Denise, U of A graduation, 1993.

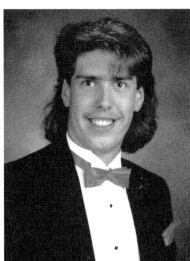

Above: *Bonnyville, about 2012. L–R: Danielle Smith-Weeks with her kids, Jayden and Mikayla Weeks.*

Left: *Mikayla Weeks at high school graduation, 2014.*

Right: *Jayden Weeks makes his debut as an award-winning drummer.*

Above: *Mack and Diane on the day of their 50th wedding anniversary, 2015.*

Opposite, top: *Bonnyville. Denise with Tom Charawich, spring, 1995.*

Opposite, bottom left: *Douglas with daughter, Arcana Shanks, about 2010. (Arcana got Doug's permission to change her surname from Smith to Shanks, her mother's maiden name.)*

Opposite, bottom right: *Doug's daughter, Arcana, high school graduation, 2015.*

Sid and Shirley Smith Family

Opposite: *1983. Sid and Shirley Smith family. Standing, L–R: Shirley, Sid, Kim. Sitting: Heather.*

Left: *L–R: Kim, age 4, Heather age 5.*

Below, left: *1986. Heather, grade 12.*

Below, right: *Kim, grade 10.*

Left: *Parenteau home, 2015. Sid and Shirley's grandkids at a pool table. L–R: Amy Parenteau, Halle Hebert, Dylan Hebert, Macie Parenteau.*

Left: Rife, Sid and Shirley's growing extended family, 2015. Parenteau home, June 2015, prior to Samantha Smith and Brian Mare's wedding. Back row, L–R: Ray Parenteau, Heather (Smith) Hebert, Sid Smith. Front row: Halle Hebert, Amy Parenteau, Kim (Smith) Parenteau, Dylan Hebert, Shirley Smith, Macie Parenteau.

Below: Rife, 2015. Sid and Shirley with their daughters.

Rick and Janet Smith Family

Above, left: *Glendon, 1983. Rick and Janet's family. Standing, L–R: Terry, Rick. Sitting, L–R: LeeAnn, Janet.*

Above, right, top: *Rife home, Christmas, 1980. LeeAnn at age 1½, Terry at age 8.*

Above, right, bottom: *Samantha in sun hat, about 1995. Samantha was our first great-grandchild.*

Opposite, top: *Rife, Rick and Janet's yard, about 1998. Standing: L–R: Marci, Rick, Janet. Sitting, L–R: Terry, Danny, me. On little chairs in front: Samantha, Kyd.*

Opposite, bottom: *Bonnyville, 1995. Dinner with Rick, Janet, LeeAnn.*

Above: Rife or Bonnyville, about 2005. Terry and Marci Smith family. Back row, L–R: Terry, Kyd, Marci, Samantha. In front: Anson.
Below: Rife or Bonnyville, 2013. Samantha and Brian extend the family. L–R: Anson; Samantha; Brian Mare, holding Kaylee Mare; Kyd.

Above: *Rife, LeeAnn and Vern Vachon family. At Parenteau home prior to Samantha's wedding, 2015. Back row, L–R: LeeAnn and Vern Vachon. Front row: Brooklyn and Jerzey Vachon.*

Left: *Bonnyville, December 2016. Brooklyn Vachon as flag bearer for the Western Canada hockey team in the World Junior A Challenge in Bonnyville.*

SMITH–GREENING DESCENDANTS

Esther (Ettie); Margaret; Charles (aka Bill Davis); Joseph (died as a baby); Jack (died as a young adult); Thomas; Daniel; Reginald; MacDonald, aka Allan.

*Ettie and Lawrence Spence Family

Probably Leeds, about 1930. Ettie and Lawrence Spence family. Standing: Lawrence Spence. Sitting, L–R: Ettie Spence, Joyce Spence, Stella Spence.

Descendants of Esther Smith[1] (1898–1989) m. Lawrence Spence (died 1960)

Stella Spence[2] (about 1925–1995) m. Ralph Mills[3]
   Ruth Devlin (Stella's daughter)
      Barry Devlin
      Grant Devlin
   Heather Mills[4] (1956–1981)
   Diane Mills[5] (about 1958) m. Colin Livingstone
      Ivan Garth Livingstone (Dec 1993)

Joyce Spence m. Ron Barnes
   David Barnes m. Geraldine Barnes
      Three children

[1] Trained and worked as nurse and midwife

[2] Trained and worked as nurse and midwife; also worked as "health visitor" for children and seniors

[3] Worked as civil servant in communications, three times served 3-year tours with family in Hong Kong

[4] BA in International Relations; MA in Oriental and African Studies, London University; killed in car accident, age 25

[5] Trained as nurse with special qualifications at Charing Cross Hospital, worked in New Zealand, returned in 1992 to UK (Wales) with artist husband

Left: *Leeds or Leighton, Welshpool, 1988. Ralph and Stella Mills family. L–R: Ettie (Smith) Spence, Stella (Spence) Mills, Colin Livingstone (groom), Diana (Mills) Livingstone, Ralph Mills.*

*Margaret and Reginald Metcalfe Family

Leighton, about 1950. Margaret and Reg Metcalfe Family. Back row, L–R: David Metcalfe, Joan Metcalfe, Margaret (Smith) Metcalfe, Reg Metcalfe. Front row: Peter Metcalfe, Pauline Metcalfe.

Margaret Smith (Aug 5, 1901–Feb 19, 1985) m. Reginald Metcalfe[1] (Nov 25, 1895–1974)

Margaret and Reg's offspring are Joan (1927), David (1931–1997), Peter (1940), and Pauline (1945–1965). Peter was the only one to marry and have descendants. Accounts of the lives of David and Pauline are in Chapter 14, and photos are used here to tell something of Joan's and David's careers.

Peter Metcalfe[2] m. Alice Joan Botham[3]
   Roger Mark Metcalfe[4] (Sep 9, 1963) m. Joanne Hanson
     Aimee Sally Metcalfe (Jun 8, 1989) m. Anthony MacIntyre
     Robert Mark Metcalfe (Mar 30, 1991)
   Lesley Ann Metcalfe (Feb 18, 1966) m. Paul Phenix
     Katy Phenix-Norman[5] (Dec 20, 1992) m. Adam Phenix-Norman[6]
       Edwin Shaun Phenix-Norman[7] (Feb 23, 2015)
     Lucy Emma Phenix (Sep 18, 1997)

Richard John Metcalfe (Nov 27, 1968) m. Helen Miles (divorced)
    Emily Kate Metcalfe (Feb 8, 1997)
    Andrew John Metcalfe (Jul 17, 1998)

After divorcing, Richard married Sarah Tiffin (Dalby) Metcalfe and acquired a stepson, James.

[1] Reginald's parents: Thomas Metcalfe (1869) and Emma (Broadbent) Metcalfe (1870); Reginald's sisters: Julia (Metcalfe) Lamb and Cissie (Metcalfe) Innes.

[2] Three years in RAF on Signals Intelligence; joined Police Force as Constable, Retired as Chief Superintendent of Police for Cleveland

[3] Joan's parents: Sidney Botham and Irene Underwood; History honours degree

[4] Developed an engineering company for CNC manufacture of components for a range of industries; retired at age 50 to pursue other interests

[5] Honours degree in history

[6] After marriage Katy Phenix and Adam Norman both changed their surnames by deed poll to Phenix-Norman.

[7] First great-grandchild for Peter and Joan

Joan Metcalfe's Career

Her Majesty requires that Joan, a nurse in the Royal Air Force, maintain good order and discipline among the airmen and airwomen in her charge. To that end the Queen commands all such people to obey Joan as their superior officer.

Elizabeth R

Elizabeth II, *by the Grace of God* OF THE UNITED KINGDOM OF GREAT BRITAIN AND NORTHERN IRELAND AND OF HER OTHER REALMS AND TERRITORIES QUEEN, HEAD OF THE COMMONWEALTH, DEFENDER OF THE FAITH.

To Our Trusty and well beloved   Joan Metcalfe   Greeting :

WE, *reposing especial Trust and Confidence in your Loyalty, Courage, and good Conduct, do by these Presents Constitute and Appoint you to be an Officer in Our Royal Air Force from the First day of February 1956 . You are therefore carefully and diligently to discharge your Duty as such in the Rank of Flying Officer or in such other Rank as We may from time to time hereafter be pleased to promote or appoint you to and you are in such manner and on such occasions as may be prescribed by Us to exercise and well discipline in their duties such Officers, Airmen and Airwomen as may be placed under your orders from time to time and use your best endeavours to keep them in good Order and Discipline. And We do hereby Command them to Obey you as their superior Officer and you to Observe and follow such Orders and Directions as from time to time you shall receive from Us, or any superior Officer, according to the Rules and Discipline of War, in pursuance of the Trust hereby reposed in you.*

GIVEN at Our Court, at Saint James's the Sixth day of March 1956, in the Fifth Year of Our Reign

By Her Majesty's Command

Left: Buckingham Palace, March 1956. Queen Elizabeth signs the document appointing Joan Metcalfe to command as Flying Officer.

Above: *London, 1966. Joan was awarded the Royal Red Cross Medal (left). The other medal is for Service in Cyprus during instability there.*

Right: *London, Buckingham Palace Gate, mid-1960s. At a ceremony at the Palace, Joan Metcalfe, by then a Squadron Officer, was given a Queen's Birthday honours medal. L–R: Reginald Metcalfe, Joan Metcalfe, Margaret (Smith) Metcalfe.*

Opposite: *Saltburn, July 23, 1995. L–R around circle: Lesley Phenix, Roger Metcalfe, Joanne Metcalfe, Richard Metcalfe, Helen Metcalfe, Aimee Metcalfe (on lap), Joan Metcalfe. Children in front: Robert Metcalfe, Katy Phenix. Photo by Jeff Mottershead.*

Despite severe problems with his eyes, David had a long career as a gardener and eventually a chef. When Danny and I met him at his parents' home, he gave a lovely slide show of flowers he had grown at the Castle.

David Metcalfe's Career

Left: David Metcalfe, probably at Swinton Castle garden, where he worked. About 1965.

Peter and Joan Metcalfe Family

Above: *Peter Metcalfe with wife, Joan Metcalfe.*

Right, top: *Probably in Cleveland, about 2015. A picnic with Lesley's family. Standing, L–R: Peter Metcalfe, Paul Phenix, Lesley Phenix, Lucy Phenix. Sitting: Adam Phenix-Norman, Katy Phenix-Norman, friend of Katy, Joan Metcalfe.*

Right, centre: *Probably Saltburn, about 2015. Roger Metcalfe family. L–R: Aimee, Roger, Joanne, Robert Metcalfe.*

Right, bottom: *Probably Saltburn, about 2015. Richard Metcalfe family: L–R: Andrew, Sarah, Emily, Richard, stepson James.*

Above: Saltburn, 1995. Peter Metcalfe tosses Katy Phenix. Background, L–R: Joan Metcalfe, Peter's wife; Joan Metcalfe, Peter's sister; Mottersheads—Jean, Don, Blair.

Left: Katy Phenix-Norman with son, Teddy, who is Peter and Joan's first great-grandchild.

Below, left: Hutton-le-Hole, July 1995. L–R: Blair Mottershead; Joan and Peter Metcalfe; Jean with Jeff Mottershead. Such an enchanting place!

Below, right: 1993. Peter Metcalfe, Chief Superintendent in Cleveland Constabulary.

*Bill and Florence Davis Family (Bill aka Charles Smith)

Above, left: *Probably California about 1950. Charles Smith aka Bill Davis.*
Above, right: *Probably California, about 1950: Florence (Dahl) Davis.*

Charles Smith aka Bill Davis[1] (1903–1969) m. Florence Dahl
   Mary Davis[2] (stage name Rebecca Seefeltd)
   Glen Davis

[1] Charles was the first member of the Smith family member to emigrate from England. He went to the United States, lived in Michigan, California, and Nevada. His main career was in real estate, but soon after he landed in the new country, he worked as a cowboy in rodeos, where he acquired his new name.

[2] Had career as model and actress

*Tom and Amelia Smith Family

St. Paul, July 15, 1992. Tommy and Amelia Smith family. L–R: Joan (Smith) Doonanco, Tom Smith, Amelia Smith, Frances (Smith) Kuori.

**Thomas Smith (Apr 10, 1911–Apr 3, 2000) m.
Amelia Pauline Wilkowski[1] (Jan 22, 1907–Mar 31, 1993)**

Joan Florence Smith (Jan 17, 1933) m. John Ivan Doonanco[2]
   Darlene Amelia Doonanco (Jul 31, 1958) m. Gary Kindrat (divorced)
   (Darlene has a partner, Steve Pelkey.)

[1] Amelia's parents: Edmond Wilkowski and Anastasia Morris. Tommy
and Amelia's baby Kathleen Smith died at birth, 1938.
[2] Johnny's parents: Paul Doonanco and Elise Raymond, a Parisienne; Fish
and Wildlife Officer and Manager; flew single-engine plane at work.
John Doonanco was murdered Oct 31, 1992. Several years later Joan
married long-time friend Robert (Bob) Gray. After a decade or so of
happy marriage with Joan, Bob died of cancer.

(continued overleaf)

Joan Florence Smith (Jan 17, 1933) m. John Ivan Doonanco *(continued)*
  David John Doonanco (Jul 23, 1961) m. Agathe Joly
    Ryan Doonanco (Sep 6, 1986)
    Taryn Doonanco (Jul 17, 1989)
    Andrew Doonanco (Oct 28, 1993)
  Dwaine Thomas Doonanco (Feb 1, 1964) m. Joanne Foisy (divorced)
    Braylon Doonanco (Sep 5, 1994)
    Caiben Doonanco (Jul 17, 1996)

Frances Mary Smith[3] (Jun 27, 1941) m. Stanley Kuori (divorced)
  Dean Allen Kuori (Nov 21, 1971) m. Desiree (Des) McFarlane
  Robin Carla Kuori (Nov 21, 1974) m. Mr. Supernant
    Carley Frances Supernant (Aug 11, 1997)
      Raelyn Robin Amelia Supernant[4] (May 26, 2016–Aug 8, 2016)
    Reese Kuori (Dec 16, 2004)

[3] Worked 11 years as hospital operating room technician in Saudi Arabia, elsewhere as LPN
[4] Baby Raelyn Supernant's obituary is in Chapter 14.

Right:
Truman, 1947. Back row, L–R: Reg, Velva, me, Joan, Mama, Amelia, Tommy. Front row, L–R: Mervin, Jeep, Elaine, Mack, Jean, Sid, Frances.

*Reg and Velva Smith Family

Glendon, about 1963. Standing, L–R: Mervin, Elaine, Allan (Jeep). Sitting, L–R: Reg and Velva.

Reginald Edwin Smith (Dec 5, 1917–1995) m. Velva May Ross[1] (May 12, 1917–2013)

Reginald Mervin Smith (May 31, 1942) m. Rejeanne Marie Gagne[2]
   Gail Marie Smith[3] (Apr 17, 1969) m. Wayne Thoben (divorced)
   (Gail is now Gail Hachey, married to Francis Hachey.)
      Chelsey Lynn Thoben (Mar 12, 1993)
      Brittney Anne Thoben (Oct 5, 1995) m. Chase Burshtinski
         Kye Walter Burshtinski (May 11, 2015)
   Shelly May Smith[4] (Aug 20, 1972) m. David Lotsberg
      Ole Mervin Lotsberg (Apr 30, 1993)
      Kasey May Lotsberg (Jul 6, 1995)

[1] Velva's parents: John Ross and Mary Jane Sharpe; Executive Member of Glendon Hospital Board Women's Auxiliary; Volunteer with Meals on Wheels
[2] Rejeanne's parents: Rene Gagne and Marie Anne (Brisson) Gagne
[3] District family counsellor
[4] Works at my residence, Bonny Lodge; much appreciated by elderly people here

(continued overleaf)

Reginald Mervin Smith (May 31, 1942) m. Rejeanne Marie Gagne *(continued)*
   Tina Marie Smith[5] (Mar, 1975) m. Parry DeBusschere
      Regen Rejeanne Mae DeBusschcrc (Jul 22, 1997)
      Heidi Marie DeBusschere (Dec 29, 1999)
      Nolen Victor DeBusschere (Nov 22, 2004)
   Reginald Rene Smith (Oct 10, 1978) m. Mandy Connor
      Peyton Velva-Rose Smith (Oct 14, 2009)
      Ellyanna Del-Marie Smith (Aug 3, 2011)
      Zoey Rejon Smith (Feb 8, 2016)

Elaine May Smith[6] (Nov 11, 1943) m. Peter Cornelius Doonanco[7]
   Rockwell Jack Reginald Doonanco[8] (Mar 22, 1966) m. Rhonda Rezel[9]
      Miranda Nikita Hassan (Jul 12, 1992)
      Blake Everett Hassan (Feb 28, 1996)
      Carson Reginald Cash Doonanco (Jun 3,1999)
      Georgia Laine Doonanco (Nov 7, 2001)
   Byron Montgomery Doonanco[10] (Jul 25, 1970) m. Koreen Karas[11]
      Kassidy Oksana Doonanco (March 5, 1997)
      Wyatt Timothy Doonanco (May 31,1999)
      Nikkita Nadia-Ann Doonanco (Oct 18, 2002)
      Dalton Walker Doonanco (Sep 16, 2004)

Allan "Jeep" Leroy Smith[12] (Jul 2, 1945) m. Grace Elaine Erickson[13]
   Donna Mae Knapp (Mar 31, 1959) m. Daniel Wizniuk
      Danica Dawn Wizniuk (Jul 29, 1980) and Adam Siewert
         Natasha Lyn Siewert (Sep 22, 2003)
         Ashley Madison Siewert (Nov 12, 2005)
         Tyson Aubrey Siewert (Dec 12, 2008)
      Dana Dawn Wizniuk (Oct 15, 1981) m. Travis Chisholm
      Daylan Daniel George Wizniuk (Feb 11, 1990)
   Daryl Mervin Knapp (Aug 19, 1962) m. Lorraine Hebert
      Adam Rodrique Knapp (Dec 2, 1989)
      Evan Allen Knapp (Jul 15, 1991)
      Emily Lorraine Knapp (Jul 4, 1996)

[5] Works at St. Paul Crisis Centre
[6] MEd Psych; Director of Glendon and District Historical Society
[7] Peter's parents: Jack Frederick Doonanco and Helen Taschuk; retired principal of Glendon School; former town councillor; president of Glendon and District Seniors Organization

8 Owner of Rockwell Telecom Ltd., which does fibre optics installations in Prairie provinces; Communications Engineering Technologist

9 Accounting and Safety for Rockwell Telecom

10 Owner's Worksite Representative; Registered Engineering Technologist

11 Safety instructor and school teacher

12 Director of Glendon and District Historical Society

13 Grace's parents: Glen James Erickson and Bernice Elaine Cunningham; Treasurer of Glendon and District Historical Society; Assistant Editor of Glendon district history book, *So Soon Forgotten*

Left: Glendon, 1954. A visit from Grandma Esther Smith Sonnichson (new married name). Back row, L–R: Sonnich Sonnichson, Grandmother Esther, Elaine Smith. Front row, L–R: Allan "Jeep" Smith, Mervin Smith.

Left, bottom: Glendon, 2008. Reg and Velva Smith family, adult siblings with their widowed mother. Standing, L–R: Mervin, Jeep. Seated, L–R: Elaine, Velva.

Mervin and Rejeanne Smith Family

Opposite, top: *Glendon, 2008, on the occasion of Reginald Smith's wedding. Rejeanne and Mervin Smith's children: L–R: "Reggie" Smith, Tina (Smith) DeBusschere, Shelly (Smith) Lotsberg, Gail (Smith/Thoben) Hachey, Rejeanne (Gagne) Smith, Mervin Smith.*

Opposite, bottom: *Glendon, 2008. Extended family of Rejeanne and Mervin Smith. (Double) back row, L–R: Parry DeBusschere, Tina DeBusschere, Ole Lotsberg (peeking), David Lotsberg, Shelly Lotsberg, Francis Hachey, Gail Hachey, Mervin Smith, Rejeanne Smith, Reggie Smith (groom), Mandy (Connor) Smith (bride). Kneeling, L–R: Heidi DeBusschere, Regen DeBusschere, Nolen DeBusschere, Kasey Lotsberg, Brittany Thoben, Chelsey Thoben.*

Above: *Glendon, 2015. L–R: Jeep, Rejeanne, Mervin. Mervin and Jeep are long-time partners in farming on a big scale.*

Elaine and Peter Doonanco Family

Glendon, 1988, Monty's high school graduation. Standing, L–R: Montgomery Doonanco, Rockwell Doonanco. Sitting: Elaine (Smith) Doonanco and Peter Doonanco.

Above, left: *Glendon, November 30, 1995. Marriage of Koreen Tracy Karas and Byron Montgomery Royle Doonanco.*

Above, right: *Glendon, 2013. Elaine with grandchildren, all with Doonanco surname. In tree: Nikkita. Back row, L–R: Elaine, Carson. Middle row, L–R: Georgia, Wyatt, Kassidy. Front: Dalton.*

Left: *Glendon, 2008. Elaine and Peter Doonanco family. Standing, L–R: Rhonda (Rezel) Doonanco, Rocky Doonanco, Monty Doonanco, Koreen (Karas) Doonanco. Sitting, L–R: Peter Doonanco, Elaine (Smith) Doonanco.*

Jeep and Grace Smith

Near Franchere, 2008. Grace (Erickson) Smith and Jeep Smith on their farm.

*Allan and Charlotte Smith Family

**Allan MacDonald Smith (Mar 2, 1920–2010) m.
Charlotte Leeds Harper (Mar 29, 1924–2007)**

Allan Smith (May 3, 1946) m. Carol Tuff
   Lisa Marie Smith (May 16, 1967)
   Troy Douglas Smith (Jul 4, 1969) m. Laurel Bray
      Dyllon Allan Smith (Mar 29, 1991)
   Christopher Smith (Feb 2, 1972)

Charles Smith (Sep 11, 1950) m. Cathy Ross
   Ryan Smith (Dec 15, 1975)
   Ramona Dawn Smith (Jan 15, 1980)
   Angala Marie Smith (Jun 24, 1981)

Above, left: *Glendon, about
1990. Allan and Charlotte visit
Alberta.*

Above, right: *Possibly
Vancouver dock, about 1954.
L–R: Grandfather Charles
Smith, holding hand of grandson
Charles Smith; Charlotte
(Harper) Smith; Allan Smith Jr.
Photo probably taken by Allan
Smith Sr.*

CHAPTER 16

Enjoying the Present and Looking Forward

Reviewing Good Times

I t's time to bring this memoir to a close. Writing it has taken me back in time on a mainly pleasant but occasionally sad trip. I relived happy memories of my girlhood with my twin brother as my companion. In my mind I tagged along with my older sister and her boyfriend, Ray, her true love. We went to dances, those whirling mixes of music, athleticism, grace, flirtation, tension, courtship, box lunches, adventure, and exhaustion. I relived the suspense of my long romance with Danny, the joy of marriage, and the amazing arrival of babies in our home and in the homes of my sister, brother, and Danny's brothers. How quickly the babies grew up and had fancy weddings and more babies!

Such good times we had along the way—many of them involving dancing. I think of the wedding dance of Laurie "Louie" Ross to Donna Black at Rocky Mountain House in 1975. Emcee Peter Doonanco set the tone for the evening—pure fun. How the dance hall rocked when the orchestra struck up "An Okie from Muskokie"!

Opposite: *Rife, September. 2016. Five generations. Back, L–R: Terry; Samantha (Smith) Mare; Rick. Front: me (seated); Kaylee Mare (standing). Photo by Jean Mottershead. I recently had the pleasure of sitting for a five-generation photo at Rick and Janet's home. Knowing that everyone in the photo comes from a happy home makes me feel grateful.*

Left: *Rocky Mountain House, 1975. Wedding of Louie Ross and Donna Black.*

My most special memories come from the 50-year anniversary celebration for Danny and me in 1990. When the grandkids acted out our story, I saw, for the first time, Danny wiping tears from his eyes. And then we danced.

Five years later, at the wedding dance of Denise Smith and Tom Charawich, in 1995, Danny and I were older, but we still had a good time dancing to the lively music. I vividly remember dancing out the door as we left for home. That was the last time Danny danced.

Fort Kent Catholic Church, 1995. Mack Smith takes his daughter Denise down the aisle to marry Tom Charawich. We danced quite a lot that night.

Danny and I had four good years together at Bonny Lodge. We had two rooms—a bedroom, and a living room—where we loved to have visitors and offer them refreshments. The space was tiny compared with the Browning house, but it was enough.

For nearly ten years now, I have lived alone and happy in my big bright room at Bonny Lodge. Being the last of my siblings and last of Danny's generation of Smiths, I could feel sad, like "The Last Rose of Summer." Instead I look on the bright side of my life and feel thankful. I have been exceptionally lucky—happy nearly every day of my life. I have not struggled with illness or deprivation, nor have I endured tragedy such as the loss of a child.

From the day Danny and I moved into the lodge, Mack, and his wife, Diane, have been our most frequent visitors. They have cheerfully taken us—now just me—to more doctor's appointments, done more errands, and fixed the TV more times than I could possibly count. I also want to say that during all my years at the lodge, I've had the pleasure, almost daily, of seeing my grandniece Shelly Lotsberg. She is a competent, caring person and a ray of sunshine here.

My Reasons to be Remain Upbeat

Mack and Diane, my most frequent visitors.

Life at Bonny Lodge suits me very well. I enjoy many friendships here, some with people I've known for many decades, some with new friends. I enjoy the excellent meals and many activities and outings arranged for us. What brightens a day most of all is a visit from family members, be it sons, daughter, grandchildren, nieces, nephews, or their spouses.

I enjoy having many visitors to the lodge—to my room and the piano room. I see all three of my sons or their wives now and then, and every summer Jean comes from Quadra for a week. Don and Jean's sons have also come from BC to visit me. Blair came in 2013, after I broke a femur—while dancing. Jeff and his family keep in touch with me. They came from BC to visit me in 2014 and 2016. This summer eight-year-old Devlin treated me to a medley of songs on the piano. In July 2016 I had the pleasure of holding another musical soiree with Pat and Ian Perry and Eileen and Phil Walker. Pat often comes to sing with me or watch a movie.

My room at the lodge, February 22, 2010. L–R: Jerzey Vachon, me, LeeAnn (Smith) Vachon, Brooklyn Vachon, on LeeAnn's lap. I love to see my descendants.

Top: *Grandson Blair Mottershead in our living room at the lodge, about 2004.*
Bottom: *University of British Columbia, 2012. Grandson Jeff with his mother, my daughter, Jean.*

About the only negative thought I have about myself is that I am not contributing very much to society by simply living a long time. I was therefore delighted in 2015 when Notre Dame Elementary School gave me an opportunity to work with children learning to read. I so enjoyed being with the charming young people and feeling useful. This year, once a month, I have the pleasure of playing children's songs for a group of young mothers with babies. The babies seem entranced as their mothers casually sing along. And I feel useful.

Above: Bonnyville, 2015. Working with school children.
Opposite, bottom left: Rife, Rick and Janet's, 2016. L–R: Kaylee Mare, Brooklyn Vachon, and me at piano while Jerzey looks on.
Opposite, bottom right: Fort Kent Catholic Church, 1995. Me preparing to play "Here Comes the Bride" for Denise's walk down the aisle.

Music is still a big part of my life, and I am pleased that most of my descendants play instruments and sing. In his teens Rick played with a band called "Neon Sign," and for a decade or two Sid and Shirley were popular entertainers at the Bonnyville Grand Opry.

Left: *Bonnyville, about 1992. Newspaper clipping from the* Bonnyville Nouvelle, *featuring Sid and Shirley Smith performing at the Bonnyville Country Opry in Lyle Victor Alberta Hall. Reprinted with permission.*

In 2006, thanks to my granddaughter Danielle and her husband, Jeff Weeks, I had a recording session at Lyle Victor Albert Hall. There I played a medley of popular songs on a beautiful grand piano. The resulting CD, produced with Jeff's expert sound management, was a gift I enjoyed giving to my descendants. I am pleased my music can be heard after I am gone.

The older I get, the more attention I get from politicians and people planning school reunions and the like. I am always pleased to chat with these people. I include a photo from the *Bonnyville Nouvelle* of mc chatting with Alberta Government Minister Sigurdson.

Bonnyville, Spring, 2016. Meeting with Alberta's NDP Minister of Seniors and Housing, Lori Sigurdson. Photo by Eric Bowlin, first published in the Bonnyville Nouvelle. *Reprinted with permission.*

I am fortunate to be able to enjoy special family gatherings outside the lodge. At Thanksgiving, Christmas, and Easter, without fail, I am invited to a sumptuous feast at the home of Rick and Janet or LeeAnn and Vern Vachon or Samantha and Brian Mare.

Eastbourne Hall, 1990. My kids the way I still see them. (They are actually a little more wrinkled now, but I resist seeing them as old people.) L–R: Mack, Jean, Rick, Sid.

Impact of Technology on Agriculture

When I look beyond my own small world, I am more concerned than ever before about the future of the world. I have seen the march of generations for nearly a hundred years. I have seen how one generation holds sway for a while then gradually gives way to a younger generation with new ideas, new technologies. In my lifetime, tractors, cars, planes, radios, and phones became common. In the last few decades computers and cell phones have revolutionized nearly everything everywhere.

Considering the importance of food, technology's influence on agriculture is significant in many ways. In my early years I saw a parade of new machines that at first seemed only to make work easier for farmers. In subtle ways, however, they were changing farming so that fewer and fewer farmers would be needed. Rural areas lost much of their population. Neighbourliness lost the importance it had in pioneer days. According to some demographers, over the last century—that is, in approximately my lifetime—the number of Canadians directly involved in various aspects of agriculture dropped from 95% to 5% of the population.

The revolution continues. Huge multinational corporations are involved in agriculture. I hear about new machines, such as the "no-till drill," which eliminate the need for farmers to prepare for seeding by cultivating soil to loosen it and uproot weeds. What about the weeds? They are sprayed by gigantic million-dollar sprayers at appropriate intervals. What chemicals are in the spray? I cannot tell you, but it worries me.

Life goes on—at least it has for millennia. We of the older generations unknowingly overloaded the world with carbon dioxide. Now the world needs, perhaps desperately, new generations and technologies to keep lands fertile and productive. Not only do we need to stop polluting water and soil. We also need to stop rising temperatures and rising oceans. I hear about using the sun, wind, and tide to produce electricity that might stave off disaster. But all that is work for younger generations.

Principles for a Good Life

I humbly offer some principles, born of my life experience, that might be useful to someone reading this memoir.

1. Live by the golden rule: "Do unto others as you would have them do unto you." Be kind, tolerant, and helpful. Be fair in your dealings with others. Tell the truth unless it is more hurtful than helpful. Do your share of the work. Keep your promises.

2. If you make a mistake and do something to hurt someone, try to make amends. Figure out how to avoid making the same mistake again. Then forgive yourself.

3. Do not damage your own life by dwelling too much on a wrong that someone has done to you. Be willing to forgive and get on with more satisfying and productive concerns.

4. Accomplish something worthwhile in your life. Develop your talents, whatever they are, to contribute to the wellbeing of others. If you want a great challenge, educate yourself as much as you can to help identify practices that degrade the environment, and, if you can, help eliminate them. You can also better the world just by recycling. Musicians and artists give something of value to the world. So do people who wash the dishes and sweep the floors. There are many ways to accomplish something worthwhile.

5. Maintain connections to other people—your family, a circle of friends, an organization, a community. Belonging somewhere helps you find happiness.

6. Notice the good things each day brings.

7. Do not let money be your primary source of satisfaction.

A Cup of Kindness

As I look over my "principles for a good life," the golden rule stands out above the others, especially the part about kindness. I recall the time Peter and Elaine Doonanco discovered me trying to arrange public transportation home from summer school. They simply insisted on driving me home. I stored away the happy memory.

Finally, in celebration of wonderful hospitality and the completion of this book, I include a photo of a recent gathering of Smith cousins and me.

Glendon, Elaine and Peter Doonanco's home, September, 2016. Standing, L–R: Jean (Smith) Mottershead; Elaine (Smith) Doonanco. Sitting L–R: me, Catherine (Ross) Smith; Frances (Smith) Kuori; Janet (Lay) Smith; Joan (Smith) Doonanco-Gray. Photo by Peter Doonanco.

Index of Names

Smith, Allan MacDonald
("Mac"/"Allan") *(continued)*
  relationship with his father, 130,
    249–50, *311*
  at family gatherings, *127*, 243
  death of, 244
Smith, Amelia Pauline (Wilkowski),
  123, *159*, 165, 243, 301, *301*, *302*
Smith, Angala Marie, 311
Smith, Anson William, *72*, 204, *230*,
  276, *290*
Smith, Catherine Anna (Ross)
  ("Cathie")
  birth of, 3, 32
  in Smith–Ross family, 275
  as a child, 36, 37, 39–40, 44, 45,
    78, 81, 85–86
  as a child, in photos, *16*, *21*, *32*,
    35, *36*, *38*, *46*, *49*
  dancing, 146, 148, 150–51,
    313–14
  as a young adult, 152–53, 154–56
  relationship with and marriage
    to Danny, *viii*, 18, 125, *140*,
    141, 146–58, *161*, 221. *See also*
    Smith, Catherine Anna (Ross)
    ("Cathie"): anniversaries
  early in marriage, 57, 166–67
  as a mother, *162*, 166, 172, *172*,
    192
  move to and life in BC, 173–75,
    177–78, 179–83
  as a teacher, 89, 193, *193*, 194
  relationship with Vivi and Ray,
    184
  at Browning house, 187, 205, *209*
  retirement of, 205–6
  anniversaries, *viii*, 211, 221, 222,
    223, 227, *227*, *228*
  travels of, 4, 9–10, 114, 197–200,
    205
  at family gatherings, 17, 18, 191,
    208, 210–11, 220–21, 243
  at family gatherings, in photos, *16*,
    17, *65*, *66*, *67*, *68*, *71*, *101*, *145*,
    175, *209*, 211, 212, 219, 220,
    223, 225, 230, 274, 275, 288,
    302, 313, 324

Smith, Catherine Anna (Ross)
  ("Cathie") *(continued)*
  at Bonny Lodge, 38, 229, *231*,
    238, 315–18, 320
  during Danny's final days, 231–34
  at Danny's memorial, 234–36
  and music, 43, 96, 171, 206, *206*,
    318–19
  on technology and agriculture, 322
  principles for a good life, 323
  in other photos, *89*, *316*, *317*,
    318, *320*
Smith, Charles (Danny's father,
  b. 1877)
  early life, 107
  marriage, 109, 111, 117–18
  life in Canada, 103–6, 113–15,
    117–18
  as a parent, 111–12
  relationship with Margaret, 118,
    119
  letter to Danny, 118–19
  relationship with Allan and
    Charlotte, 119–20, 249–50, *311*
  death of, 249–50
  in other photos, *110*, *112*, *250*
Smith, Charles (aka Bill Davis,
  b. 1903). *See* Davis, Bill (aka
  Charles Smith)
Smith, Charles (Allan and Charlotte's
  son, b. 1950), 311, *311*
Smith, Charlotte Leeds (Harper),
  107, 129–30, 179, 244, 249–50,
  311
  in photos, *162*, *179*, *311*
Smith, Christopher, 311
Smith, Daniel ("Danny")
  in Smith–Ross family, 275
  as a child, *103*, 178
  immigration to Canada, 103–6,
    115
  relationship with his father, 118–
    19, 249
  dancing, 146, 148, 150–51,
    313–14
  as a young adult, *122–24*, *134*,
    141, *142*, 157

Smith, Daniel ("Danny") *(continued)*
  relationship with and marriage to
    Cathie, 18, 125, *140*, 146–58,
    161, 231. *See also* Smith, Daniel
    ("Danny"): anniversaries
  early in marriage, 57, *57*, 166–67
  as a father, *162*, 166, 190, 192,
    194
  working on the farm, 123, 125,
    165, 167–68, 183, 186, 194,
    226, *226*
  working off the farm, 158, 173,
    177–79, 197
  move to and life in BC, 173–75,
    177–78, 179–83
  friendship with Ray and Vivi, 146,
    184, 236
  back surgery, 173
  at Browning house, *187–89*, *205*,
    209, *217*
  anniversaries, *viii*, 211, 221, *221*,
    222, 223, 227, *227*, *228*
  and music, 171
  travels of, *9–10*, *114*, *190*, *197–*
    200, *205*
  at family gatherings, 18, 208,
    210–11, 220–21, 224, 243
  at family gatherings, in photos, *17*,
    60, *66*, *67*, *101*, *175*, *180*, *198*,
    211, *212*, *217*, *219*, *220*, *223*,
    225, *227*, *228*, *230*, *275*, *288*
  in Bonny Lodge, 229, *231*, *317*
  final days, 231–34
  death of, 234, 244
  memorial for, 234–36
  in other photos, *103*, *124*, *125*,
    129
Smith, Daniel MacKinnon ("Mack")
  birth of, 167
  naming of, 9
  in Smith–Ross family, 276
  as a child, 170, 177, 183, 186–87,
    190
  as a child, in photos, *17*, *58*, *162*,
    168, *171*, *177*, *238*, *275*, *302*
  working on the farm, 194
  wedding of, 194, *194*
  house of, 204
  during Danny's final days, 231–34

White, Vivian (Ross) ("Vivi")
  (continued)
    relationship with and marriage to
      Ray, 143–45, 150
    as a mother, *77*
    move to and life in BC, 173–75,
      177–78, 180
    relationship with Cathie and
      Danny, 184. *see also* White,
      Vivian (Ross) ("Vivi"): as a sister
    retirement of, 182
    relationship with Aunt Alice, 251
    and music, 43, 171
    and poetry, 87
    at family gatherings, 17, 18, 191,
      208, 240
    death of, 240–41
    in photos, *16, 17, 21, 26, 27, 46,*
      89, 145, 209, 212, 258, 274
White, William Raymond Edgar
  ("Edgar"/"Ed"), 18, 165, 167, 178,
  208, 234, 241, 253, 258
    in photos, *17, 31, 77, 131, 209,*
      225, 236, 258, 260, 269
Whysk, Annie, 135
Whysk, William, 134
Wilkowski, Edmond, 301
Williams, Patricia ("Pat"), *20*, 233,
  233, 259, *266*
Williamson, Ben, 5
Williamson, Mary Ethel (McClure),
  5, 154
Wilson (later McClure), Martha Ann,
  3, 15
Wirgen, Mr., *26*
Wizniuk, Danica Dawn, 304
Wizniuk, Daniel, 304
Wizniuk, Daylan Daniel George, 304
Wizniuk, Donna Mae (Knapp), 304

Z
Zamzul, Clara (Haland), 187

CPSIA information can be obtained
at www.ICGtesting.com
Printed in the USA
LVOW05s1044020417
529313LV00003B/3/P